MEDIA BLIGHT AND THE DEHUMANIZING OF AMERICA

MEDIA BLIGHT
AND THE
DEHUMANIZING
OF
AMERICA

William K. Shrader

PRAEGER

New York
Westport, Connecticut
London

Copyright Acknowledgments

The author and publisher are grateful for permission to use the following material:

Excerpts reprinted with permission of The Free Press, a Division of Macmillan, Inc., from *The Birth and Death of Meaning* by Ernest Becker. Copyright © 1962, 1971 by The Free Press.

Excerpts from *The Birth and Death of Meaning* by Ernest Becker (Penguin Books, Second edition, 1972), copyright © The Free Press, 1962, 1971. Reproduced by permission of Penguin Books Ltd.

Excerpts from *Feelings: Our Vital Signs* by Willard Gaylin. Copyright 1979 by Willard Gaylin. Reprinted by permission of HarperCollins Publishers.

Excerpts from *Teaching as a Conserving Activity* by Neil Postman. Copyright 1979 by Neil Postman. Used by permission of Dell Books, a division of Bantam Doubleday Dell Publishing Group, Inc.

Excerpts from *Zen Buddhism and Psychoanalysis* by D. T. Suzuki, Erich Fromm, and Richard DeMartino. New York: Grove Press, 1960. Used by permission of Grove Press.

Exerpts from *The Narcissistic Condition: A Fact of Our Time* edited by Marie Nelson. New York: Human Sciences Press, 1977. Used by permission of Human Sciences Press, Inc.

Every reasonable effort has been made to trace the owners of copyright materials in this book, but in some instances this has proven impossible. The author and publisher will be glad to receive information leading to more complete acknowledgments in subsequent printings of the book and in the meantime extend their apologies for any omissions.

Library of Congress Cataloging-in-Publication Data

Shrader, William K.
  Media blight and the dehumanizing of America / William K. Shrader.
    p. cm.
  Includes bibliographical references and index.
  ISBN 0-275-94119-1 (alk. paper)
  1. Mass media—Social aspects—United States. 2. Mass media
—United States—Psychological aspects. 3. Television broadcasting
—United States—Influence. 4. United States—Moral conditions.
  I. Title.
  HN90.M3S47 1992
  302.23—dc20   91-28653

British Library Cataloguing in Publication Data is available.

Copyright © 1992 by William K. Shrader

Library of Congress Catalog Card Number: 91-28653
ISBN: 0-275-94119-1

First published in 1992

Praeger Publishers, One Madison Avenue, New York, NY 10010
An imprint of Greenwood Publishing Group, Inc.

Printed in the United States of America

The paper used in this book complies with the
Permanent Paper Standard issued by the National
Information Standards Organization (Z39.48–1984).

10 9 8 7 6 5 4 3 2 1

To Betty and Tom,
and Davy in memoriam

The moral flabbiness born of the exclusive worship of the bitch-goddess SUCCESS. That—with the squalid cash interpretation put on the word "success"—is our national illness.

William James to H. G. Wells
September 9, 1906

We have grown literally afraid to be poor. We despise anyone who elects to be poor in order to simplify and save his inner life. . . . We have lost the power even of imagining what the ancient idealization of poverty could have meant: the liberation from material attachments, the unbribed soul, the manlier indifference, the paying our way by what we are and do and not by what we have, the right to fling away our life at any moment, irresponsibly—the more athletic trim, in short, the moral fighting shape.

William James, *The Varieties of Religious Experience*,
Gifford Lectures, no. 14,
delivered at Edinburgh, Scotland, 1902

Contents

Preface

Ever since its advent in the late 1940s there has always been a TV in my home. I can distinctly remember my parents watching, without fail, the weekly installments of "I Remember Mama," a benign serial about the adventures of a newly arrived family of Swedish immigrants to the United States. This, of course, was in TV's early "black and white" days, before the coming of color and around-the-clock programming, and at the very outset of its technical and social evolution—two positively accelerating aspects of its inexorable presence in contemporary America. In those days, in my youthfully naive appreciation of things, America was unshakable in its preeminence among the world's nations, and its future as international leader was absolutely secure. The TV was another interesting technological gadget, having vast promise as a source of entertainment, and being another symbol of American superiority. Like so many of my peers I watched it sporadically, with varying degrees of amusement. It was not nearly as critical within my life-space as were women, sports, education, and the budding future.

Since those halcyon days a lot has changed. I have experienced the vicissitudes of early adulthood and middle age and am beginning to get the first glimpses of "hoary eld." In the process I have become, like most of my peers, a sadder, and perhaps, wiser man. Over the years, as I began to look around me, paying a bit more attention than I did at 16, I have become aware of a complex and disturbing phenomenon gradually, but perceptibly, emerging. On the one hand, America has progressively sunk deeper and deeper into a sea of troubles that was utterly unanticipated by the majority of us who grew into adulthood during the 1950s. On the other hand, TV, as the avatar of the electronic media, has enjoyed a meteoric rise within American society, to the extent that new slang terms such as "couch potato," characterizing the behavior of persons literally addicted to its hedonistically mesmeric appeal, have become fixtures of our everyday vernacular. I am convinced that there is a causal connection between these two contiguous, but seemingly disparate, phenomena. I am convinced that the growth of the electronic media is serving as a powerful—though not sole, nor sufficient—determinant contributing to America's waning health, vigor, and competitiveness as a citizenry, and thus to its diminishing prospects as a leader among the sovereign nations preparing for the rigors of the twenty-first century.

I realize that the relationship between media influence and the wider sociocultural health and vigor has been investigated and written about frequently. But, as a clinical psychologist, I am also aware of the tendency of humans to live in their heads, so to speak, rather than in the external reality. To put it differently, I know that we humans interpret the data of everyday experience in terms of our fears and wishes, rather than objectively registering them, as a camera does. To the extent that our subjective bases for interpreting the flux of our daily experience are filled with unreality, our interpretations and the overt acts flowing from them are apt to have damaging repercussions for us, for our immediate affiliates, and ultimately for the wider society. That the electronic media are filling the heads of regular viewers, particularly our children, with unrealistic and tasteless drivel is a given. How, and why, these daily media inputs are undermining our inner bases for interpreting experience in ways that, normally, would motivate us to various acts of kindness, cooperation, and social cohesion are the subjects of this book.

This is not meant to be a doomsday book. However, it addresses what is to me a serious and growing problem, one that will not go away by itself. I have written it in the hope of focusing attention on the issue of media blight and motivating concerned people, particularly parents of young children, to consider ways of parrying the insidious influence of same on themselves and their vulnerable, impressionable offspring. Time is not exactly short yet, but it is slipping away faster than most people seem to think. We need to act!

I would like to express my gratitude to a number of persons who have helped me in the preparation of the manuscript. Being both friends and/or professional associates, they all have freely offered intangibles in the form of encouragement and emotional support, as well as tangibles such as help in typing and specific advice in regard to my next, at the time, unsurmountable obstacle. They include Dr. Michael Fiore, Elizabeth Lum,

Dr. Carolyn Eastman, Arlene Coleman, Donna Hammergran, Dr. Harry Keyishian, Dr. Robert Francouer, and Michael Jones.

Special thanks are also due Janie St. Peter, Ken Mulligan, and Bob Hibbett. All thinkers, all friends, they have provided me with valuable intellectual feedback and emotional support over the time span of my project, as well as before.

In addition, I would like to express my gratitude to those at Praeger who were actively involved in bringing my project to fruition for their patient, kindly, efficient, and unerringly professional assistance, two of whom I have met, and two I have not. In the first dyad are Anne Kiefer, sociology/communications editor, and Bert Yaeger, project editor. In the second are Wanda Giles, copy editor, and Mary Dorazio, proofreader.

Last but not least, I want to express my gratitude to Betty Shrader, my better half and a busy professional educator herself, who, over the years, has listened to my ideas and offered me typically tight, cogent intellectual feedback, put up with my foibles and idiosyncracies, helped me—as I hope I helped her—survive one of life's bleakest tragedies, and kept the homefires burning.

Introduction

I come home from work at about 5:00 in the evening and, like most Americans, automatically switch on the TV. "Live at Five," NBC's New York City evening news, is just beginning, or, if I'm a few minutes late, in full swing. In the background of the audiovisual phantasmagoria is music with an intense, rapid, attention-riveting beat, together with a fascinating kaleidoscope of brilliant color. The leading figures, the anchorpersons, are exceptionally attractive, typically well-dressed, articulate, poised, and, so it would appear, extremely knowledgeable. To top things off, they project an air of witty, controlled ease, as they move flawlessly through their nightly performances. The subordinate figures—the sports and weather announcers and those on special assignment—while possibly not burning with as much candlepower as the star anchors, also make their own smooth, precise, often witty contributions to the program's aura of seamless professionalism. It is the same on the 6:00 news program and those coming later in the evening, in New York and in other large and medium-sized cities across the nation.

Ironically, the subject matter on these evening TV-news programs can be broken down into essentially four categories: sports, weather, miscellaneous catastrophes, and crime. Further, the bulk of the news program, night after night, is devoted to the last category. All of this professional talent and technological wizardry focused primarily on reporting the destructive and violent interactions of ordinary persons in American society! This weighting is incongruous and demoralizing, to say the least.

I use the words "incongruous" and "demoralizing" with special purpose here. I believe that evening city TV-news programs present an example, in microcosm, of a pervasive incongruity in the lives of millions of Americans. This incongruity is, in turn, feeding an equally pervasive personal demoralization. It is because of this less obvious, psychic demoralization that the dehumanization of America is occurring. The mass media, particularly the electronic media, are integral to the incongruity, which, from the wider societal perspective, can be seen as structural. "Media blight" is the term I use to describe much of the mass media's increasing presence and influence in American society.

According to the *Random House Dictionary of the English Language*, the verb "demoralize" has two essential meanings: (1) "to deprive [a person or persons] of spirit, courage, discipline, etc., destroy the morale of"; and (2) "to throw [a person] into disorder or confusion, bewilder".[1] Thus, demoralization is defined essentially as a state of dispirited confusion—a combination of emotional and cognitive factors lying at the heart of classical definitions of psychopathology. When personal demoralization is severe, it tends to express itself overtly in a variety of aberrant behaviors. Such behavior patterns can have dire consequences for individuals, their immediate social affiliations, and the culture at large.

I believe, at this point, that it is accurate to speak of America as a demoralized society. While it is many things, a society is an aggregate of interdependent and interacting persons in various degrees of relationship, communication, and mutual responsibility, just as the human body is an aggregate of interdependent and interacting cells. And by a process analogous to the development of organic disease, the wider society is weakened to the extent that its individual members' own inner workings are thrown out of equilibrium. My purpose in this book is to examine the widespread affliction of personal demoralization, suggest some of its basic causes, and delineate some of its deeper psychological and social ramifications.

The signs and symptoms of personal demoralization are ubiquitous in contemporary America. We are bombarded daily with descriptions and statistical reports indicative of this condition. Serious crime, alcoholism, drug abuse, wife beating, rape, child abuse, vandalism, work sabotage, and innumerable other forms of antisocial behavior appear to be the norm rather than the exception. Frank and frightening craziness seems to be everywhere nowadays, rather than on the lonely and eerie fringes, as in past eras.

Among the ranks of healthier persons who manage to remain free of serious antisocial symptoms, there are pervasive, though subtler, signs of this demoralization. Cynicism so thick it can be cut with a knife, suggesting latent paranoia, permeates the atmosphere of the office, the shop, the home, and the social gathering. Terms like "rip-off" and "scam" gain instant currency in the contemporary vernacular, and conversations in all circles abound with references to the corruption and self-aggrandizement of others. While usually not severe enough to lead to suicide, hospitalization, or prolonged treatment, depression is epidemic in contemporary America. In fact, among psychotherapists and mental health specialists it is referred to as the "common cold of mental illness."

The connections are less obvious, but a cluster of socioeconomic issues that have come into focus in the past decade further imply widespread personal demoralization. I speak here of the mountain of personal, corporate, and public debt; the decline in national productivity and industrial competitiveness; and the loss of quality in modern life. Though all three are complexly determined, it can be argued that they are reflective of a progressive weakening of the productive, as opposed to the consumptive, orientation in the public mentality. All three reflect a growing parasitic attitude toward the system, a preoccupation with taking from it without proportionate concern for conserving or developing it. They are particularly ominous because they represent a major shift in dimension, a translation of personal psychological problems into broader and more difficult societal ones.

The factors contributing to widespread personal demoralization in contemporary America are legion. Rather than a detailed listing of specific factors at this point in the discussion, an indication of the burgeoning pace and complexity of daily life as the two basic conditions pressing people into their demoralization is sufficient. Alvin Toffler's concept of "future shock" is apposite here. According to Toffler, the overwhelming rate of social change, caused primarily by science and runaway technology, is taxing the individual's coping mechanisms to the limit. Too many things are happening too fast; pace and complexity are increasing at positively accelerated rates.

As Toffler theorizes, technology is plying people with a superabundance of choice and convenience, subtly "future shocking" them. But it also has a more dramatically sinister side. Technological wonders such as the thermonuclear bomb and biological weapons can kill millions of people quickly and efficiently, perhaps even destroy civilization in its entirety. Less dramatic, but no less lethal, is technology's capacity to change the very planet we all live on, and in the process pollute the atmosphere, irreparably damage the delicate ecosystem, and plunder the planet's dwindling supply of nonrenewable raw materials. To the extent that awareness of these threats impinges on people's consciousness, it can be seen to feed insecurity and cynical consumerism, a "get it while the getting's good" attitude.

More to the focus of this discussion, the illusory quality of much of life feeds the pervasive demoralization in a special way. And this, too, is a product of recent developments in communications technology. As a populace, we are subject to an endless flow of illusory images produced by the mass media. I call this collective phenomenon the "imagery of unreality" because so much of it is shot through with subtle deception and distortion, while being presented in the guise of reality. All of the electronic and print media contribute to this surging river of illusions, although the electronic advertising and entertainment media, piped in over the TV, are its principal source. It is endless, omnipresent, and invasive. Referring to a major segment of this imagery in an article entitled "The Decline of Quality," Barbara Tuchman stated that advertising is the air we breathe. The imagery of unreality contributes to the demoralization under discussion by fostering expectations that cannot be realized, thus predisposing naive and impressionable viewers to chronic frustration and self-dissatisfaction. As we will see, the self-dissatisfaction is particularly noxious psychologically, and integral to the demoralization.

But there is another aspect of the imagery of unreality that greatly intensifies its capacity to feed widespread personal demoralization. It constitutes a major aspect of something I call the "experiential bind." The experiential bind is rooted in the incongruity between the two juxtaposed realms of firsthand and vicarious experience. It is an internal subjective phenomenon arising out of the flux of daily experience. That experience, in turn, is conditioned by external factors existing in contemporary America that contribute to a pervasive incongruity between the two experiential realms. In a sense they tend to split or fracture the totality of experience. The firsthand, proximate realm is the realm of immediate, active experience—of work, responsibility, and the daily struggle for survival, meaning, and success. The vicarious realm is the realm of passive experience at one remove, the realm of attending to others as they perform, the realm of dreams and fantasies. Humans have always spent time and energy in both realms. But with the development of the electronic media in the past sixty years or so, the vicarious realm has grown enormously, presently rivaling the firsthand realm for dominance in the totality of daily experience. Illustrating this point is the statistic indicating that by the age of 18 the average American adolescent has spent about 12,000 hours in school and about 15,000 hours watching television—not to speak of the additional time spent watching movies and listening to radio and musical recordings.[2]

I believe that the experiential bind is literally tearing people apart psychologically. In the firsthand realm, they are smothered by feelings of insignificance and impotence. Simultaneously, in the vicarious realm they are titillated by an endless flow of glitzy, glamorous, fantastic images—the imagery of unreality—causing their heads to swim with grandiose illusions. People face this bind, live within it, from day to day. It frustrates and confuses them and forces them, on an unconscious level, into corrosive doubt about their potency and value as human beings.

Put differently, it constantly undermines their self-esteem, that fragile and pivotal affirmation of self that is so critical to mental health and emotional stability. The spreading demoralization, with all of its associated symptoms and abuses, is a sign that people in contemporary America are losing the battle to maintain their self-esteem, are sagging under the leaden weight of the experiential bind.

Guilt is the deeper intrapsychic cause of the demoralization. Further, guilt undermines self-esteem. Self-esteem is based on self-affirmation, on positive self-regard, whereas guilt is a form of negative self-regard. Willard Gaylin speaks to this with especial clarity in his fine commentary on feelings.

Guilt, then, is a form of self-disappointment. It is the sense of anguish that we did not achieve our standards of what we ought to be. We have fallen short. We have somehow or other betrayed some internal sense of potential self. This is why guilt is the most internalized and personal of emotions. You-against-you allows no buffer—and no villains except oneself. . . . It is why guilt is so painful to endure.[3]

In regard to guilt's capacity to motivate the sufferer to defensive or compensatory measures, he adds, ''The readiness to avoid the emotion is testament to the discomfort, and therefore the driving force of the emotion. To avoid it we may avoid the behavior that generates it—or, short of that, expiate for it.''[4]

Guilt is usually thought of in religious terms, in connection with the transgressing of some moral-ethical law or value. However, guilt, as described by Gaylin, can have a purely secular bias. People can feel just as much anguished self-disappointment for having failed to achieve or accumulate sufficient (to them) wealth or worldly success as they would for having sinned in a variety of ways—cheated, fornicated, stolen, physically aggressed, or even murdered. Humans necessarily form ideals, secular or religious, and react with the painful and intensely personal emotion of guilt when they feel they have fallen short of their inner standards. And because the values in modern America are overwhelmingly materialistic and hedonistic, the inevitable guilt endured by millions of people is of a secular bias. I say inevitable because the imagery of unreality, beaming out from the various mass media, proffers an endless stream of fantastic illusions that have an enormously powerful capacity to foment unattainable ideals among much of the viewing public. To return to Barbara Tuchman's metaphor, from the standpoint of psychological health the air we breathe in the vicarious realm of experience is foul. It is permeated with elements conducive to the development of unrealistic standards of human achievement. When people internalize such standards, a sense of failure and pathological guilt, to one degree or another, are the natural results.

Guilt is a uniquely human emotion. As far as we know, no other creature in the animal kingdom is subject to it. And as Gaylin also points out, it can have both a benign and a baleful effect on human behavior. It may serve to motivate humans in their highest acts of altruism, being an elemental part of such noble character traits as compassion, fair-mindedness, and devotion to duty. More specifically, guilt is integral to human beings' unique inner self-reflectiveness, particularly in connection with the pursuit of ideals. However, when ideals are unrealistic or unattainable and, as a consequence, guilt is severe and unrelenting, it has the potential for wreaking havoc with inner peace and mental health. Where such morbid guilt exists, it can either stifle people in their attempts at maintaining mature, productive, socially approved patterns of behavior, or, contrarily, drive them into socially destructive patterns. Serious study of abnormal psychology shows that pathological guilt is central to all forms of functional mental illness, that is, mental illness without organic brain disease.

Guilt is a uniquely human emotion because values are unique to the human situation. Humans are the only species within the animal kingdom who have highly developed systems of value, systems that define the good and the bad, the desirable and the undesirable. In fact, the capacity to conceptualize values and ideals, and to pursue them energetically throughout a lifetime, would seem to be the crowning characteristic of humanness. Other animals possess intelligence, social instincts, and habits. They show devotion to their young. It is only humans who, individually and collectively, erect abstract value hierarchies and enjoy self-affirmation or suffer guilt, depending on the immediate outcome of their goal-oriented efforts. Thus, the subject of values is central to this discussion. It is the key to the whole concatenated series of problems running from personal demoralization to the larger, related, societal issues.

Humans are pulled forward in life by their values, motivated by them, in psychological parlance. As a species we seem to be essentially teleological at our core—purposive, goal-oriented, appetitive—rather than rational, as traditional Western philosophy, stemming from the Greeks, asserted for the better part of 2,500 years. William James in his classic *Principles of Psychology*, which was published a hundred years ago and is still considered by many to be the finest book on psychology ever written, conceptualized mental life as being characterized by the choosing of means appropriate to the attainment of desired goals.[5] Consistent with this concept he described attention as selective, as guided by interests. In the eloquent prose that has come to be associated with his name, he was formulating the well-known, intuitively sensed psychological law stating that we see (attend to) that which we want to see.

Values constitute the more permanent soil, out of which momentary interests grow. With respect to attentive focus, materialists live in a world of sleek new cars and luxurious homes; intellectuals in one of important books and stimulating thinkers; spiritualists in one replete with manifestations of the deity particular to their religion or creed. Despite the fact that persons immersed in these three value categories may live in the same city, their subjective worlds will be quite different, as will their more enduring patterns of behavior. Further, if the goals springing from their values and interests are essentially unattainable, then the stage is set for personal demoralization involving guilt, diminished self-esteem, and the lurking propensity of aberrant forms of behavior. When, in the individual case, these deeper psychological factors escalate to some critical, unpredictable flash-point and begin to cause erratic and antisocial patterns of overt behavior, as they appear to be doing at an alarming and increasing scale, the wider society may then begin to sputter and malfunction in response to the widespread personal demoralization. There is considerable evidence in support of such a second-order societal demoralization, as manifested in America's diminishing economic-industrial competitiveness on the international scene.

As suggested earlier, the parallel with organic illness is instructive. Clinical pathology, which may eventually be fatal, begins with disequilibrium at the cellular level. At the onset of the disease process the disequilibrium is undetectable to all but the medical specialist. Only as it spreads and becomes more virulent does it begin to clearly show its potential for seriously damaging or destroying the host organism.

There is, in addition, another interesting parallel between the development of a prevalent form of organic disease and the widespread vulnerability to personal demoralization under analysis here. It is well known that cardiovascular disease is the commonest form of physical illness in America. In fact, it has been called the disease of Western society. In terms of etiology, it is also patently clear by now that this disease is generally caused by ingestion of an overly rich diet. Here is where the curious etiological parallel with the pervasive demoralization exists. The demoralization, also, can be seen to stem ultimately from excessive wants, from a taste for experiences—psychical nutriments—that are generally unattainable for the average person, that are, in a word, too rich.

It is my firm belief that these excessive wants are continuously and powerfully reinforced by the imagery of unreality flowing out from the mass media. This imagery, omnipresent and aided by the arcane wizardry of modern communications technology, has an enormous potential for creating values, interests, and wants among the viewing masses. It is virtually limitless in its mind-bending capacity.

The dominant values—I might say the gods—of present-day America are overwhelmingly materialistic-hedonistic, and much of the imagery of unreality, particularly television commercials, can be thought of as having iconic significance. The TV is the real altar at which contemporary

America worships. Tony Schwartz, a recognized expert in media communications, wrote a book a few years ago entitled *Media: The Second God*. In it he commented, "The analogy between the electronic media and God obviously has its limits, and I don't want to carry it too far. However, let me suggest quite seriously that media have influenced our lives and shaped our beliefs as profoundly as any religion."[6]

To go back to my illustration concerning the differing perceptual worlds of the materialist, the intellectual, and the spiritualist, we are becoming a nation of demoralized, hedonistic materialists. It is my contention that we are being lured into this collective state of mind largely by the insidious, but pervasive influence of the imagery of unreality. Neil Postman, professor of education at New York University, in essential agreement with Tony Schwartz, put it thus:

Specifically, the purpose of media ecology is to tell . . . about the consequences of technology; to tell how media environments create contexts that may change the way we think or organize our social life, or make us better or worse, or smarter of dumber, or freer or more enslaved. . . . the power of communications technology to give shape to people's lives is not a matter that comes easily to the forefront of people's consciousness, though we live in an age when our lives—whether we like it or not—have been submitted to the demanding sovereignty of new media.[7]

There is nothing new about the materialism. America's valuative bias has been materialistic since the pilgrims landed. Nor is there anything inherently bad about materialism, at least a realistic, balanced materialism. But in America, since the end of World War II, the materialistic emphasis has increased tremendously. Because of the development and growth of the electronic media, the volume, to use an apt term, has been turned way up. As a consequence, the effect of the incongruity between the firsthand and vicarious experiential realms, which exists in all societies, has undergone something like a qualitative intensification. The subtly noxious intrapsychic stress borne daily by Americans as they face the experiential bind—with their feet on the hard pavements of the firsthand realm and their heads in the beguiling, media-spawned images of the vicarious realm—is well calculated to induce a pandemic combination of frustration, discouragement, and bewilderment (i.e., demoralization). Average people in modern America find themselves in a position analogous to that of a frail and tired beast of burden, with a heavy load on behind and a succulent carrot dangling in front—tantalizingly visible, but always just out of reach. The carrot and the load are symbolic of the two sides of the bind. The carrot is the dazzling imagery dancing constantly on the periphery, frequently in the center, of their consciousness; the load is the tiring, often numbing, round of daily firsthand experience.

And because it is virtually impossible to escape either experiential realm, most people are doomed to their plight.

The reader might ask, "What is the connection between the experiential bind and the guilt-demoralization?" or "How does facing the bind cause the guilt?" Two very relevant questions. Earlier, I referred to the bind as an inner psychological phenomenon that is fed by external structures and institutions existing in contemporary America. Further, I suggested that these external factors tend to split or fracture the totality of experience into incongruous, difficult to synthesize, aspects. But what is important here is the fact that such external factors can, and often do, leave a permanent mark or imprint on the personality. In psychological terminology they become internalized. They contribute to the formation of psychological structure. A good deal of human experience is like this. It does not bounce harmlessly off the psyche, but, rather, penetrates it, and in the process alters its total configuration. This is the principal danger of the bind psychologically speaking. It is being internalized on a societal scale. In this process of internalization, experience in the first-hand realm is generally serving to deflate peoples' sense of actual value and potency. Simultaneously, experience within the burgeoning vicarious realm is serving to inflate their sense of what they could, or ought to, or would like to, be. As a result, the dilemma is molding, slowly and insidiously, a new modal personality that has as one of its fundamental elements a serious structural weakness—an irritated and intractable self-ideal discrepancy. Chronic, corrosive guilt is the unavoidable reaction to an intractable self-ideal discrepancy. This psychodynamic structure, once it becomes fixed in the psyche, sets the stage for depleted self-esteem, demoralization, and a latent potential for erratic patterns of overt behavior.

Thus, an external societal incongruity is being internalized, on a broad scale, into a dangerous intrapsychic disharmony. This is leading to widespread personal demoralization. In addition, if we care to look, we can also see signs of the translation of these personal psychological problems into broader socio-politico-economic issues. The cellular disequilibrium is already producing symptoms in the host organism. Further, we can anticipate the development of a troubling vicious cycle: widespread demoralization leading to macro-level societal problems which weaken the nation on the international scene, will eventually result in a reduced overall standard of living which will tend to deepen the demoralization, and so on. In this case, life in the firsthand realm will become more difficult. With no mitigation in the imagery of unreality, the bind will be intensified. And one can predict with reasonable surety that this imagery will continue to dazzle Americans, no matter what the general status of their more mundane reality is.

There are no efficient panaceas for the widespread personal demoralization or the incipient second-order societal demoralization under discussion here. That is to say, there are no sweeping answers or solutions, just as there are none for the problems of poverty, ignorance, or inequality. However, a variety of techniques, attitudes, pursuits and ideologies may help persons in their individual efforts to parry the influence of the experiential bind and transcend their personal demoralization. These will be treated in detail in a later chapter.

But, in the last analysis, the individual may be the only valid approach to this thorny issue. While society, as an aggregate of interacting persons, can be seen to have numerous dynamisms of its own—economic, social, political, religious—the individual is the primary bearer of life. In order to improve the vitality of the larger society, rehabilitative efforts may well begin with individuals. To the extent that individual people can rejuvenate themselves, societal rejuvenation may come as a matter of course. Once again, the parallel with organic healing is apparent.

NOTES

1. *The Random House Dictionary of the English Language: The Unabridged Edition*, ed. Jess Stein and Laurence Urdang (New York: Random House, 1966), 365.

2. Neil Postman, *Teaching as a Conserving Activity* (New York: Delacorte Press, 1979), 50.

3. Willard Gaylin, *Feelings: Our Vital Signs* (New York: Harper & Row, 1979), 52.

4. Ibid., 53.

5. William James, *The Principles of Psychology* (Chicago: Encyclopedia Britannica, 1952), 7. While I quote this specific passage in a later chapter, James states at the end of his first chapter, "The Scope of Psychology," that "no actions but such are done for an end, and show a choice of means, can be called indubitable acts of mind"(7). This assumption was basic to his understanding of human behavior.

6. Tony Schwartz, *Media: The Second God* (New York: Random House, 1981), 9.

7. Neil Postman, *Conscientious Objections* (New York: Alfred A. Knopf, 1988), 18–19.

MEDIA BLIGHT
AND THE
DEHUMANIZING
OF
AMERICA

1

The Experiential Bind

In understanding the principal cause of demoralization of America, it is important to recall the experiential bind that is permeating life here and now. To recapitulate, an insistent incongruity between proximate, first-hand experience on the one hand and vicarious experience on the other is, on a daily basis, reinforcing a simultaneous deflation of the actual self and inflation of the ideal self in the psyche of the average person. Thus, the principal experiential pressures acting upon that psyche are dual, and in a vectorial sense, essentially divergent, creating tension within the total self analogous to that within the rope used in a tug-of-war. This analogy is appropriate because in both cases there is the tendency to an increase in internal pressure. In a tug-of-war, the opposing groups struggle to exert more and more force in their efforts to win. With the passage of time, the experiential bind can be expected to intensify, primarily because of the growth, and increased societal influence, of the mass media. The result in the general case will be a steady increase in intrapsychic tension and, hence, a mounting threat to the integrity of the personality structure. Such mounting intrapsychic tension is the familiar and predictable antecedent to troublesome psychological changes, often overtly expressed in patterns of aberrant and antisocial behavior.

Specifically, these divergent experiential pressures contribute to a chronically irritated self-ideal discrepancy that is the nuclear intrapsychic dynamic underlying the demoralization. Further, it is my contention that while the forces contributing to both sides of the experiential bind are potentially pathogenic, the more serious are those relating to vicarious experience. This is the realm in which the dangerously inflated and unrealistic standards of material achievement and success, characteristic of the collective American ideal self, are being forged.

THE IMAGERY OF UNREALITY TYPE A: FANTASY IMAGERY

There are other factors in American society feeding these unrealistic inner personal standards, but certainly the various mass media are the archculprits in the vicarious realm of experience. Within this group the electronic advertising and entertainment media are especially blameworthy. These two agencies of mass communication, aided enormously by television in the past forty years, reach into every nook and cranny of our society, creating illusions and insidiously portraying fantasy in the guise of reality.

Advertisements in general, but particularly on television, continually massage viewers with images of a "good life," that is, in effect, one that is inaccessible to most ordinary people, even though it is temptingly depicted as being just a hop, skip, and a down-payment away. Further, the lure of the endless stream of goods, services, and experiences is amplified by the fantastic atmosphere that typically surrounds the product itself—beautiful, sexy young women; dashing, forceful, super-masculine men; healthy, charming, exuberant children; exotic, glamorous settings; instantly successful and effortless outcomes; clever, comic situations; gorgeous homes; and so on ad infinitum. In sum, the product is seldom employed or experienced by ordinary people in ordinary circumstances, and viewers are constantly reminded that they could have more than they actually have, and be more than they actually are. In addition, there is an underlying element of exhortation to the entire advertising genre, a suggestion that consumers "should" purchase the goods and services being shown. This imperative nuance is contributed to by both the sender and the receiver of the message. With respect to the former, it is central to the economic pitch. With respect to the latter, communications appealing to ideals, whatever the valuative category, are inevitably received in the imperative mood. This stems from the fact that, reflecting ideals, they naturally tend to stimulate conscious and unconscious guilts in the mind of the recipient. While it can be argued that there is an aspect of truth and economic utility in the basic advertising message, it becomes pathogenic by virtue of its omnipresence and incessant repetition in the media and by the subtle distortions of reality that riddle modern advertisements.

It is relevant to note here that in general the product itself is only incidental to the main theme of the television commercial, which usually centers around such topics as sexual attractiveness, popularity, masculine adequacy, economic success, youthfulness, and robust health. Products such as Pepsi-Cola, Jordache Jeans, Hondas, and Scot Tissues acquire positive valence in viewers' minds by virtue of their artful association with value, themes that are extremely vital to people in this culture. Thus, television commercials are really not about products so much as human achievements and personal relationships. It is the incessant and sensationalized presentation of such themes that make the real appeal to the ideal self. Although, there is an added hook in the suggestion that success in these vital areas of life can be achieved through mere consumerism.

Advertising in general, and particularly on television, provides a prime example of the imagery of unreality. Existing to create spurious needs in the viewing public, and shot through with hedonistic and romantic illusions, it tends to foster expectations that the products and services depicted can in no way fulfill. Advertisements in earlier times, until approximately 1920, were largely devoted to providing potential consumers with factual information about the product in question. Today, most TV ads provide little or noting by way of technical, practical, useful information. The current advertising genre, creating psychological pressure by association, and occurring with particular power on television—with its audiovisual special effects, its minidramatizations, and its omnipresence in daily life—can be seen as a form of subtle deception par excellence.

While he is expressly concerned with the problem of rampant narcissism, Christopher Lasch's discussion of the effects of modern advertising on the individual psyche coalesces closely with my thesis concerning the influence of the imagery of unreality upon the individual's ideal self, and hence upon the problem of widespread demoralization:

Strictly considered, however, modern advertising seeks to promote not so much self-indulgence as self-doubt. It seeks to create needs, not to fulfill them; to generate new anxieties instead of allaying old ones. By surrounding the consumer with images of the good life, and by associating them with the glamour of celebrity and success, mass culture encourages the ordinary man to cultivate extraordinary tastes, to identify himself with the privileged minority against the rest, and to join them, in his fantasies, in a life of exquisite comfort and sensual refinement. Yet the propaganda of commodities simultaneously makes him acutely unhappy with his lot. By fostering grandiose aspirations, it also fosters self-denigration and self-contempt.[1]

Writing on the same problem of narcissism, Aaron Stern reaches similar conclusions concerning the advertising media's penchant for bombarding the ordinary person with images of the unattainable.

In time those who managed the media realized they could see not only things but also people. So they generated celebrities. Celebrities have become an integral part of the American way of life. No society in the world is more solicitous of them than we are. We give them too much power, we pay them too much, and we give them too much credence. . . . Celebrity power has spun out of control in this country.[2]

While these two writers view much media imagery as contributing directly to widespread narcissism, I see it as contributing to a sense of personal demoralization that in turn feeds compensatory, defensive, guilt-driven narcissism. Such narcissism poses a serious societal problem, as writers Lasch and Stern, among others, realize. However, it is its rootedness in guilt that gives the narcissism its compulsive, tenacious quality. And because the guilt, in turn, is fed by the experiential bind, the narcissism can be expected to intensify as the bind and the underlying guilt worsen.

Turning now from TV advertising to the general run of TV entertainment programs, we again encounter the imagery of unreality in unending and flagrant measure. In most television dramas—and movies, as well—an aura of superhuman achievement and prowess is substituted for the pedestrian efforts of real people. Fearless detectives (of both sexes); unflinching marshals; nerveless pilots and flight attendants; cool, incisive physicians; efficient psychotherapists, portrayed as sensitive, folksy, paragons of normalcy; recondite scientists; suave diplomats; selfless, imaginative educators; strangely eloquent blue-collar workers, all function and pursue their objectives in a manner that their counterparts in real life could not possibly approach, let alone equal. And by and large, this is all enacted by beautiful people in a temporal context of instant gratification. It is indeed fantasyland. But it is insidiously presented as being true to life.

This fantasyland is possible on carefully prepared films and videotapes because it is free of all of the antagonistic and countervailing pressures that constantly confront the striving person in the firsthand realm of experience. Actual fantasy, daydreaming, is the other mental space, so to speak, where humans can pursue their innermost desires to be free of the constraints of external reality. However, excessive involvement in fantasy can be symptomatic of severe forms of psychopathology, particularly when the turn to fantasy is uncontrollable and a function of the inability to cope with reality. And whether the reason for the immersion in fantasy is intrapsychic conflict or environmental stimulation, one consequence may well be a marked reduction in the capacity for coping with reality, which is invariably fraught with difficulties. But enough of this for now. The deeper psychodynamic consequences of media blight will be discussed in detail in a later chapter.

In addition to these dramatic excursions into fantasyland there is much on regular network television which openly parades the glamorous and spectacular, thus stimulating mental sets and expectations that are unrealistic and unreachable for most people. Some common examples include pop-music extravaganzas, all-star variety shows, movie and television awards shows, beauty contests, and sports programs involving special competition between celebrity athletes. I am not referring here to scheduled league games, which are played seriously, are relatively free of media hype, and do not involve concentrations of sports celebrities competing in irrelevant events (e.g., army obstacle courses). All such TV extravaganzas create an atmosphere featuring special effects, special accomplishments, and special people. And in a manner similar to both advertisements and dramatic productions they remind millions of ordinary people in the audience that life out there, somewhere else, is being lived at a much higher plane of glitz, glamour, and excitement. Although such programs are open in their portrayal of the fantastic and the extraordinary, thus lacking much of the distortion inherent in the dramas, they certainly contribute to the inflationary pressure acting upon the expectations of the collective American ideal self.

Even television news programs can be seen to contribute to the pressure. Despite their orientation to serious coverage of local, national, and international news, there is a strong tendency to report on the comings and goings of celebrities and "beautiful people"—their travels, accomplishments, romances, momentary tribulations, and particularly their earnings. Such coverage exposes the viewing public to ever more titillating imagery of dazzling life one step removed, existing close by but always outside one's actual grasp. I remember noting, in the mid- and late-1970s, the effects on the thinking of my own two adolescent sons of such repeated commentary about the earnings of top professional athletes. With salaries ranging from $200,000 to $800,000 a year—in that fiscally quaint and modest era—frequently waved before their eyes, they tended to react with naive contempt for the pay scales they could realistically expect as educated professionals in science, education, or law. To the boys, these more modest earnings came over as paltry recompense for so much training and effort, and I had the feeling that my comments concerning realistic plans and expectations fell, at the time, on relatively deaf ears. And why not? The sensationalistic images created by the tube, plus the omnipotence of youth, combined to effectively strip my warnings of any real meaning.

Television sitcoms and comic movies, while not necessarily emphasizing glamour and the spectacular, also add to the manifold illusions. Steeped in farce, burlesque, and rapid-fire humor, they tend to depict life and human relationships as frivolous and harmless. Whatever the plot, the characters invariably emerge from their predicaments safe and happy, aided frequently by outrageous good fortune. It is all good fun, achieved effortlessly and speedily, and it contrasts sharply with the toil and routine that characterizes much of the time spent in the firsthand experiential realm. This is not to pan humor and comedy, which serve to ease the unavoidable toil. But the volume of such programming in the mass media can also serve to obscure life's more serious side and contribute to false expectations in the minds of many regular, but undiscerning young viewers.

Aside from these specific examples of sensationalism and distortion, an atmosphere of magic tends to pervade the electronic media. Both in movies and television dramas the pace of the action is preternaturally swift and intense, with all manner of scene changes occurring effortlessly, at precisely the right moment. Further, the unpleasant, noisome, often traumatic conditions of reality—bureaucratic red tape, time spent waiting in lines, interpersonal incivilities, dirty dishes, freezing cold, sweltering heat, burned debris, violence, blood and gore—all vanish as the scenes change and the story proceeds. All are experienced in a vicariously anesthetic atmosphere, which helps to whet the viewer's appetite for ever more morbid sensationalism. This element of ease and speed in the progression from scene to scene as the story unfolds brings to mind one of William James's insights into the complexities of experience. For James, it was the relations between, or the transitions to, perceived objects that constituted much of the experiential flux, as well as our registration of it in the "stream of thought." In this regard, he states

As we take, in fact, a general view of the wonderful stream of our consciousness, what strikes us first is the different pace of its parts. Like a bird's life, it seems to be made of an alternation of flights and perchings. . . . Let us call the resting-places the 'substantive parts' [objects], and the places of flight the 'transitive parts,' of the stream of thought. It then appears that the main end of our thinking is at all times the attainment of some other substantive part than the one from which we have just been dislodged. And we may say that the main use of the transitive parts is to lead us from one substantive conclusion to another.[3]

If James's theory holds, then the lurid hedonism and the revved-up quality characterizing the thinking and behavior of many Americans, particularly the young, can be seen to receive steady reinforcement from daily exposure to this unreal pace of events inherent in media programming. On the tube, time spent on any "perching" of a pedestrian nature is inevitably cut to the point of virtual nonexistence, while the more sensational perchings, the goals, are emphasized and drawn out in an equally unrealistic and misleading manner. Finally, there is the fact that the program, whatever its content, is invariably rehearsed or rigged so that individual performances, as well as the overall presentation itself, are carried off without flaw. All of this lends a gloss to life within the electronic media that is in sharp contrast to the hard-won, yet imperfect, accomplishments of men and women in the firsthand realm of experience.

Readers might raise the point that rehearsal, skillful editing, special effects, and beautiful, talented people are necessary if the programming is to be sufficiently gripping to hold the attention of a mass audience. They might also argue that the central purpose of much entertainment is to allow the audience momentary escape from the tribulations of hard reality. Both points are valid. But the fact remains that the electronic media have the capacity to influence people profoundly, and in television's case this is greatly enhanced by its virtual omnipresence. Consider the additional fact that younger viewers, who tend to choose the more lurid and flamboyant programs, and at whom much of this kind of programming is purposely aimed by the networks, are generally less able than adults to distinguish reality from unreality. With these considerations in mind, the electronic media, with their inherent tendencies to gloss over and distort life, loom ever more ominously as potentially dangerous shapers of the public mentality.

Neil Postman, cited in the introduction, has written extensively and insightfully on the problem of media ecology. In one of his eloquently crafted works directed at the problems faced by our public schools, he distinguishes between the "first curriculum"—essentially the spectrum of entertainment programming directed at school-aged children and youth by the TV networks—and the "second curriculum"—the traditional classroom curriculum. In his analysis he shows convincingly that the second curriculum simply cannot compete with the first curriculum in the ability to entice, and rivet, the attention of this youthful audience. No one states his case more lucidly and powerfully than Postman. To me, the answer to the recurrent, worrisome question concerning the failure of public education in America—which, ironically, is aired periodically on TV—is clear. The second curriculum is difficult and at times boring; the first curriculum is effortless, exciting, and always available. Except for the rare egghead or science nerd, what average American child or adolescent is going to turn regularly and willingly to the study of geometry or American history when "Star Trek" or MTV is waiting a switchflick away? Yet all educated people know that education and literacy are a neverending process, and that they grow and deepen primarily through active individual effort—reading, writing, talking, and concerted problem-related thinking. As Postman points out, no developed nation in the world has anywhere near as much unregulated commercial TV programming available to the viewing public as America. In the terms of the present discussion, this suggests that no other citizenry is as endlessly lulled and transported by the imagery of unreality as Americans. Thus, is there any mystery to our younger generation's growing educational inadequacies, or our equally worrisome national decline in the industrial sphere?

So far, in discussing the imagery of unreality, I have concentrated on that part of it produced by the electronic advertising and entertainment media. Because of its availability and its electronic special effects, this is the most hypnotic and mind-bending strain of the wider media-spawned phenomenon.

However, elements within the printed media contribute steadily to the flood of illusions. Prime examples come from the plethora of polished "good-life" pictorial magazines that appeal primarily to highly motivated, educated, young adults, the so-called yuppies. Most of these proffer lurid imagery of the good life, with a particularly heavy sensual-sexual slant. If a person who had been kept in some remote place since birth were allowed to read only magazines of this genre, she/he would gain the distinct impression that most women are shatteringly beautiful and voluptuous; most men are muscularly well proportioned, boyishly handsome, yet determined and purposive, as implied by their facial expressions; most automobiles are either racy sports models or long, elegant limousines; most meals consumed by humans are exotically sumptuous; most people dress in utter sartorial splendor; most homes are opulent mansions situated in breathtaking surroundings; and most human relationships center around romantic adventures occurring in far-off, idyllic places.

Less polished and sophisticated are the many movies and cheesecake photo magazines appealing to perhaps a less-educated and younger segment of the viewing public. Emphasizing female pulchritude and celebrity, they would give our hypothetical isolated reader an equally narrow, possibly more tawdry, perspective on life in this society.

Of course, no one really lives in total seclusion and spends each day poring over photo magazines. But more than a few Americans spend a lot of time with them. This applies particularly to middle- and lower-class adolescents who tend to prefer the more garish movie-girlie magazines, such as *Hustler* and the *National Enquirer*, and whose tastes for such stimulation are apt to exist in a near vacuum in regard to good art, good literature, serious nonfiction, and the thought-provoking aspects of everyday reality. As all of these viewers casually leaf through the pages and ponder the banquet within, their appetites are likely to be whetted, and their expectations concerning entry into that life-style gently, but firmly fanned. In psychodynamic terms, many of them are unconsciously identifying with the depicted figures. But because, in truth, these readers are really not at all like those fictitious figures on the page, they are courting disillusionment, inadvertently opening themselves to personal demoralization.

On the subject of magazines, it should be noted that other more respectable publications also contribute to the flood of imagery, albeit in subtler, less lurid, ways. Women's magazines of the *Better Homes and Gardens*, *Good Housekeeping*, and *McCalls* variety literally bulge with arresting images—beautiful homes, tastefully decorated rooms, exotic dishes, romantic vacation settings, the latest and most stylish apparel modeled by perfectly proportioned men and women—in the form of advertisements and illustrations for feature articles. Central to the unreality of this imagery is the covert suggestion that this domestic cornucopia is within reach of all interested consumers.

Admittedly, I have listed only a few examples of elements within the printed media that contribute to the imagery of unreality impinging upon Americans on a daily basis. There are many more. In general, however, it is the pictorial magazines, presenting their messages in arresting images, as the electronic media do, that add to the illusory quality of life in contemporary America. Magazines emphasizing written materials contribute much less to this illusory atmosphere, as is also the case with newspapers, which are heavily verbal in spite of their revolutionary use of photos in this century.

Carefully crafted visual images are more immediately interesting and spellbinding than are passages of words, at least at the outset before the respondent has had a chance to study the passage and allow its meaning to sink in. The adage that a picture is worth a thousand words is apposite here, particularly in our fast-paced society where everybody is in a hurry. Furthermore, pictures, as analogic symbols, appeal more to the right hemisphere of the cerebral cortex, the so-called right brain, which is more primitive evolutionary, and which is neurologically more involved in the integration of relatively primitive emotional and appetitive behavior patterns than is the left cerebral hemisphere, which, in turn, is both more advanced evolutionally and neurologically more involved in the higher mental processes of humans—speech, abstraction, analytical thinking. Registration of a picture's message is essentially effortless, as well as instantaneous. Reading the meaning out of a printed passage, which entails active decoding of digital symbols, is basically more difficult and slower. Thus, there appears to be an ironic mixture of mutually reinforcing factors contributing to the illusory character of life in contemporary America, and to the general acceptance of the imagery of unreality therein. Technology has quickened the pace of life; the message of pictures is easier and quicker of apprehension than that of word chains; pictures appeal to a less discriminating, more wishful, aspect of our basic mentality. The irony lies in the fact that the development of the underlying technology required inordinate amounts of the higher, more discriminating and disciplined, aspect of that same mentality.

But applications of technological advances are a matter of societal values, and the imagery of unreality is a result of the overriding hedonistic materialism that pervades the present American ethos. However, this ethos did not originate with the coming of media technology. It has deeper, older roots, roots that from the standpoint of history can be seen to have fostered Western science and technology. Now, perversely, some of the fruit of that technology is lending itself to the virulent spread of these values and, in this process, to the dehumanizing of Western culture. This development brings to mind Norman Cousins's famous essay "Modern Man Is Obsolete," published in 1945, just after the end of World War II.[4] Cousins's thesis was that modern humans are capable of inventing technologies that they are not able to effectively restrict to ethical, socially beneficial uses. That is, their moral development is obsolete compared with their burgeoning intellectual prowess. It would appear that Cousins's thoughts on this subject have shown rare prescience and stood up well to the test of time.

In considering the source of the imagery of unreality, I have laid the essential blame at the feet of the mass media. In the interest of accuracy, however, the analysis needs qualification. The media are a fundamental part of the structure of modern postindustrial society, and in the future they are destined to grow steadily. They are the basic information system of postindustrial society, and for many citizens the TV provides the principal window onto the world around. And certainly, a good deal of what they produce affords education, entertainment, and news in accordance with the highest standards of quality and taste.

Nevertheless, I believe that my analysis is essentially correct, supporting the conclusion that much, far too much, of what the media disseminate to the public on a daily basis can be seen to have a deleterious effect on society at large, can be seen as a form of airwave pollution. If one thinks of experience as psychical nutriment analogous to food as physical nutriment—a tenable analogy that has been used by other writers—then the specter of media-produced airwave pollution takes on serious implications in connection with the mental health of the general public. The point is that the health and development of the human psyche is largely dependent on the quality of the individual's experience, and a steady diet of unrealistic vicarious experience may serve to undermine psychological health in much the same way that an unbalanced food diet may serve to undermine physical health. Put somewhat simply, it follows that physically, people are what they have eaten; and psychically, they are what they have experienced. Although this nutritional analogy is perhaps crude, it does have a certain utility in alerting the reader to the mind-bending capacities of the mass media. They are powerful and potentially dangerous, and it is naive to toss them off as harmless diversions. C. Wright Mills sees this clearly, and his comments are instructive:

The media have not only filtered into our experience of external realities, they have also entered our very experience of ourselves. They have provided us with new identities and new aspirations of what we should like to be, and what we should like to appear to be. They have provided in the models of conduct they hold out to us a new and a larger and more flexible set of appraisals of our very selves. . . . we may say the media bring the reader, listener, viewer, into the sight of larger, higher reference groups—groups real or imagined, up-close or vicarious, personally known or distractedly glimpsed—which are looking glasses for his self-image. More than that: (1) the media tell the man in the mass who he is—they give him identity; (2) they tell him what he wants to be—they give him aspirations; (3) they tell him how to get that way—they give him technique; and (4) they tell him how to feel that he is that way even when he is not—they give him escape. The gaps between the identity and aspiration lead to technique or escape. That is probably the basic psychological formula of the mass media today. But, as a formula, it is not attuned to the development of the human being. It is the formula of a pseudoworld which the media invent and sustain.[5]

The statistics concerning public use of the electronic media grow with every year. Recently, while driving to work and listening to the radio, I learned that the average amount of time Americans spend, per day, watching TV is seven hours. This indicates that the portion of each day devoted to experience within the vicarious realm is almost equal to that devoted to work, the principal activity within the proximate realm for most adults. And because TV programs can combine both visual and auditory stimulation with dramatic presentation and special effects, this experience, though wholly passive, can have deep and lasting psychological impact. In fact, it is conceivable that much media experience has more psychological impact than firsthand experience, because of the artificial intensities pumped into it by special effects and related technology.

This particular kind of vicarious experience is uniquely capable of influencing the ideal self, which naturally tends to form itself around heroic models and achievements perceived at a distance. While the details will be discussed in the next chapter, I believe that a good deal of this media-based vicarious experience stimulates the process of individual identification with the characters and activities appearing on the screen, as well as with the values implied. In this process, which is fundamental to personality change throughout the life cycle, people begin to mold themselves, consciously or unconsciously, after the imagery in question, and as a consequence structural changes are apt to occur within their ideal selves. While there are individual differences among viewers in the extent to which this identification takes place, in all too many cases—especially among the young and uneducated—it can be seen as a basic source of the pathological inflation occurring within the collective American ideal self.

Evidence for this contention is gained from the impression that the whole society is vibrating in sympathy with the media, such that echoes of the imagery of unreality constantly impinge on the individual from all sides. People in every age group reflect their preoccupation with it in their dress and social behavior.

Among many of the young there is a transparent effort to resemble Hollywood celebrities or "beautiful people," and the illusion is fostered with the help of stylish sunglasses, formfitting clothes, flamboyant hairdos, cosmetics, and exercise and diet regimens. In this age group much social behavior is fraught with one-upmanship and affectation. An unwritten, but intuitively sensed code forbids open admission of ignorance on a subject, along with careless expressions of exuberance, amusement, and amiability. Every effort, it seems, is devoted to maintaining a "cool" and sophisticated image.

In the older group, conspicuous consumption and an often pitiable attempt to remain forever young, attractive, and chic are common examples of the societal echoes under focus. Aware of this same phenomenon, David Fischer describes, with a touch of irony, the ludicrous consequences of middle-aged adults attempting to project the image of youth.

This historian observed a Boston matron on the far side of fifty, who might have worn a graceful palla in ancient Rome, dressed in a miniskirt and leather boots. He saw a man in his sixties, who might have draped himself in the dignity of a toga, wearing hiphugger jeans and a tie-dyed T-shirt. He witnessed a conservative businessman, who in an earlier generation might have hesitated each morning, wondering whether to wear black or charcoal gray, going to the office in white plastic shoes, chartreuse trousers and cerise shirt, purple aviator glasses, and a Prince Valiant haircut. Most astonishing were college professors who put aside their Harris tweeds and adopted every passing adolescent fad with an enthusiasm all out of proportion to their years. One season it was the Nehru jacket; another, dashikis; the next, railroad overalls. In the early 1970s it was love beads and leather jackets. Every twist and turn of teenage fashion revolutionized their costumes. But always, old was out and young was in.[6]

Such examples of individual posturing and groping, while representing minute bits of the illusory atmosphere within American society, can also be seen in many instances as symptoms of underlying feelings of inadequacy, which are integral to the demoralization. Thus, we can see an example on a societal scale of the well-known neurotic vicious cycle, in which successive elements within a response loop tend to reinforce one another and perpetuate the maladaptive loop. In this case, posturing and affectation on the part of countless people, who are themselves struggling with feelings of inadequacy, tend to perpetuate the illusions that induce similar feelings and behaviors in yet other people.

Why, if we take the trouble to look, do we see so much posturing and affectation among the young, and strained, often pathetic, groping for youth and beauty among so many of the middle-aged and elderly? And why are feelings of personal inadequacy so prevalent among people in modern America? A major part of the answer to these two question lies in an understanding of the effects produced by the imagery of unreality as it shoots out from the mass media and ricochets from person to person throughout the wider society. Admittedly, the young have always postured and strutted, while those of advancing years have always yearned for their fading youth; and in both cases, feelings of inadequacy have undoubtedly been at least part of the underlying motivation for such behavior. But one gets the impression that somehow in America in the last four decades or so all of this reaching and straining has greatly increased, that somehow the "volume"—to repeat the electronic metaphor used earlier—has been turned way up. And that is precisely what has happened. The volume of the imagery has increased enormously, and in proportionate measure, the volume of natural human reaction to that imagery has likewise increased.

THE FIRSTHAND EXPERIENTIAL REALM

In recapitulating the experiential bind at the beginning of this chapter, I relegated the realms of firsthand, proximate experience to a secondary position in terms of its contribution to the underlying dynamics of the demoralization. In my mind, it is the realm of vicarious experience, superheated by the mass media, that is causing the individual self the more acute internal stress. Further, it is the explosion of experience in this realm that is peculiar to modern postindustrial society, and unique historically.

However, much experience within the juxtaposed firsthand, proximate realm is also psychologically stressful, even noxious, to huge numbers of people in modern America and is capable in its own right of causing the self internal stress. In terms of its implications for individual self-regard, much of this experience, when boiled down and stripped of appearances, carries a hard lesson for great numbers of average people in America today. Reinforced daily, this lesson instructs them that, as individuals, they are insignificant within the larger scheme of things; they are relatively powerless; and that in the end they matter to only a precious few. In the course of time, this general message is internalized by most average people and becomes the ineradicable and inescapable ground of their sense of themselves as they actually are. The mechanism of internalization, in this case, is simple conditioning that has been steadily reinforced for however long the person has been seriously involved in the firsthand realm.

Of course, this occurs idiosyncratically with each person, so that the individual's actual self retains unique elements, while bearing this common stamp. Also, I do not mean to suggest that for the average person in modern America, all experience has this psychologically deflating quality. Just as it is possible to escape the imagery of unreality in the vicarious realm, so can one experience much in the firsthand realm that is genuinely satisfying, and elevating to his/her actual self. But the situations and conditions of life serving to humble or deflate the actual self are widespread and deeply rooted in the structure of our society.

It is really the pace and complexity of life in postindustrial society that are the root sources of self-deflation in the firsthand realm. All of the following specific examples are intimately bound up with these two fundamentals. Specialization and automation in the workplace, huge business or industrial organizations, confusing technical systems, insensitive bureaucracies, mushrooming governments, sprawling and deteriorating urban environments, overcrowded highways and shopping areas, frenetic schedules, and the overarching fact of increasing social-interpersonal alienation are all potential sources of a quality of self-experienced daily phenomena that naturally erodes the individual's sense of personal value and potency.

Specialization and automation tend to rob work of much of its enjoyment and meaning; recent reports indicate that boredom and dissatisfaction are commonplace in jobs across the entire occupational spectrum.[7] Complex technical systems used in business, industry, government, and education confuse most people, even those working within them on a regular basis, and as a consequence engender generalized feelings of insecurity and personal inadequacy. Many, if not most, people in the work force are employed by huge organizations that create a sense of anonymity among their employees. Increasingly, the individual worker's identity within the organization is marked by a number, and a man or a woman's record of employment is coded in nothing more personal than a succession of electronic bytes in the memory disk of a computer. Public agencies characterized by insensitive and time-consuming bureaucratic procedures induce frustration, mistrust, and feelings of helplessness among those unfortunate persons immediately dependent on them, and thus subjected to their maddening inertia. At a distance from the average person, but still highly visible, are mushrooming state and national governments that seem to have great power in the lives of people but which appear to bristle with a mixture of dishonest politicians, incomprehensible legal codes, and ineffective machinery. It is a well-known fact that governments in modern society tend to elicit pervasive feelings of mistrust within the citizenry, and this is clearly the case in America. People seem to sense that the social, economic, and political systems around them run by themselves, and that neither their votes nor the promises and programs of political leaders have any real effect on the established momentum. Even broader and more basic than any of the foregoing factors is the cold, uncivil quality of transitory interpersonal relationships. At the office, in shopping malls, at large public gatherings, in public agencies, at transportation terminals, on the sidewalk, and particularly on the roadways, interpersonal relationships are characterized by a disheartening combination of indifference, impatience, and frank hostility. In the more intimate and perduring spheres of marriage and family, human relationships are increasingly tinged with alienation, conflict, and chronic dissatisfaction; and largely because of this deteriorating interpersonal climate such basic and necessary human connections are being severed at an alarming rate.

While reactions such as boredom, dissatisfaction, mistrust, helplessness, alienation, confusion, and impotent anger are subjectively distressing, even painful, it is the imprint left by such experience on the self-regard of the individual that is the more serious consequence of this general state of affairs. Repeated experience, day after day and year after year, molds individual self-regard, producing within the person deep, enduring assumptions about his/her real worth as a human. If the tone of that experience is consistently negative, it will unavoidably tend to deflate and undermine this pivotal element of personality.

As with my rather cursory treatment of the vicarious realm, this sketch of the firsthand realm is also brief. The list of potentially self-deflating experiences is by no means exhaustive. But it really doesn't seem necessary to meticulously catalog and analyze all of the probable situations and circumstances of this unavoidable realm of activity in which the average person has, or can have, experiences that deflate his/her actual self. Besides, this whole concept is familiar. It is widely recognized that in modern mass society—as compared to older cultures, or contemporary rural societies—the individual tends to be diminished, sort of lost in the shuffle, and in the process is apt to incur lasting psychological scars. Again, C. Wright Mills's reflections on this issue are pertinent.

And in the mass, he [man] loses the self-confidence of the human being—if indeed he ever had it. For life in a society of masses implants insecurity and furthers impotence; it makes men uneasy and vaguely anxious; it isolates the individual from the solid group; it destroys firm group standards. Acting without goals, the man in the mass just feels pointless.[8]

The plight of the average person in modern mass society has long been the concern of serious observers and thinkers. The term alienation—referring to a combination of estrangement, isolation, and chronic feelings of powerlessness—has come to symbolize modern humanity's generalized psychological malaise. Depending on the individual writer's background and bias, this condition has been attributed to such factors as the machine, mass communications, the size of modern communities, the transition from gemeinschaft to gesellschaft, capitalist commodity production, loss of traditional religion, and original sin.

In regard to postindustrial society, the latest phase of modern mass society, Alvin Toffler's concept of future shock provides special insight into the contemporary human predicament. Emphasizing the overwhelming and accelerating rate of technology-driven social change, he states:

"Rising rates of change thus compel us not merely to cope with a faster flow, but with more and more situations to which previous experience does not apply. And the psychological implications of this simple fact . . . are nothing short of explosive."[9] A bit further along in the same discussion he adds, "Relationships that once endured for long spans of time now have shorter life expectancies. It is this abbreviation, this compression, that gives rise to an almost tangible feeling that we live rootless and uncertain, among shifting dunes."[10]

All of this is bad enough. But the experiential bind can be seen to add another dimension to the manifold forces tearing at the total self of contemporary Americans. In a sense it raises the stress quotient to a second power. Since the onset of media saturation—dating back to the coming of television, roughly 1950—a set of societal stressors operating on one vector and primarily influencing the actual self have been complicated by another equally strong set of stressors operating on the opposite vector and primarily influencing the ideal self.

Of course, it goes without saying that all societies in all historical periods confront the individual with models and standards that exert a pull on the ideal self and also raise personal expectations. However, in modern postindustrial society the media magnification of this idealizing process has resulted in something like qualitative change, or a quantum leap in the terms of modern physics. As a consequence the experiential bind has become intensified to the point that it is now capable of fomenting the pervasive personal demoralization under discussion.

Consider the hordes of average citizens—accountants, engineers, machinists, secretaries, salesclerks, housewives, social workers, truck drivers, students, unemployed workers, members of a minority group— plodding anonymously, but steadily, through their daily routines. The chances are very good that they worry about money, and in fact have no real surplus; find their regular work or study activities rather monotonous and seemingly irrelevant; are vaguely aware that they exist in and depend on a complex life-support system about which they understand next to nothing; distractedly follow the machinations of local, state, national, and international governments with a mixture of confusion, distrust, and helpless anger; view their spouses, children, relatives, and themselves as normal and healthy, but not beautiful or charismatic, people; frequently encounter functionaries in agencies and business firms who, in the impersonal administration of affairs, make them feel more like shadows than human beings; are living from day to day with no grand design or compelling goal; and know, in the back of their minds, that in not too many years they will go the way of all flesh, unnoticed and unmourned, except by a very few.

Acting in counterpoint to all of this is the imagery of fantasy, with its lure of luxury and abundance, and its incessant portrayal of celebrity, glamour, and success. Intruding constantly and from all sides, whether in bright beams direct from the electronic media or by way of softer reflections from individual posturing and affectation, it tantalizes average people, and at the same time, by comparison, puts the hard facts of their lives into a dim, pedestrian light. Caught in this inescapable experiential bind, it is inevitable that many such people will begin to doubt themselves, and will begin implicitly asking the painful and perplexing questions, "What is wrong with me? Why can't I make it?" This is the essential negative self-regard within the demoralization; and these generic questions express the corrosive guilt underlying the demoralization. The incongruity between vicarious experience and firsthand experience has been internalized into the condition of chronically irritated self-ideal discrepancy. With the acquisition of this pathogenic intrapsychic structure, the demoralization will be internally fed and, thus, self-perpetuating.

The truth of the matter is, when measured by the facts of reality rather than by perceptions of the imagery of unreality, there is little wrong with them. Compared with most human beings on earth, either now or in ages past, they are making it, and with considerable margin. Mesmerized by the imagery, though, they cannot see this; and they cannot transcend their painful, guilt-driven demoralization.

THE IMAGERY OF UNREALITY TYPE B: DOOM IMAGERY

In discussing the principal vicarious determinant of the pervasive demoralization hovering over the American public, I have heaped much blame at the feet of the mass media and their dubious creation: the imagery of fantasy. But this endless, hypnotic flow of garishly hedonistic images, together with its supporting dialogue and/or propaganda, is really only one aspect of the broader phenomenon of media blight. The other principal aspect, which constantly proffers a different strain of airwave pollution, might be called the imagery of doom. Its main source is the collective news media. Its main form is a wearying, sensationalized preoccupation with tragedy and crime as news subjects, what Paul Harvey, the syndicated radio newscaster has aptly referred to as "the bleak, the black, and the bloody."

While this imagery does not directly feed the demoralization in question via irritation of normal self-ideal discrepancy, it can be seen to contribute indirectly by inflaming general fears and insecurities among the viewing public. In this sense, its intrapsychic imprint can be seen to contribute more to deflation of the actual self than inflation of the ideal self. Hence, treatment of this aspect of media blight would seem to belong here in the discussion, despite the fact that personal engagement with this imagery is essentially vicarious experience.

These two aspects of media blight, which on television in particular occur in dizzying kaleidoscopic mixture, regularly confront viewers with violent perceptual incongruities. One instant, as part of the body of the news program, it is a live audiovisual report of murder, arson, rape, or political terrorism; the next instant, as a commercial is programmed in, it is a romantic idyll in a Caribbean lagoon, replete with brilliant sun, shining sea, beautiful people, background music, and so on, in endless procession.

Physiologically, this kind of swift, violent change creates great stress, and it is conducive to various forms of bodily depletion—weight, energy, coordination—as well as illness. I am suggesting a parallel in the psychological sphere. The rapid and random alternation of elements of the imagery of fantasy with those of the imagery of doom is psychologically stressful because it is confusing and difficult to integrate emotionally. It creates an atmosphere of dissonance, shock, and uncanny variation that undermines security and our sense of the predictable. Put differently, it lends a subtle quality of surrealism to life around us. That it is conducive to demoralization seems abundantly clear. In fact, it brings the term schizophrenogenic to mind. This term, used in theories of the psychogenesis of schizophrenia, refers to experiences occurring in the infant's life that might predispose it to the development of this severe form of functional psychosis. Carl Jung, the great Swiss psychiatrist and one of Sigmund Freud's early disciples, described the schizophrenic's waking state as similar to the normal person's dream, which is typically surrealistic. It does not seem overly farfetched to suggest that the electronic news and advertising media, in contributing to this quality of environmental surrealism, are inadvertently lending a kind of schizophrenogenic element to society at large. The common symptom of schizophrenic "blunting" provides some support for this idea. Blunting, a quality of emotional flatness, is interpreted by psychiatrists as a self-protective form of withdrawal from the mental turmoil characteristic of the acute schizophrenic breakdown. It tends to typify the symptom picture in chronic schizophrenia, which generally follows the acute phase in severe, intractable cases of this illness. While I do not want to overdraw this connection, and am not for a moment suggesting that the media cause schizophrenia, parallels can be instructive. Perhaps there is a functional connection between the tendency of many contemporary Americans to show indifference to suffering and violence, and the presence, on a daily basis, of this surrealistic imagery on the omnipresent tube. And perhaps, too, there is a remote self-protective parallel between this "normal" indifference and schizophrenic blunting. Bruno Bettleheim and Victor Frankl, in their psychological analyses of life in the Nazi concentration camps, described a similar form of indifference to the suffering of others as a common reaction among the helpless prisoners. Both of these psychiatrists, who were themselves inmates of the camps, interpreted this emotional blunting as a primitive psychological survival mechanism, necessitated by the atmosphere of sadistic, yet random and unpredictable, violence into which these formerly normal humans had been thrown.

Like the imagery of fantasy, the imagery of doom is pervasive in modern America. Its principal sources are television, radio, newspapers, and weekly news magazines. These conduits spew forth an endless and surging river of bad news. Newspaper headlines and daily radio and TV news broadcasts overflow with brief, staccato reports of natural disasters, bizarre accidents, murder, arson, rape, theft, drug abuse, child abuse, corruption in government, shady business deals, miscalculations by scientists and other supposedly learned authorities, inflation, recession, environmental pollution, political terrorism, local warfare, nuclear threat, international crises, and so on, ad nauseam. Newspaper editorials, special programs on TV, and serious articles in magazines, constantly criticize, expose, lampoon, and second-guess. A recently added genre, tabloid television, contributes a sensationalized, quasi-voyeuristic ripple to the river of bad tidings, as if the purpose of the program were to ghoulishly offer the audience an intimate peek at the latest example of human degradation. Which, of course, is precisely the case. Virtually every politician and leader is depicted as corrupt or inept. Virtually every program in government, business, science, and education is described as somehow ill conceived, wasteful, obsolete, or inadequate. Issues on the international scene are invariably portrayed as being on the brink of collapse, while at the same time managed by hapless or singularly self-aggrandizing leaders.

Alvin Toffler, whose book *Future Shock* I have cited, has published another thought-provoking social analysis entitled *The Third Wave*. His basic thesis is that second-wave civilization, industrialism, is in its death throes and is being superseded by third-wave civilization. Because it has not yet fully manifested itself, Toffler does not try to label third-wave civilization. However, he does spend a great deal of time adumbrating it and describing its probable features. He devotes an entire chapter to the breakdown and paralysis of our present, second-wave political and governmental structures. In his discussion he remarks:

Today, although its gravity is not yet recognized, we are witnessing a profound crisis not of this or that government but of representative democracy itself, in all its forms. In one country after another, the political technology of the second wave is sputtering, groaning and malfunctioning dangerously.[11]

While Toffler attributes this dysfunction to a variety of trends integral to the demise of second-wave civilization, it seems clear that a compulsively critical press, aided by the power of the electronic media, is a significant factor. Toffler's comments suggest this, and I quote him liberally.

Watching Second Wave politicians stumble and flail drunkenly at the problems arising from the emergence of the Third Wave, millions of people, spurred on by the press, have arrived at a single, easy-to-understand explanation of our woes: the "failure of leadership." If only a messiah would appear on the political horizon and put things back together again.[12]

Similarly, the "honeymoon" with the press that the new president once enjoyed was truncated in time. Carter, even before inauguration, was blasted for his cabinet selections and forced to withdraw his choice for head of the CIA.[13]

Our so-called "contemporary" political systems are copied from models invented before the advent of the factory system—before canned food, refrigeration, gaslight or photography, before the Bessemer furnace. . . . before radio and television began working their alchemy on our minds.[14]

The term "negative alchemy" seems more appropriate. How can any leader, public figure, program, or plan maintain credibility in the face of this ceaseless barrage of criticism and pejorative innuendo? Or, from the standpoint of the viewing public, how are average people to maintain any semblance of faith in leaders and institutions in the face of the same assault? Toffler speaks of a collapse of consensus, a splintering of the electorate into a multiplicity of special interest groups that keep changing identity and purpose.

Thus the rise of diversity means that, although our political systems are theoretically founded on majority rule, it may be impossible to form a majority even on issues critical to survival. In turn, this collapse of consensus means that more and more governments are minority governments, based on shifting and uncertain conditions.[15]

Considering the omnipresent influence of the imagery of doom, this development is not hard to understand, at least in part. When the ship is going down, or appears to be, people rush around clutching at anything and everything, and they are apt to discard numerous objects of survival in their frantic search for the safest thing. While this metaphor may be a bit overdrawn, and while the imagery of doom may be but one of a multiplicity of factors contributing to this growing loss of political consensus, I believe that this imagery is feeding distrust and unrest, even mild paranoia, among the electorate. In a representative democracy this can only shackle elected leaders and impede the system.

I understand the importance of a free press and an informed electorate in the fruitful functioning of our democratic political process. And I am aware that one of the principal roles of the press in a democracy is that of watchdog in relation to the agencies of government and other concentrations of wealth and power. Further, I believe that power tends to corrupt, and that absolute power tends to corrupt absolutely. But there is something to be said for balance, for perspective, for affirmative reporting—for good news. Surely, some of our leaders are capable people; sometimes they have good days and good ideas; some aspects of important plans and programs, whatever the institution, are valuable and successful. And surely, there are other things to report, within the daily routine of local, city, national, and international events, than murder, arson, rape, theft, senatorial sex scandals, localized foreign insurgencies, international drug cartels, and the like.

I have frequently had the experience of either watching a television news program or listening to its equivalent on the radio and gaining the distinct impression that civilization is literally coming apart at the seams, self-destructing; but then, diverting my attention to life around me, receiving the fresh and reassuring impression that, in my own immediate sphere at least, things are still working—people are courteous, automobiles glide smoothly down the street at safe speeds, the water in the faucets is potable, and there are no atomic mushroom clouds on the horizon. These moments of vivid incongruity between personal experience and media-induced vicarious experience illustrate, to me, the intense illusion-creating power of the electronic media. As I sit here and think about them, I am reminded of Barbara Tuchman's comment to the effect that everything appearing on TV is magnified by a factor of ten in the minds of the viewing public.

Speaking of wrenching incongruities, I am bemused each night at the antics of the various television news teams. While deluging the audience with reports of every conceivable crime, malfeasance, and tragedy, the members of the team are apt to quip and joke with one another like college students at a beach party, and then at the end of the program heartily wish everyone a happy and tranquil evening. It is as incongruous as a team of physicians bantering with one another as they inform their patient that he/she has terminal cancer and then cheerfully telling him/her to rest easy as the consultation ends. True, it would be too much to have the nightly installment of morbid news delivered in dour tones by grim-faced announcers. That is no solution, particularly from the standpoint of audience appeal. But a certain amount of good news, other than in the areas of sports and weather when the home team has won and the sun is going to shine, would balance out the bad news and complement the feel-good presentation of the newscasters.

Why do the news media inundate us with so much bad news? A number of plausible reasons come readily to mind. One, bad news has a curious attraction to people, and because of this it raises the probability of a large audience for the nightly news, a prime consideration of the commercial interests backing the program. I have mentioned Paul Harvey, the syndicated radio news reporter, who threw light on this during one of his own broadcasts, wondering about the preponderance of the ''bleak, black, and bloody'' in the daily news, as well as to why the public is willing to tolerate it. His answer to the second part of his query reflected the maxim that misery loves company. Bad news is intriguing to many people because it suggests to them that they are not alone in their troubles. When people have the sense of spinning their wheels in the mud, it is subtly gratifying to hear of others who are caught in similar or deeper ruts. When others are pulled down by circumstance or their own poor judgment, we are elevated in relation to them. This egoistic malevolence lurking below the more amicable social surface of normal humans is well known to psychologists, and its propensity is heightened in a culture wherein the fundamental interpersonal mode is individual competition. Further, it would be an expectable concomitant of the demoralized personality, with its chronic self-dissatisfaction and lingering suspicion that somehow one is not keeping pace with those who are considered the successful people. Such an attitude is calculated to feed a morbid interest in bad news, because such news serves to allay or mitigate this lurking suspicion. My hunch is that in countless instances the widespread, guilt-driven, demoralization is working in just this manner in regard to the imagery of doom, thereby providing it with an irrefutable public sanction. After all, what the public wants and is willing to pay for, is what goes in a free-market, capitalistic economy.

Secondly, bad news has an element of the sensational to it. Even without the above malevolence operating, it captures our attention in a way that much good news does not. One cannot really talk about unconscious malevolence in examining the fascination with natural disasters such as the San Francisco earthquake. But there is probably something of the ''There, but for the grace of God, go I'' sentiment lying at the root of the fascination. This sentiment, though not really malevolent, is congruent with our primordial survival instincts. And this basic instinctual interest, also, gives bad news ready marketability.

But this is no excuse for allowing it to saturate the news media. The task of a responsible press is to inform the public in regard to all new developments: good, indifferent, and bad. Just as educators in the past twenty-five years have been challenged to make their materials relevant and interesting to students, so must the news media seek ways to enliven coverage of things that may be simultaneously less sensational but more representative of the range of daily events. If this could be achieved, then the news would be more educative, and absorption of it would enable citizens to keep their fingers realistically on the pulse of the area being reported on. No history teacher worth his/her salt would limit lectures on the Roman Empire to an enumeration of massacres at the Colosseum, failed military campaigns, and senatorial scandals and murders. There simply was much more to the Roman Empire or it would never have existed, let alone enduring for 1,000 years. Similarly, there is much more to the contemporary world scene than the daily installment of the imagery of doom would suggest.

A third factor applies more to special news programs, magazine articles, and editorials, which abound with criticism and denigration, no matter what their subject. This compulsion to negative analysis can be partly attributed to a combination of impotence and a related compensatory need to appear knowledgeable and sagacious, that is, to maintain a prestigious image. In this sense, the media pundits find themselves in a position analogous to that of psychiatrists and other mental health specialists, particularly those working in past eras. Lacking effective therapies and working from naive models of mental health, the common recourse of such specialists, both in dealing with the situation and maintaining their professional image, was to apply clinical terms and labels that were essentially demeaning to the patient. Thus, a perplexing set of habits and reactions became pseudo-neurotic schizophrenia, with pre-Oedipal libidinal fixations, weak ego boundaries, pan-anxiety, unstable object-cathexes, and poor reality testing. It would border on professional incompetence for the wise doctor not to find something wrong, or to be unable to present his findings in lengthy, esoteric terms. For him to plead ignorance and suggest that all concerned back off and leave well enough alone, at least for the moment, would be out of the question. An implicit rule similar to Murphy's Rule or Parkinson's Law suggests itself here: If an expert cannot help, he must be able to find something seriously wrong. The news analysts appear to react accordingly. Reporting on issues they really do not understand—in terms of a firsthand confrontation with the complexities and pressures involved—and having no workable solutions to offer, they fall back on endless criticism. After all, things aren't proceeding neatly and efficiently. There must be something terribly wrong: stupidity, corruption, weak leadership. Like the descriptive psychiatrists of yesterday, they render little help. And while I cannot prove it, I believe they are worsening things. Although he was referring to a different group in a different context and time frame, they bring to mind Spiro Agnew's "nattering nabobs of negativity."

I can imagine an amused reporter or television commentator reading this and thinking, "The fool is an ostrich. He wants the whole country to stick its head in the sand and pretend that the danger is not there." Not at all! But, within this discussion, there is a firm plea for balance and perspective, for an accurate and representative sampling of events in the subject matter of the daily news.

Another member of the press might also point out that if people know where to look, they can find a profusion of scholarly analyses of current events that do treat their subjects with balance and perspective. I do not doubt this. But average American citizens do not read scholarly articles in such magazines as the *Atlantic* or *Harper's*, let alone the more academic professional journals. Above all, they watch television and read their daily newspapers, and less frequently, they browse idly through news magazines such as *Time* and *Newsweek*. They get their information—in fact, their basic picture of the world around them—from the mass media. And it is in the mass media, particularly television, that the communications blight under discussion abounds.

It is a safe assumption that most executives within the electronic media have little understanding of the mind-bending power of their industry, particularly in regard to its capacity to foment widespread individual unrest, even psychopathology, and thus to weaken the adaptive capacity, the very life force, of the larger society and the nation. Oh, yes, they're familiar with the marketing potential of clever advertisements, as well as the profitability inherent in fantasy-rich dramas that appeal to the lowest common denominator of public taste, and hence to the largest audiences. But awareness of the power of the electronic media in motivating people to spend their money would be expected of industry executives. It is syntonic with their own success motives. However, this narrow awareness is distinct from insights into their industry's darker potentials in connection with the public's mental health. Further, it can literally suppress such insights. As William James taught so long ago, people see (perceive) what they want to see and unconsciously ignore that which controverts their deeper interests.

Although the main thrust of a review by George Comstock and others supports the contention that violence on television tends to foster a predisposition to violence and aggression among viewers, other related influences are also indicated. A number of these studies suggest that many people, especially the young and the poor, believe that television accurately reflects the world around them. In a staff report to the National Committee on the Causes and Prevention of Violence, A. E. Siegel concluded:

Television is an especially authentic medium because of its vividness and apparent fidelity in portraying what is before the camera. This makes television news especially credible, and much evidence indicates that television entertainment often is perceived as credible—as a reasonable representation of the way people behave. . . . Adults as well as children may imitate what they observe. The immediate increase in airline bomb threats following the television showing of "The Doomsday Flight," which involved a bomb on an airliner, is an example. . . . Television may be particularly influential in shaping the behavior of younger children because they are unable to distinguish fact from fiction when each is presented with similar fidelity, as occurs on television. Nevertheless, adults too, may be affected, as the "Doomsday" experience indicates.[16]

In another study on the influence of media violence on children's role expectations, Siegel concluded that her data support the hypothesis that audiences generalize from the content of the mass media to their social world.[17] B. S. Greenberg and B. Dervin, studying the use of the mass media by the urban poor, found that, compared to a higher-income group, children and teenagers from lower-income families and black families reported devoting more time to TV and expressed greater belief that TV accurately portrays real life.[18] Researching television's impact on everyday life, J. P. Robinson and P. E. Converse found that ownership of a television set influenced the way people spend their time (watching) far more than ownership of an automobile (driving) or ownership of a major appliance (doing housework). Robinson and Converse concluded, "Thus, at least in a temporal sense, television appears to have had greater influence on the structure of daily life than any other innovation in this century."[19]

A few years back, *Time* magazine ran an article on unemployment in the urban ghettos. A photograph within the text of this piece depicted two men in a littered doorway in Harlem drinking and idling their time away. The caption underneath addressed their predicament and ended with the statement, "Their only window to America is the television set."[20] If this is accurate, it is not hard to understand, from the psychological standpoint, why many persons living in these circumstances fail to show realistic initiative and imagination in regard to bettering their plight and making some contribution to society. Continuously subjected to the most virulent strains of media blight, and assumedly receiving relatively little by way of corrective information, it is no wonder that such unfortunates lose faith in both themselves and their society. Television news in particular seems well calculated to suggest to people in a ghetto that much of modern America is but a distant continuation of the upheaval and degeneration that they live in. On the other hand, in surrealistic counterpoint to the stream of jarring news bits are the ads, and on most other prime-time network programs, a mixture of more ads and an unwavering melange of sex, violence, and general derring-do. All of the latter serve to tantalize these have-nots with images of a life-style of action, excitement, exquisite comfort, and sensual refinement that, while existing out there, somewhere, is ultimately barred to them. Mindless engrossment in television, occurring within the unremitting squalor and deprivation of the ghetto, constitutes the experiential bind at its demoralizing worst. In the face of such a predicament, what is the point of struggle, sacrifice, and delay of gratification?

The urban ghetto in America is the result of many forces, both historical and contemporary, and this discussion is in no way an attempt to lay the full weight of blame, or even a major part of it, on either television or the collective mass media. But purely from the standpoint of psychology, a heavy diet of television, with relatively little by way of compensating experience, puts such people at a terrible disadvantage. For one thing, they cannot counteract the steady emotional undertow of the imagery of doom by turning away to the pleasantries of their immediate surroundings, as many middle- and upper-class persons can. For another, research indicates that ghetto dwellers, in watching television, tend to concentrate on the news and network entertainment programs, the two purest founts of the imageries of doom and fantasy. The demoralization under analysis here is undoubtedly most severe among the urban poor. Together with such related attitudes as insecurity, chronic rage, and a generalized mistrust of established societal institutions, it can permanently kill initiative and the capacity for realistic personal growth.

The combination of television and the ghetto is extreme in terms of the general psychopathological impact of the imagery of unreality. Television is the most powerful of all media forms, and ghetto dwellers are especially susceptible to its mesmeric appeal. Other forms of the media are less invasive, and, as mentioned above, other socioeconomic groups have better resources with which to counterbalance its reality-distorting influence, particularly in regard to either weighing or ignoring the daily torrent of depressing news and negative analysis. But it seems clear that the imagery of doom has troublesome potential across all social classes. Even persons within the news media are aware of the danger. According to *Time* magazine in an article at the outset of the 1980s, no less a figure than the veteran newscaster Lowell Thomas complained of the current of bad news and promised that his own upcoming series would place greater emphasis on the positive in the selection of news stories.[21]

On this same note, the experiential bind can be seen to foster another widespread mental set that is not restricted to the lower socioeconomic classes, and which carries dire implications for the nation's status in the intensely competitive arena of international relations predicted for the twenty-first century. I speak here of the winner-loser dichotomy that is so prevalent in the self-evaluative thinking of contemporary Americans.

The principal danger of dichotomous thought lies in its black-white absoluteness, its tendency to classify in terms of polar opposites and in the process to overlook the infinite continuum of steps that actually exists between the extremes in any realm of activity or value in the real world. It ignores the shades of gray that are interspersed between black and white. However, the gray area, the middle ground, is the area within which most of us fluctuate in the manifold day-to-day activities of our lives. In the flux of most human experience and achievement, actual differences are subtle and shifting, regressing constantly to the middle ground, and less glaring than appearances would suggest. Dichotomous thinking ignores this fundamental reality, and as a result, it tends to exacerbate guilt when individuals find themselves in a lesser position vis-à-vis the immediately relevant situation and/or other person(s). Momentarily forced by circumstances or by lack of effectiveness into this dread position, and thus plunged into guilt, people tend to react to themselves as dumb, ugly, unlovable, inferior, and worthless, that is, as losers. These maladaptive extremes of self-devaluation, borne up by dichotomous thinking, and distorting the individual's moment-by-moment performance within the flux of events, perpetuate and deepen the guilt and cause it to feed on itself.

Pathological guilt is thus the intermediate element in the chain of causation between the experiential bind and the winner-loser dichotomy characterizing American self-appraisal. By engendering pathological guilt, which is basic to all functional psychopathology, the bind simultaneously predisposes individuals to this rigid, indiscriminate mode of self-reflective thought. Both are manifestations of regression or arrested development. Persons in the grip of guilt are apt to grab impulsively and irrationally for things that promise quick surcease from their inner distress, because as Gaylin tells us, the pain and driving force of this unique human emotion requires either expiation or avoidance of the behavior generating it. In modern America, persons feeling like losers want, and need, to feel like winners. They want and need quick, powerful, unequivocal redemption, of the kind that, like salvation, comes from without, from the gods. But the gods of contemporary America are overwhelmingly materialistic-hedonistic, and their manna is money!

I believe that the above analysis illuminates, from the standpoint of psychology, an alarming behavioral trend in America today: the growing addiction to gambling. More and more people struggle with difficult reality and are titillated by both the messages of the imageries of fantasy ("There's much more out there if you can find the key, or get lucky") and voices of doom ("Everyone's a crook at heart, or at least cheating") And they are seduced into feeling that hard work, planning, and self-discipline are beside the point. Money is the answer to life's problems, and taking a long chance seem to be the most meaningful modus-operandi to a growing number of Americans: "If I can win big bucks, presto, I'm a winner in life. Work is for losers!" But statisticians tell us that the probability, in the individual case, of winning the purple ribbon in most of the big state lotteries is about the same as that of being struck by lightning. It is essentially nonexistent.

Of course, this desperate, irrational quest for monetary salvation wreaks its worst havoc in the ghetto, where the dire psychological effects of the experiential bind are severest. There people gamble not only discretionary funds, but monies badly needed for food, shelter, clothing, medical care, and other necessaries of life. So, in the short run, this behavior is ironically serving to mire society's real victims—a status that only in terms of the most superficial and wrongheaded analyses can be blamed on a loser mentality, hereditary laziness, lack of ability, and the like—more deeply into their socioeconomic abysses. Many are being lured by the experiential bind into irreparably self-destructive behavior patterns.

However, in its discrediting of the work ethic, this spreading preoccupation with mundane salvation via luck, with its implicit promise of immediate and painless success and happiness, is operating, on a much vaster scale within society, to undermine America's real sociopoliticoeconomic strength in the international sphere. It is common knowledge that Asian and European public-school students work harder and learn more than their American counterparts in the crucial preparatory years prior to entering the work force. David Halberstam, in his compelling book *The Reckoning*, illustrates in great detail how the Japanese post–World War II rise to primacy in the automobile industry can be traced to harder and smarter work across all echelons of a company. Halberstam studied Nissan Motors, from the workers, through the various levels of management, to the top executives, and, in America, the Ford Motor Company during a contemporaneous period.[22] Any reasonably intelligent adult knows that creativity of any significance is rooted in hard work. The maxim that genius is 98 percent perspiration and 2 percent inspiration suggests that, even at the highest levels of intellectual-artistic accomplishment, hard work and unrelenting effort and dedication lie at the core of things.

Media blight, whether it involves the imagery of fantasy or the imagery of doom, is dangerous because of its mind-bending, or perhaps better, mind-creating power. By constantly immersing the viewing public in an endless torrent of unrealistic imagery and skewed information, it is creating a vast, and growing, realm of vicarious experience, thus creating a kind of public psyche. As suggested earlier, experience is the essential nutriment of the psyche, as food is the essential nutriment of the brain. Not all experience is internalized, but that which is leaves a lasting mark. Whether such experience is internalized in the form of identifications, memories, or technical skills, it adds to or modifies the existing constellation of images, thoughts, and motivations that comprise the individual psyche. Further, by a subtle process of association, each individual psyche contributes indirectly to a public psyche. Thus, we can speak with an element of veridicality, as Luigi Barzini does, of the imperturbable British, the mutable Germans, the quarrelsome French, the flexible Italians, the careful Dutch, and the baffling (baffled?) Americans.[23]

Granted, media blight is but one source of personal experience in contemporary America. Further, we know from developmental psychology that certain kinds of experience have greater and more lasting impact on the psyche than do others, particularly in regard to their deeper-lying emotional and motivational significance. Experiences in infancy are more critical to personality formation than those occurring after independence and maturity have been attained. Experience in connection with intimates, primarily within the family of origin, is generally more critical than that in connection with strangers or persons to whom we are indifferent. It would be naive to suggest that the mass media have more overall psychological influence on individuals than do parents, siblings, spouses, admired mentors, and personal models, or that they typically take precedence over such basic life involvements as formal education and career. But because of certain inherent qualities, especially in the case of television, media stimulation has a unique potential for differentially influencing the individual psyche, as well as its collective analog. This amounts to the assertion that the mass media are not only capable of, but actually are, changing the face of America.

These mind-bending qualities of the electronic media have already been touched on, and in the main they involve vicariousness, sensationalism, glamourization, and omnipresence. This latter is particularly important. For millions of Americans, television provides either figure or ground stimulation virtually all of the time during waking hours. This fact brings to mind the action of river or a stream on its underlying terrain. Working without letup, even the gentlest of currents can in time alter the shape of, or cut through, the hardest rock. In modern America, media input has this quality of incessance. Further, much of it is more like a wild and turbulent river than a gentle stream.

NOTES

1. Christopher Lasch, *The Culture of Narcissism* (New York: W. W. Norton, 1978), 180.

2. Aaron Stern, *Me: The Narcissistic American* (New York: Ballantine Books, 1979), 136.

3. William James, *The Principles of Psychology* (Chicago: Encyclopedia Britannica, 1952), 158.

4. Norman Cousins, ''Modern Man Is Obsolete,'' *Saturday Review of Literature* 28 August 18, 1945: 5–9.

5. C. Wright Mills, *The Power Elite* (New York: Oxford University Press, 1956), 314.

6. David Fischer, *Growing Old in America* (New York: Oxford University Press, 1977), 132–34.

7. See, for example, W. E. Upjohn Institute for Employment Research, *Work in America: Report of a Special Task Force to the Secretary of Health, Education and Welfare* (Cambridge: MIT Press, 1972).

8. Mills, *The Power Elite*, 323.

9. Alvin Toffler, *Future Shock* (New York: Random House, 1970), 31.

10. Ibid., 40.

11. Alvin Toffler, *The Third Wave* (New York: William Morrow, 1980), 408–9.

12. Ibid., 415–16.

13. Ibid., 423.

14. Ibid., 430.

15. Ibid., 426.

16. A. E. Siegel, in G. Comstock et al., *Television and Human Behavior: The Key Studies* (Santa Monica: RAND Corporation, 1975), 223–24.

17. Ibid., 223.

18. B. S. Greenberg and B. Dervin, *Television and Human Behavior*, in G. Comstock et al., 158–59.

19. J. P. Robinson and P. E. Converse, *Television and Human Behavior: The Key Studies*, 215–16.

20. "N.Y. Budget Squeeze," *Time*, June 16, 1980, 23.

21. "Good News from Lowell Thomas," *Newsweek*, July 7, 1980, 9.

22. David Halberstam, *The Reckoning* (New York: William Morrow, 1986).

23. Luigi Barzini, *The Europeans* (New York: Simon and Schuster, 1983).

2

Psychodynamic Considerations

My purpose in this chapter will be to suggest the general psychodynamics of the widespread demoralization, and to show how the experiential bind is contributing to these intrapsychic forces in the minds of millions of Americans.

THE SELF-CONSTRUCT

The self, as a central integrating element within the personality, has a long history in both academia and applied psychologies and in related disciplines devoted to the study of humans and their environments. Before the turn of the century William James wrote his famous chapter on the self in his classic *Principles of Psychology*, and since that time the construct has been given a central role in a diversity of works attempting to illumine the intricacies and vagaries of human behavior. In regard to the explanatory and predictive value of the construct, Arthur Combs and Donald Snygg assert: "Indeed, the phenomenal self is so important in the economy of each human that it gives continuity to his personality. It provides the central core around which all perceptions are organized. When the individual's phenomenal self is understood, the various and diverse behaviors of people become consistent and predictable."[1]

A key consideration in self theory has to do with the role of the sociocultural backdrop in the development of the individual's self-construct. Concerning this critical relationship, Arthur Combs and Donald Snygg add: "For practical purposes, however, the culture in which we move is so inextricably a part of our experience as to overshadow all else in determining the nature of the concepts of self developed by each of its members."[2]

Along this same vein, G. H. Mead suggested that the relationship between the individual self and the social backdrop is so intimate that the integrity of the former mirrors, or reflects, that of the latter. Thus his comment that "the self, as that which can be an object of itself, is essentially a social structure, and it arises in social experience . . . it is impossible to conceive of the self as arising outside social experience."[3] A bit further on he adds, "The unity and structure of the complete self reflects the unity and structure of the social process as a whole; and each of the elementary selves of which it is composed reflects the unity and structure of the various aspects of that process in which the individual is implicated."[4]

Self theories, typified by the work of Carl Rogers, tend to divide the total self into two major components: an actual self and an ideal self. As the terms suggest, the actual self reflects the individual's perceptions, in all their complexity, of what he/she is at any point in time. This is the empirical "Me" in James's earlier scheme, and it extends from the physical body, personal traits, and abilities to family, friends, material possessions, vocation, avocations, and much else. The ideal self suggests, again complexly, what the person would like to be or needs to be. As with the actual self, the ideal self has many facets. These facets are arranged in a crude hierarchy of priority in accordance with individual experience and the values that have consequently been internalized.

This division of the self, or its correlative, also occurs in most traditional psychodynamic theories of personality. Freud spoke of the relationships between the "ego" and the "ego-ideal"; Karen Horney between the "real self" and the "idealized self"; and Alfred Adler, between the "self" and the "guiding self-ideal." Integral to this division within the self, in all of the theoretical systems, is the notion that surveillance of the actual component is a primary function of the ideal component. In reference to this Freud wrote:

From analysis of the delusion of observation we have come to the conclusion that in the ego there exists a faculty that incessantly watches, criticizes, and compares, and in this way is set against the other part of the ego. In our opinion, therefore, the patient reveals a truth which has not been appreciated as such when he complains that at every step he is spied upon and observed, that his very thought is known and examined. He has erred only in attributing this disagreeable power to something outside him and foreign to him; he perceives within his ego the rule of a faculty which measures his actual ego and all his activities by an ego-ideal, which he has created for himself in the course of his development.[5]

Freud made this comment in connection with a psychopathological condition (delusion of observation associated with narcissistic disorder). However, the principle of incessant self-observation holds in all cases, both pathological and healthy. Further, while this capacity for internal surveillance is normal and necessary for human beings, it also carries the potential for causing much emotional trouble and unhappiness.

It is when a serious and unbridgeable discrepancy exists between the actual and ideal aspects of the total self, and when, as a direct consequence, the criticism of the actual by the ideal is relentlessly harsh and punitive, that the stage is set for the development of clinical psychopathology. All theories of personality and abnormal psychology hold that the condition of severe and chronic self-ideal discrepancy—superego tension in psychoanalytic parlance—is potentially pathological, and it is widely invoked in psychodynamic explanations of various forms of neurotic, borderline, and psychotic maladjustment. This is particularly true with respect to most forms of functional depression, wherein an aggravated self-ideal discrepancy is seen as a principal dynamic.

Although a certain tension, or discrepancy, between the two aspects of the self is normal and unavoidable, I am suggesting that this discrepancy is being dangerously exacerbated by the experiential bind that confronts and envelops modern Americans on a day-to-day basis. Once the condition of chronically irritated self-ideal discrepancy becomes structured within the psyche, it naturally feeds depleted self-esteem, guilt, and demoralization. Put differently, once the experiential bind becomes internalized, as parental figures were earlier internalized, then the inner self-criticism is apt to become frankly tyrannical. Persons harboring this self-punitive intrapsychic dynamic may appear to others as being excessively ambitious and driven in their pursuit of success. Or, where erratic and antisocial behaviors are in the fore, their mania with achievement and accumulation may appear to spring from deeper, darker psychical forces, such as pathological greed and vanity. In truth, many of them, driven by their guilt, are running away from themselves, as much as they are running after the trappings of success.

Self-theories also differentiate between the self-as-object and the self-as-process. The self-as-object is essentially a person's self-appraisal—again, the empirical "Me" in James's conceptualization. The self-as-process is an aggregate of mental processes, organized around the self-as-object, which are largely devoted to the enhancement and defense of the latter. These processes consist of such things as perception, thinking, memory, judgment, and the initiation of action. The self-as-process is, in many respects, analogous to the Freudian ego, especially in its coping and defensive functions.

These two aspects of the self are intimately linked, so that disturbance in one is very likely to spread to the other. With the demoralization under discussion, this contagion, so to speak, moves from the self-as-object to the self-as-process. That is, as self-esteem is depleted, both defensive mechanisms and coping skills begin to falter. The disturbance of self-regard that is basic to the demoralization tends, with time, to impair ego function. This in turn makes it increasingly difficult for such demoralized individuals to extricate themselves from their predicament, tends to lock them into it.

Percival Symonds has devoted considerable attention to the interrelationship between self-as-object and self-as-process, between self and ego in his system. As he puts it,

The ego functions best when the self is valued, whereas self-depreciation is usually accompanied by a falling off of the effectiveness of ego-functioning. Self-evaluation determines the kind of behavior that will take place. It sets the stage for effective functioning and gives the cue for an output of energy. When the self is valued, behavior becomes more organized, consistent, more forward-moving, more effective, realistic and planful.[6]

He even goes on to say that mental health depends in large measure on the degree and kind of self-evaluation, and that lack of self-esteem is one sign of mental illness. Thus, persons in the grip of the bind-induced demoralization are not only preoccupied with illusions, but because of the self-devaluation that these illusions naturally cause, they are also apt to be employing maladaptive methods in dealing with many of the real demands of their lives.

IDENTIFICATION

While both the actual self and the ideal self are acquired through experience, theories of personality teach that the ideal self is nurtured primarily by the normative and authoritative figures of the surrounding culture—parents, parent surrogates, glamorous adults, culture heroes, and imaginary figures—as they are perceived and interpreted by the individual. This being the case, it follows that the actual self will be influenced more by first-hand daily experience, while the ideal self will be influenced more by vicarious experience stimulated by images of persons and objects existing at a distance and cloaked in various auras of power, beauty, intelligence and general charisma. In modern America, these distant figures affecting the ideal self are all too often blatant fictions served up in the guise of reality by the media, particularly the electronic advertising and entertainment media.

The reader might question whether vicariously experienced media figures, who are always distant and frequently fanciful, are really capable of influencing structural elements within the personality. I believe that they are, and both psychological theory and research data support my contention. The linkup between elements within the imagery of unreality and the ideal selves of millions of Americans involves the mechanism of identification.

Robert Goldenson, in his *Encyclopedia of Human Behavior: Psychology, Psychiatry, and Mental Health*, refers to identification as "the tendency to incorporate or adopt the attitudes and behavior of other individuals or groups." In his commentary he states,

Identification is probably the most important factor in shaping the personality and establishing standards and goals. The boy takes on masculine traits by identifying with his father, the girl acquires feminine traits from her mother.[7]

Willard Gaylin's comments on identification are particularly clear and useful in this discussion:

Identification is seen as literally internalizing—swallowing up—another person and his attributes, or, if not that person, some idealized image of the way you thought he was, or the way he ought to have been. . . . It is not imitation, although it may lead to it. It is much more an unconscious and unwilled process. Identification leads to manners, form, taste, attitudes—all the behavior that makes little English boys seem to English, and French boys so preciously Gallic. The same procedure allows us to incorporate a model of proper moral behavior. The model exists—in our unconscious, unbeknownst to our conscious self—as an ideal against which we measure ourselves. This ego-ideal becomes fundamental to the self-respect mechanisms of the individual.[8]

While Gaylin specifically mentions the incorporation of moral models via identification, we know that the mechanism operates in connection with a much wider range of figures and values. In this regard, Calvin Hall and Gardiner Lindzey state:

We choose as models those who seem more successful in gratifying their needs than we are. The child identifies with his parents because they appear to him to be omnipotent, at least during the early years of childhood. As the child grows older, he finds other people to identify with whose accomplishments are more in line with his current wishes. Each period tends to have its own characteristic identification figures. Needless to say, most of this identification takes place unconsciously and not, as it may sound, with conscious intention. . . . It is not necessary for a person to identify with someone else in every respect. He usually selects and incorporates just those features which he believes will help him achieve a desired goal. . . . One may identify with animals, imaginary characters, institutions, abstract ideas, and inanimate objects as well as with other human beings.[9]

In this same vein, Goldenson's thoughts provide yet further understanding of this complex psychological mechanism.

> The process of identification may work for ill as well as good. Parental models may leave much to be desired. Groups or gangs outside the family may foster distorted values and objectionable behavior. We may also reach too high and identify ourselves with unrealistic or unattainable models. Identification can go even further awry and become a factor in psychiatric disorder.[10]

Although, as these excerpts suggest, identifications contributing to the formation of the ideal self occur primarily in infancy vis-à-vis parents and older siblings, they continue on into subsequent phases of the life cycle. Further, as maturation proceeds, the objects of personal identification tend to range outward, from those more immediate and concrete to those more distant and abstract. A study by Robert Havighurst, Myra Robinson, and Mildred Dorr done with children and adolescents to investigate formation of the ideal self illustrates this point. Students at various ages from 10 to 17 were asked to write an essay titled "The Person I Would Like to Be." Later on, the procedure was repeated for purposes of a validity check. In analyzing the essays the following categories of models were used: (1) parents and relatives; (2) parent surrogates; (3) glamorous adults; (4) cultural heroes; (5) attractive successful young adults; (6) composite or imaginary characters; (7) age mates and youths; and (8) miscellaneous, not classifiable. One conclusion drawn by the authors is that the responses fall mainly into categories 1, 3, 5, and 6 (parents and relatives, glamorous adults, attractive young adults, and composite or imaginary characters). A second conclusion supported by the data is that an age sequence exists, moving outward from the family circle, becoming more abstract, and culminating in the composite imaginary character. A third general conclusion is that the social environment affects choice of the ideal self; children in families of lower socioeconomic status name a higher proportion of glamorous adults as their identification figures.[11]

While the broader topic of media violence will be treated later in more detail, some research reported by Albert Bandura has relevance to the present discussion concerning identification and the ideal self. Bandura's research suggests that learning—in this case having to do with aggression in children—can occur through simple observation of peers, models, and other figures, even though the activity in question is not practiced and rewarded. Referring to something he calls vicarious, or "no-trial," learning, Bandura concludes that children may acquire behavior patterns merely by observing them, such as in films or on television. Along this vein Bandura hypothesizes that an observed response becomes learned when stimuli elicit mental representations of the behavior, which in turn are incorporated into a symbolic pattern by the child.[12] In another article, entitled "Social-Learning Theory of the Identification Process," he concludes that children acquire the capability to behave in new ways not only through direct instruction, but also through observing the behavior of others, such as parents, teachers, peers, and television and film characters. Further, he suggests that as children come to spend more time observing television and film models and as communications technology improves, it is highly probable that parents and teachers may become comparatively less influential as models for behavior.[13] In yet another article, entitled "Social Learning through Imitation," Bandura again suggests that television's wide availability has probably increased the role of visual and symbolic models in children's learning how to behave, as compared to live models experienced directly.[14] In sum, according to Bandura's conclusions, a wholly passive vicarious experience such as that provided by television can result in "no-trial" learning, in which a pattern of potential behavior is acquired in lieu of active practice and reinforcement. Worse yet, his studies provide reason to suspect that experiences of this nature may, in the case of the growing child, be displacing experiences with real persons as the primary source of behavioral models.

Although Bandura's research, which hails from the behaviorist point of view, focuses on the vicarious learning of responses that can influence subsequent behavior patterns, it requires but a small step to apply his findings to the problem of self-construct formation. There is every reason to assume that the same vicarious experience underlying "no-trial" learning of potential behaviors can also promote identifications that affect the ideal self. Indeed, these two vital processes are probably in most instances indissolubly linked, representing but different elements within the larger process of psychological growth and change. That is, as individuals vicariously record new response possibilities, they are more than likely simultaneously, and unconsciously, modifying their burgeoning ideal selves in such a way as to harmonize them with the response patterns in question.

Identification, then, is the mechanism by which the characteristics of models and their standards of behavior are unconsciously taken into the personality, shaping and reshaping the ideal self throughout the life cycle. But it is critical to bear in mind the idea that these identifications very often, if not always, have an element of necessity to them. Once established, they require that individuals live up to the standard in question in their daily performance. If the person fails to do so, guilt and self-devaluation are the probable, if not inevitable, consequences. Where the demands of the ideal self are involved, the person is usually not let off the hook easily. What is more, the self-devaluation is incessant and inescapable. As Gaylin points out, under the painful emotion of guilt it is a case of you against you, with no possible buffers and no villains except oneself. Thus we begin to see why the imagery of fantasy is potentially so dangerous. It constantly confronts people with unrealistic models and standards of behavior which, through the mechanism of identification, are apt to be taken into the ideal self. While there is great individual variation in terms of the degree to which people are internalizing this imagery. I believe that the phenomenon is pervasive in our media-saturated society.

SELF-ESTEEM

Of the many psychological dangers associated with life in modern postindustrial society, particularly America, it is above all the difficulty in maintaining a solid core of self-esteem that predisposes the average person to chronic demoralization. More often than not, the demoralization indicates a deeper and more serious problem for individuals: the inability to perceive themselves as objects of primary value in a world of meaning, to feel truly good about themselves on a regular day-to-day basis. Despite a material abundance unmatched in the history of civilization, life in our society appears to breed epidemic self-doubt, and self-devaluation. The experiential bind is intimately linked to this enigma, and herein lies its principal danger to the individual. It undermines self-esteem, attacks the psyche at one of its most critical and vulnerable points.

The difficulty in maintaining healthy self-esteem in the face of the experiential bind is related to human idealism, the capacity to envision situations and achievements that surpass the realities of the present. This unique capacity is both boon and bane to humans. Although it is a principal factor in their ability to change, grow, and transcend themselves, it also lies behind their innate self-dissatisfaction, their troublesome inability to accept themselves on any kind of permanent basis. Humans constantly compare their realities to their ideals, and, with near equal frequency, reject the realities, and themselves, because they fall short of the ideals. This predicament is intensified in modern society partly because the imagery swirling about peoples' heads—which serves to stimulate their imaginations and whet their appetites—operates without letup, while at the same time it is shot through with subtle distortion and deception, with unreality. And while this phantasmagoria may have its stimulating and entertaining side, it also predisposes individuals to self-doubt, self-devaluation, and self-loathing because it fosters the formation of unrealistic and unattainable ideals. Self-doubt, self-devaluation, and self-loathing are antithetical to self-esteem. To the extent that they exist within the personality, self-esteem is impossible.

It is critical to grasp the importance of self-esteem in understanding mental health, emotional well-being, and adaptive, productive living in general. Theorists in the field of developmental psychology conceptualize it as a basic structural defense against pathological anxiety, as well as a central element underlying most coping mechanisms and interpersonal skills. Ernest Becker wrote at length on self-esteem, discussing its pivotal role in mental health, its fragility, and its need for constant renewal through appropriate social interaction. In connection with the first aspect, he stated:

We can see then that the seemingly trite words "self-esteem" are at *the very core of human adaptation*. They do not represent an extra self-indulgence, or a mere vanity, but a matter of life and death. The qualitative feeling of self-value is the basic predicate for human action, precisely because it epitomizes the whole development of the ego.[15]

In reference to its dependence on the social backdrop, he made the following comment:

Ever since the early sociologists discovered that man was dependent on society for the fashioning of his self, his identity, we began to turn our attention to what was really going on. We began to understand that the individual's view of himself depended hopelessly on the general reflection he received back from society.[16]

Erich Fromm and Alfred Adler, coming from somewhat different positions within orthodox depth psychology, have both written on the importance of self-esteem, particularly in regard to the expression of socially mature, altruistic attitudes. In a brief, but classic, statement on the art of loving, Fromm asserts that self-love is a necessary component in the capacity to truly love others. Of course, he is talking about an affirmation of self that is grounded in a realistic appraisal of one's capacities and natural human rights.

The idea expressed in the Biblical "Love thy neighbor as thyself" implies that respect for one's own integrity and uniqueness, love for and understanding of one's self, cannot be separated from respect and love and understanding of another individual. The love for my own self is inseparably connected with the love for any other being.[17]

Further on in his discussion he suggests that the overt expression of selfishness is the result not of an excess of self-love, but rather its opposite, self-contempt. Thus, "Selfishness and self-love, far from being identical, are actually opposites. The selfish person does not love himself too much but too little; in fact he hates himself."[18]

Adler saw the maintenance of self-esteem as the supreme law of psychical life. For him, the essence of neurotic and psychotic behavior lay in an exaggerated, yet fruitless, preoccupation with personal superiority, which was ultimately rooted in a profound feeling of inferiority. According to Adler, "Nothing stands more in the way of social interest than increased inferiority feeling."[19]

In his characteristic combination of eloquence and realism, William James penned these thoughts, among others, on self-esteem:

Not that I would not, if I could, be both handsome and fat and well-dressed, and a great athlete, and make a million a year, be a wit, a bon-vivant, and a lady-killer, as well as a philosopher; a philanthropist, statesman, warrior, and African explorer, as well as a "tone-poet" and saint. But the thing is simply impossible. The millionaire's work would run counter to the saint's; the bon-vivant and the philanthropist would trip each other up; the philosopher and the lady-killer could not keep house in the same tenement of clay. . . . So our self-feeling in this world depends entirely on what we *back* ourselves to be and do. It is determined by the ratio of our actualities to our supposed potentialities; a fraction of which our pretensions are the denominator and the numerator our success; thus, $\text{Self-esteem} = \dfrac{\text{Success}}{\text{Pretensions}}$. Such a fraction may be increased as well by diminishing the denominator as by increasing the numerator. To give up pretensions is as blessed a relief as to get them gratified; and where disappointment is incessant and the struggle unending, that is what men will always do. . . . Yet still the emotion that beckons me on is undubitably the pursuit of an ideal social self, a self that is at least worthy of approving recognition by the highest possible judging companion, if such a companion there be.[20]

The experiential bind influences self-esteem because it influences the self. Self-esteem is inseparably linked to conditions within the self or, more specifically, to relationships between the components of the total self. When certain dislocations within the self occur, healthy self-esteem becomes difficult, perhaps impossible, to regulate and maintain. In this state the person is apt to be in serious trouble psychologically and susceptible to the development of a wide variety of symptoms.

THE IMAGERY OF UNREALITY AND THE IDEAL SELF

It cannot be overemphasized that maintenance of a positive sense of self is critical to humans' well-being and their ability to contribute meaningfully to their society. This theme occurs again and again in the writings of self theorists. According to Combs and Snygg, "human beings are continually and insatiably engaged in a never-ending attempt to achieve an adequate sense of self."[21] In the same vein Ernest Becker argued that in order to live with any degree of security and effectiveness each person must have a core of basic self-esteem.[22]

The relationship between self-esteem and behavioral competence is, as we have seen, rooted in the interdependency of the self-as-object and the self-as-process, or stated differently, between the self and the ego. In reference to this interdependency Symonds states that "the integrative functions of the ego are largely determined by the integrative character of the self. If there are areas of the self which we dislike and do not want to admit to as real and true, then we are liable to threats and open to conflict."[23]

In the preceding chapter I attempted to show how the experiential bind, in feeding the condition of chronically irritated self-ideal discrepancy, is undermining normal self-esteem and fostering unconscious self-devaluation in huge numbers of average people in contemporary America. In this section I would like to explore this phenomenon further, particularly in regard to the ways in which the widespread demoralization is weakening the social fabric in America. I have used the disease-nutritional analogy to suggest the dangers involved. Becker seemed to be thinking along similar lines when he remarked

But man is not just a blind glob of idling protoplasm, but a creature who lives in a world of symbols and dreams and not merely matter. His sense of self-worth is constituted symbolically, his cherished narcissism feeds on symbols, on the abstract idea of his own worth, an idea composed of sounds, words, and images, in the air, in the mind, on paper.[24]

As mentioned earlier in this chapter, the development of the total self is profoundly influenced by the social-cultural backdrop. But standing by itself, this general idea is truistic and not overly helpful. Of much more utility is an awareness of those social agencies and institutions that have especial influence on the self, together with an understanding of why they have their effect. The concept of need satisfaction appears to provide a key to the problem, particularly in regard to the formation of the ideal self. Those elements of the surrounding society that symbolize satisfaction of personal needs, and which by virtue of this association acquire value in the individual's eyes, have great potential for influencing the development of the ideal self. As Hall and Lindzey point out in discussing the mechanism of identification, we choose as models those who seem more successful in gratifying their needs than we are.[25] And as Symonds suggests in a similar discussion, "The ideal self comes from accepting the characteristics of people of prestige and honor in the community."[26]

When one stops to think about it, this connection makes absolute sense. Humans are motivated or pushed from within by a complex hierarchy of needs—biological, psychological, and social—and they are simultaneously drawn from without by figures and objects that symbolize or promise satisfaction of these needs. Achieving real need satisfaction at any point in time produces both security and pleasure. Depending on the priority of the need within the hierarchy, it also heightens self-esteem because it creates a transient sense of identity with figures who are perceived by the individual as being potent and provident. In short, it momentarily produces some degree of self-ideal congruity. Most human experience carries this twofold, objective-narcissistic, consequence. Earning a raise brings in more money to spend, but it also enables people to feel good about themselves. Being turned down for a date not only deprives the young man of his sweetheart's presence, but it also forces him into a certain amount of negative self-regard. The narcissistic consequence is a necessary aspect of most experience, and in many instances it is psychologically more critical than the objective.

Unfortunately, the second of these two examples, the disappointment, is the commoner outcome in the sphere of human enterprise. It would seem that it is human fate that the moments of well-being occur within vaster expanses of frustration and disquietude; inner peace and fulfillment are generally short-lived in the condition humaine.

However, by constructing representations of admired figures within their own psyches, that is, by identifying with them, humans are able to secure a form of substitute satisfaction that both guides and urges them across the empty spaces. This is reminiscent of a phenomenon that Freud attributed to the infant in the oral stage of psychosexual development; and this early development phenomenon may well be part of the origin of the process of identification. According to Freud, the hungry infant, after repeated feeding experiences, begins to harbor fantasies of the feeding situation that are in essence hallucinatory wish fulfillments. These wishful fantasies, while lacking full satisfaction, produce a kind of low-grade vicarious satisfaction that sustains the infant as it waits for its mother to come. This inner substitute for real gratification makes endurance of the rising oral tensions a bit easier. But that is precisely what pleasurable fantasies do in general. They provide substitute gratifications that assuage need tensions. The ideal self is an aggregate of appealing fantasies and images of persons at their future best that diminishes momentary tensions and sustains people in their various projects and involvements. In brief, because it lends a sense of value and power to them, it gives them both courage and purpose.

Hall and Lindzey suggest that the ultimate test of an identification's utility is whether or not it helps to reduce tension. Becker spoke of an "inner newsreel" that people continually run on themselves, and which passes in review the symbols that give self-esteem. He stated that, "Everyone runs the inner newsreel, even if it does not record the same symbolic events. Always it passes in review the peculiar symbols of one's choice that give him a warm feeling about himself. . . . All day long we pass these images in review, and most of us even in our sleep."[27] Thus, for Becker, the newsreel had a self-stroking function. But he was also aware of the darker side of the phenomenon. In reference to the nocturnal newsreel, the dream, he argued,

When the newsreel records a negative image . . . we immediately counter the negative image with a positive one, to try and get our self-esteem in balance and onto the favorable side. But while we are asleep the ego is not working, it has no conscious control over the images we send ourselves about our sense of worth. Our deeper experience may have on record that we really feel worthless, helpless, dependent, mediocre, inadequate, finite: this is our unconscious speaking, and when the ego cannot oppose any positive images to counteract these negative ones, we have the nightmare, the terrible revelation of our basic uselessness.[28]

Becker's newsreel is a metaphor for humans' innate tendency to self-reflection, their penchant for comparing themselves to others, and to their own internalized standards of achievement and excellence. When the frames of their newsreels depict them in a positive, or superior, position relative to these reference points, they experience self-esteem and a momentary surcease of tension. When, on the other hand, the sequence of images and fantasies place them in a negative, or inferior, position, their self-esteem slumps and their tensions build. In the first instance they are enjoying, along with other feelings, a measure of self-ideal congruity. In the second, they are struggling with the problem of self-ideal discrepancy. In the first, the loss of tension is due largely to a sense of potency, a reassuring feeling that they can live successfully and satisfy their ever-recurring needs, no matter what the circumstances. In the second, the buildup of tension is largely due to a sense of guilty impotence, with its implicit prospect of unremitting frustration and deprivation. In this latter condition, depending on its severity and duration, demoralization may settle in, and as a consequence the struggling ego may begin to suffer serious loss of basic coping skills. Thus, the demoralization, with its underlying dynamic of chronically irritated self-ideal discrepancy, carries a potential danger to society as well as to the individual sufferer. Not only is it subjectively painful, but it also has the capacity to undermine such healthy adaptive traits as courage, purpose, determination, reason, trust, and friendliness. These are at once the traits that enable individuals to effectively extricate themselves from their demoralization and also make their real contributions to the manifold tasks of society.

We have glimpsed three factors that appear to operate in the development and modification of the ideal self. The first, an innate motivational factor, concerns need satisfaction. Throughout their lives humans are necessarily preoccupied with the problem of need satisfaction, and they quite naturally attend to and admire those figures and objects which, in their estimation, symbolize success in this critical realm of activity.

Starting with the parents and moving through a variety of seemingly charismatic figures, this combination of attention and admiration is apt to result in identifications that either momentarily or permanently shape the ideal self.

The second factor, which is perhaps best described as developmental in nature, concerns the outward-ranging tendency of the identification process. As people mature, they tend to become aware of and select increasingly distant and imaginary personal models. While this is integral to growth, with its inevitable widening of psychological horizons, there is the mounting possibility that the resulting identifications will acquire potentially troublesome elements of unreality. In this eventuality the danger to the impressionable and malleable ideal self is immediately clear.

The third factor, which is functional in nature, is intimately linked to the second. It concerns the potential influence of vicarious experience on different aspects of psychological growth and change, the development of the ideal self included. As research such as that done by Bandura suggests, imaginary figures passively perceived appear to have the power to function as behavioral models and objects of identification. Such vicarious experience is being provided in ever-increasing amounts to the viewing public by the collective media, particularly the electronic media. Further, because of constant improvements in communications technology, this media-based vicarious experience is apt to have more psychological impact than much first-hand experience. Also, in addition to the technical innovations, there is the basic fact that in the case of media images there is never any chance for the kind of face-to-face contact that reveals real persons' essential humanness, that show their weaknesses as well as their strengths.

In the electronic media all three of these factors can be seen to operate at high levels of intensity. Media heroes seldom suffer the relentless frustrations that beset ordinary people. For the sake of the drama there may be momentary reverses, but in the end—that is, in the course of half an hour or an hour—success is a certainty, and all needs are abundantly satisfied. Second, much of the imagery on media dramatizations, while instantly available, is thoroughly exotic and glamorous. It has great appeal to average viewers because it takes them away from the familiar and the monotonous. In this sense, it both broadens their horizons and dots the new landscape with interesting and appealing figures. And finally, the experience it provides is wholly vicarious, so that it always remains above the everyday contact and scrutiny that breeds both skepticism and realistic perspectives. Of course, most adults know consciously that media programming is shot through with fantasy, but this does not necessarily inhibit the process of unconscious identification. Where children, juveniles, and some adolescents are involved, there is much more implicit belief in the veridicality of the imagery, a fact that necessarily gives the identification process much freer rein.

A vast amount of research summarized by Comstock et al. suggests that the viewing of violence on television increases the tendency to anti-social and aggressive behavior, particularly where there is an existing predisposition in the personality.[29] The data indicate that this phenomenon applies more to the lower socioeconomic classes, where such reality checks as education and parental guidance are relatively lacking. Also, it applies more to children and adolescents than to adults, although it is not totally absent in this latter group.

It is my belief that a similar negative influence exists in connection with the general unreality that characterizes much content in the mass media. While social-science research in the past thirty years has concentrated primarily on the effects of television violence, it would seem highly unlikely that the broader issue of media unreality would fail to have some form of deleterious effect on the psychological development and behavior of the viewing public. However, in the latter case both the unreality and its resulting psychological effects are subtler and, hence, harder to detect and document.

While the imagery of fantasy reaches its zenith in the electronic media, it abounds throughout the collective mass media, as well as in the wider society as it vibrates in sympathy with the media. In all forms of the media the factors of illusory abundant need satisfaction, distant glamour, and vicarious experience frequently combine to exert a strong influence on the mechanism of identification and the development of the ideal self. In the case of societal echoes consisting essentially of individual posturing and affectation, the three factors still operate upon the perceiver, but in reduced degree. That is, where real people are involved, there is always some possibility of sobering face-to-face contact that invariably reduces the posturer to the human dimension. As a consequence of this contact we usually begin to see chinks in their apparent successes. It is precisely the impersonal hustle and bustle of modern urban and suburban life, wherein people commonly glimpse one another distantly and transitorily, that sustains these personal echoes. In the slower, more intimate, village atmosphere they tend to wash out.

The condition of chronically irritated self-ideal discrepancy typically causes people to have a sense of actual personal inadequacy. Although on realistic grounds they may well be quite adequate, even accomplished, they cannot see or feel this because of the unbridgeable disharmony existing between the two aspects of their total selves. What is more, because of related misinterpretations, they are apt to perceive many of their fellow humans as achieving the very levels of success and abundance that somehow, diabolically evade them. At best this is an unhappy situation. Richard DeMartino, in an analysis combining insights from both psychoanalysis and Zen Buddhism, suggests why and how it carries the potential for real personal tragedy.

According to DeMartino, the ego (self) has an intrinsic limitation. It is incapable of being a subject without an object. It is circumscribed and curtailed by its own object need, and it cannot affirm itself subjectively without a satisfying, meaningful inner object. This is referred to as conditioned subjectivity. The inherent instability of the ego, overcome momentarily by identification with a satisfying object, is never permanently resolved. Its inner subjective disquietude is basically ineradicable. Given this flaw of higher self-reflective consciousness the availability of realistic, satisfying objects is critical to the life of the ego (self). As long as self-consciousness exists, the subjective aspect must have an appropriate objective counterpart. Without this it necessarily begins to lapse into a potentially intolerable emptiness, an inner vacuum that leads to anguish and demoralization. In regard to this critical issue, DeMartino states:

In its attempt as subject to cope with its task of finding itself, it (ego) envisions some object-image of itself. Through this image it hopes at once to be able both to prove itself and to gain recognition and approval from the other, or, if not the allegiance of, then to gain control over or at least independence of the other. For in its double alienation the ego encounters the absolute limitation imposed upon it by the subjectivity of the other as a challenge or, indeed a threat. . . . Relying on its projected object-image to establish itself and overcome this threat, the ego may be led to take that limited, finite impression alone to be the whole of itself, its ground, its source, and its ultimate meaning, by which it is to be sustained, and through which it is to be fulfilled. Most or perhaps all of its subjectivity is now devoted and, in effect, subordinated to the content, or contents, necessary to realize the vision—wealth, power, prestige, masculinity, femininity, knowledge, moral perfection, artistic creativity, physical beauty, popularity, individuality, or "success." Virtually identifying with these contents, it focuses exclusively upon them and upon the conception of itself which they constitute. In this fixation and attachment it easily falls prey to the arch delusion of egocentricity. Ever in search of, yet ever elusive to, itself, the ego, object-dependent and object-obstructed, comes to be object-dominated and object-deluded.[30]

And in reference to the failure to establish a satisfying object-image he adds:

Unable to sustain itself within itself, and perhaps tormented by feelings of its own undeservedness, guilt, or sin, it comes to know melancholy and despondent moments of loneliness, frustration, or despair. Inwardly plagued by restlessness, insecurity, or a contempt and even hatred of itself, outwardly it possibly manifests any number of psychological or psychosomatic disturbances. . . . Yet often the ego manages to contain these pangs of disquietude and to finish out its life in just this condition. But even as it does so, it is under the continual threat that the smoldering deep-seated uneasiness may erupt and surge forth in an anguish and dread which is uncontainable. This could occur should the ego no longer be able to rationalize away its sense of unworthiness or its sense of guilt, should it become morbidly uncertain of the divine forgiveness of its sin, or should the components necessary to maintain its object-image otherwise come to be lost, destroyed, or unavailable, or, while remaining, prove disillusioning, grow empty, or simply cease to be engaging. Finally, some ordinary occurrence in daily life can bring the abrupt traumatic realization that not only is every possible content transitory and ephemeral, but so, too, is the ego itself. Ever vulnerable, in youth and old age, to illness and infirmity in body and mind, it must die.[31]

I have quoted this admittedly difficult and somber passage at great length because it is so relevant to the central argument of this book. DeMartino is saying that the subjective vitality, perhaps the very life, of the ego is basically dependent on the image it has of itself. In effect, he is restating the corollary from self theory suggesting that disturbances in the self-as-object necessarily cause disturbances in the self-as-process. But it seems to me that his conception dramatizes the gravity, urgency, and delicacy of the problem, and in doing so it dramatizes the potential gravity of the demoralization. Chronically irritated self-ideal discrepancy, which is subjectively experienced as a worrisome sense of actual inadequacy, is no laughing matter. In this condition, people's deeper images of, and feelings about, themselves are apt to be predominantly negative. While the degree of felt inadequacy may range over time from mild to severe, in general this is precisely the situation that DeMartino warns against. The subjective aspect of the self (ego) cannot readily conjure up positive images of itself. Faced with this dearth of reassuring inner objects, it quickly begins to slide into self-devaluation and self-rejection. At the very least this increases susceptibility to such dysphoric emotions as guilt, anxiety, depression, and hostility, all of which in one way or another sap the ego's vitality and adaptive capacity. And there is no doubt in my mind that at its worst, when the personality in question is thoroughly debilitated, this paucity of reassuring inner objects can eventuate in psychosis, even suicide. Any of these outcomes have destructive implications for both the individual and society.

DeMartino's analysis informs us as to why the imagery of fantasy is potentially so dangerous. Quite simply, it is luring countless Americans into identifications with figures and models that they cannot possibly emulate or even approximate. Taken in conjunction with the facts of the average American's daily routine, it is fostering a deep, structured psychical discordance that gives rise to subjective feelings of inadequacy. In time this vexing sense of impotence, if it cannot be surmounted, naturally breeds demoralization.

In DeMartino's terms, this structured inner discordance estranges the subjective and objective aspects of the self. It deprives the subjective of a positive image of itself and thus undermines its capacity to affirm itself.

As both Becker and DeMartino suggest, the self needs constant reassurance—healthy self-esteem requires constant renewal—and in this state of deprivation and autorejection it quickly begins to lose both defensive and functional capacity. Weakened at its core, it falls prey to all manner of tensions, which, in turn, breed both symptoms and compensatory reactions.

Identification, which is the principal architect of the ideal self, is a vital but hazardous process. When it is directed toward realistic figures that the individual can successfully imitate, it molds an attainable ideal and, hence, makes possible regular experiences of self-ideal congruity. Self-ideal congruent experience invariably betokens pride, well-being, and positive self-imagery. Such experience is pure tonic to people, and it can be depended upon to invigorate them psychologically. When, on the other hand, identifications attach themselves to fantasy figures that cannot be even remotely approximated in reality, the ideal becomes unattainable, and the stage is set for chronic self-ideal discrepancy with its gloomy cast of psychic characters: guilt, depression, anxiety, and hostility. Experience in connection with self-ideal discrepancy tends to be noxious, and it can be depended upon to enervate people psychologically.

In the first instance, the process of identification not only provides people with an internal mechanism for self-affirmation, for self-love, but it also helps direct their energies along socially useful paths. By identifying with realistic personal models—parents, teachers, accomplished peers and adults—who in various ways are working productively and creatively, individuals gradually acquire the skills and purposes they need to follow in their models' footsteps, and perhaps surpass them. Slowly but surely, by this process of unconscious internalization, they are equipping themselves to become useful, responsible, and fair-minded citizens. When properly directed, the mechanism of identification operates steadily and quietly on behalf of the individual *and* society.

In the second instance, wherein fantastic, unattainable figures are internalized, identification can cause havoc for both parties. Oppressed by chronic self-ideal discrepancy, people must necessarily lack the vital capacity for periodic self-affirmation. Further, they will more than likely be deficient in socially useful skills and purposes. In this case, identification gone awry *hurts* the individual and society. Of course, most people living in our society identify with both realistic and unrealistic figures during their developmental and adult years. However, the imagery of fantasy, growing step-by-step with the growth of the mass media, can be seen to be progressively fostering the second instance.

IDEALIZATION AND IDENTIFICATION

As implied throughout this discussion, idealization is an important aspect of the process of identification. Identification figures are not only internalized, but in addition they tend to be invested with various degrees of charisma, raised up on a pedestal in the mind of the individual. This aspect of identification has important consequences for human aspiration and self-transcendence. It is also critical to social change and progress. Esther Menaker's remarks on this subject are edifying.

In the course of individuation and differentiation the ego depends for its development on the experience of the outer world of reality, on its encounter with the world, and on the internalization of significant love-objects. Were this internalization merely a duplication within the psyche of outer reality—were the parents mirrored within as they actually exist in reality, without idealization—then the element of aspiration, of progress toward higher goals, would disappear from experience. The history of man's cultural development contradicts such a possibility. Mankind has always been characterized by striving; the individual in his struggle to become individuated is always future-directed. It is because the child believes his idealization to be real that in the course of growth of his ego he has the potentiality for exceeding his predecessors. Thus the capacity for idealization through the use of creative imagination is a major factor in man's sociocultural evolution as well as in the psychological evolution of the ego. Obviously, not all identifications are used constructively in individual development, nor is the course of history a consistently progressive one. Nevertheless, it is the ability to idealize that makes for change in the direction of higher levels of organization, both in the individual and in history.[32]

Menaker is indicating the importance of the ego-ideal to growth, creativity, and transcendent effort, aspects of human behavior that contribute vitally to cultural evolution. In her view it is the passionate idealization of internalized models, such as parents, teacher, and cultural heroes, that motives people to work to carry the efforts of these models forward, and perhaps add something creatively as well. Were these figures registered graphically, as a camera registers its object, the inspirational spark would be missing, as would the self-transcending effort. If Menaker's assertions are valid, the inflated ideal self of the demoralized American again looms as a potential threat to social progress. Idealization of unrealistic fantasy figures cannot possibly help to equip people with skills useful to cultural progress in a complex technology-saturated world. In addition, the resulting personal values and motivations are apt to further inhibit the development of such arduously acquired capacities. As a practicing psychotherapist, Menaker finds considerable evidence of this problem in her clinical work. She states,

It has been my impression from recent work with patients that the fragmentation of the ego due to the pathological character of the ego-ideal and superego and the conflict between them, is as responsible for much of the inhibition which we encounter in the area of sex and work as is conflict surrounding the gratification of instinctual drives.[33]

Elaborating on these observations she adds,

The ego-ideal, as it represents the individual's aspirations, gives meaning and direction to his life, and because the individual is part of a larger social unit, as he interacts with others, his ego-ideal may come to influence society as a whole and may ultimately affect the evolution of culture itself.[34]

When one reflects on it, the thought of large numbers of today's youths idealizing garish media figures, particularly those exhibiting hair-trigger violence, is chilling to say the least. What is more, there is good reason to assume that people laboring under the demoralization in question are especially prone to the adoption of aggressive-violent thought patterns and, in many cases, behavior patterns of a similar stripe as well. Idealization of media unreality tends to stimulate imitation of media violence. The link between the two lies in the fact that hostility is a natural concomitant of irritated self-ideal discrepancy. The demoralization is intimately associated with hostility because it is a profuse breeder of actual and anticipated frustration. People suffering the demoralization seethe with free-floating hostility because they naturally anticipate and experience failure, rejection, and many other forms of frustration.

The large body of research summarized in the Comstock study indicates a relationship between the viewing of violence on television and the tendency to react with various forms of internal and overt aggression.[35] It is true, the data from the various studies are ambiguous, and in general it is not clear that violence viewing necessarily increases the incidence of such overt forms as crime, delinquency, and physical assault. However, a number of studies suggest that when a predisposition to aggression exists in the personality, television violence can serve to trigger it, as well as channel it into overt expression. P. H. Tannenbaum and B. S. Greenberg conclude that the portrayal of aggressive acts on television causes subsequent aggressive behavior on the part of children and young people, and it is especially liable to do so when aggressive acts are portrayed as justified, when the viewer is angry and frustrated, and when there is an available target against whom it would be appropriate to aggress.[36] W. Weiss concludes that the imitation of observed aggression depends in part on whether the viewed violence is followed by frustration.[37] On this topic, the principal conclusions of a study done by a scientific advisory committee to the surgeon general are as follows:

Evidence from experiments, surveys, and various other types of studies indicate that there is a causal relationship between viewing violence on television and aggressiveness on the part of children and young people. However, this conclusion can only be said to be "preliminary and tentative." Such effect of violence viewing, if indeed it occurs, may be limited to children who are "predisposed to be aggressive,'' and may depend on various circumstances surrounding exposure to the violent television content.[38]

It might occur to the reader that since so much television content is violent, identification with television figures would naturally foster aggressive behavior in the viewing public. Why, then, is it necessary to invoke the hostility that is integral to the demoralization in discussing the relationship between the imagery of fantasy and aggression? To begin with, television is only one source of this imagery. It flows out from all forms of the mass media, and in addition echoes of it rebound from person to person in the wider society. Second, its principal effect on the individual is to inculcate a sense of personal inadequacy, guilt, and deprivation. Although a certain amount of it is violent, much more of it is devoted to glamour, excitement, and material abundance. A curious paradox appears to operate here. In promoting irritated self-ideal discrepancy, imagery of a seemingly harmless, even benign, nature indirectly contributes to chronic frustrations and hostilities that are apt to produce, over time, a predisposition to aggression. In the case of the demoralization this predisposition to aggression definitely exists, and in a general sense, it fosters imitation of media violence. Where the demoralization has settled in, media unreality potentiates media violence in its effects on individual behavior. This applies more to young viewers and those from the lower classes than to other groups.

DeMartino's analysis indicates how and why the condition of irritated self-ideal discrepancy is potentially catastrophic to the individual. Deprived of a satisfying and meaningful image of itself, the struggling ego cannot regularly affirm and thus renew itself. Necessarily weakened, under extreme circumstances it may die. This is reminiscent, on the intrapsychic plane, of the condition of "marasmus" described by René Spitz. In this unfortunate condition institutionalized infants may, despite adequate physical care, waste away and expire for lack of warm personal contact with a parental (mothering) figure. Normally, in the course of healthy psychological development, realistic and loving parental figures are intimately experienced, and as a consequence they are identified with and internalized into the ideal self. Ultimately, this equips individuals with a mechanism for providing themselves with the intrapsychic equivalent of parental praise and love. Each time they live up to some facet of their inner ideal, they experience self-ideal congruity, which naturally releases the equivalent in the form of pride and self-esteem, that is, self-love. Just as the real McCoy literally helps strengthen the infant and keep it alive, so does its intrapsychic equivalent provide life-giving sustenance to the more self-sufficient, but struggling, youth and adult. While irritated self-ideal discrepancy does not usually push the individual to the brink of death, it does contribute to an emotional tone within the personality that is not unlike the cold, grim, despondent atmosphere of the public mental institution. If this seems overstated, recall that in contemporary America depression is epidemic, and suicide is, after traumatic accidents, the second leading cause of death among the 17- to 34-year-old age group.

Earlier, I made reference to the dimensions of the situations into which growing children are thrown in contemporary America. I suggested that advanced technology, particularly modern communications technology, has expanded the experiential realms of most people enormously in comparison to those of people living a scant fifty or a hundred years ago. While this expansion of personal experience, both actual and vicarious, has much that is potentially beneficial, it can be seen to foster the process of individual identification with much that is patently unrealistic. Further, this expansion of vicarious experience, taken together with the simultaneous loosening of the family structure—a concomitant development having its roots in the same technetronic soil, so to speak—can also be seen as having particularly serious consequences for the mental development of American children. In this sense it carries frankly bleak national portents, which, twenty-five years into the future, may yet erupt and supersede the less sinister, but growing multiplicity of symptoms of national malaise extant today. For if we consider a scenario in which on the one side parent-child relationships are increasingly alienated, and on the other side children are increasingly absorbed in the imagery of unreality, it is possible to see how the natural process of identification might well begin, on a national scale, to turn outward too early. And if the opportunity for meaningful, gratifying experience with real parents is lacking, or relatively so, then children, if they are still healthy enough to desire life and some form of involvement, will naturally turn elsewhere to fill the void. All too often, today, the tube flickering in the corner provides an immediate and effortless solution to the problem.

Self theorists generally agree that development of the self-construct is fundamentally influenced by the wider society. As children grow, they encounter an ever-widening sphere of influence that typically runs from the nuclear and extended families through the peer culture to the various institutions of the society at large. An important implication of the above sequence is that the earliest stages, in which children are most helpless and impressionable, are facilitated by persons who care deeply about them. Presumably, in healthy families at least, the flow and quality of experience is such that growing infants are not overwhelmed or grossly misled as they explore the inherently natural "blooming, buzzing confusion" of their unfolding worlds. I am suggesting that in modern America this timeworn sequence is being telescoped in a way that is clearly dangerous to the process of healthy self-development. In far too many instances, children are being confronted too early with too much of the distal society, the principal agent behind this premature encounter being, of course, the television set. If we consider the omnipresent tube in combination with such contemporary societal trends as working mothers, enrollments in day-care centers, broken homes, and the like, it can be assumed that in a growing number of contemporary American homes elements of the wider culture are encroaching on the traditional parental roles in the early, supercritical, phases of child rearing. From the standpoint of this discussion, the influence of television is especially troublesome because it is the chief source of the imagery of unreality under scrutiny herein.

Menaker's comments, by drawing attention to the connection between idealization of personal models and social progress, further suggest why irritated self-ideal discrepancy, which always begins on the individual level, carries ominous portents of a much broader stripe.

To maintain the meaningfulness of existence and to insure a sense of his own continuity, men sought to fulfill in reality the idealizations he created in his mind—that is, to actualize his ego-ideal. As an individual his self-esteem depends in a large measure on the extent to which he succeeds in the realization of these idealizations. For society, its cohesion and survival may depend on the commonality of its ego-ideals; its progress on a flexibility which will permit viable modifications of its ideals.[39]

Although it has different causes, the inadequacy feeling associated with the demoralization is a close variant of Adler's inferiority complex. In his unified theory of human nature, Adler saw inferiority feelings and depleted self-esteem as lying at the root of all forms of functional psychopathology—neurosis, psychosis, alcoholism, and so on. In the face of these feelings of inferiority the compensatory masculine protest, the "wanting to be a real man," becomes the prepotent dynamic force within the personality.[40] Furthermore, in Adler's view, this is only a perversion of the impetus from minus to plus, the "great upward drive." As corollary to this, the outward hallmark of all maladjustment is stunted social interest. Caught up in the masculine protest and preoccupied with his own relative superiority, the disturbed individual turns away from social challenges and responsibilities. In Adler's terms, he veers from strivings on the "commonly useful side" to those on the "commonly useless side." On this specific point he wrote,

The normal man is an individual who lives in society and whose mode of life is so adapted that, whether he wants it or not, society derives a certain advantage from his work. From the psychological point of view, he has enough energy and courage to meet the problems and difficulties as they come along. Both of these qualities are missing in abnormal persons: They are neither socially adjusted nor are they psychologically adjusted to meet the tasks of life.[41]

But, in Adler's view, there is a self-defeating aspect to the masculine protest, because all real human value comes from social contribution. In this regard he stated, "The only salvation from the continuously driving inferiority feeling is the knowledge and feeling of being valuable which originate from contribution to the common welfare."[42] Adler's comments suggest yet another dimension to the problem. He is in agreement with DeMartino and Menaker that depleted self-esteem is potentially damaging to both the individual and society. However, in his appreciation of things, it is only through appropriate social action that individuals can effectively resurrect their waning sense of personal value. While withdrawal of social interest is a natural concomitant of depleted self-esteem, such withdrawal only complicates the problem. Becker, in his reflections on self-esteem, reaches the same conclusions. In reference to the need for continuous renewal of self-esteem he remarked, "Only by proper performance in the social context does the individual fashion and renew himself by purposeful action in a world of shared meaning."[43]

The heavy irony of the imagery of fantasy continues to be noteworthy. Although it appears, on the basis of this analysis, as something of a psychological Pied Piper, leading the unsuspecting rats (Americans) over the edge of the abyss, it is certainly the product of much human industry and technological progress, and, assumedly, benign intent. However, though calculated to entertain people and spur them on to the achievement of ever-greater material abundance, in far too many instances it can be seen to backfire by contributing to an internal psychological discord that makes them particularly vulnerable to the anguish of perceived personal inadequacy and failure. This phenomenon is deadly; individuals cannot take too much of it. Nor can society.

DEEPER DYNAMICS: AN INADEQUACY COMPLEX

The idea of an inadequacy complex has explanatory value in reference to the demoralization under discussion. Although this is speculative, it is my belief that today many Americans suffer from an inadequacy complex in much the same way that psychoneurotics, as described by Freudians and Adlerians respectively, suffer from an Oedipus or inferiority complex.

Turning again to Goldenson's *Encyclopedia of Human Behavior: Psychology, Psychiatry and Mental Health*, we find the following entry under "Complex":

A group or system of related ideas which have a strong common emotional tone. Complexes operate largely if not wholly on an unconscious level and are believed to be at the core of many of our fundamental drives and conflicts. The most important of these complexes in modern psychiatry are the castration complex, the inferiority complex, and the Oedipus complex.[44]

This idea is convincing for a number of reasons: (1) inadequacy feeling is widespread; (2) once fixed in the personality, it is invasive and resistant to change; (3) it has a clear topographical dimension, with deeper dynamics influencing surface reactions and symptoms; and (4) much of it can be seen, theoretically, to stem from the experiential bind. In many cases, then, we may not be dealing simply with random, garden-variety, feelings of inadequacy, but rather with an inadequacy complex: an enduring psychical structure that is capable of operating indefinitely, influencing a wide range of behaviors, and producing, in some instances at least, serious psychopathology.

The reader might well conclude at this point that the inadequacy complex is merely a rehash of the Adlerian inferiority complex. It is true that there are parallels between the two complexes in terms of surface symptoms and deeper dynamics. However, as I view it, there are two basic characteristics of the inadequacy complex serving to differentiate it from the inferiority complex. The first has to do with etiology. Adler, in the tradition of psychodynamic depth psychologists, attributed the inferiority complex ultimately to infantile experiences occurring in the context of the nuclear family. Specifically, he saw pampering, rejection, or the presence of some physical organ deficiency as conditions capable of imbuing the infant or child with an early abnormal sense of inferiority that would predispose it to the development of an adult inferiority complex. As stated previously, I believe that the essential cause of the generic inadequacy complex is the experiential bind, which is not simply a familial phenomenon but a societal, or cultural, one. In this sense, virtually everyone in modern America is exposed to the conditions capable of causing the complex. Of course, a serious clinical complex does not develop in all persons, there being enormous individual differences between them in terms of susceptibility to it. Curiously, there is a distinct parallel here with the Freudian Oedipus complex. Virtually all people in Western culture participate early in their lives in the Oedipal triad; but by no means do all adults exhibit clear-cut evidence of the complex, although viewed through the psychoanalytic prism, neurotics do. These individual differences in terms of vulnerability to both the Oedipus and inadequacy complexes are no doubt due to a multiplicity of physical, psychological, social, and philosophical factors. And in both cases it is practically impossible at any point in time to predict in the individual case whether a serious complex will supervene. However, this unpredictability applies to all psychological complexes because, on the one hand, they are intricate in their structure and, on the other hand, they are essentially subtle, quantitative, variations on normal patterns of human behavior.

The second characteristic differentiating the two complexes has to do with a subtle, but important, nuance of the basic self-regard within the inadequacy complex. The primary subjective experience within the complex is that of a relative lack of personal value and potency, a vague but insistent impression that one does not have sufficient poise, charm, intelligence, drive, talent, education, and so on to live as fully and effectively *as other people appear to*. Its cutting edge is a sense of deficiency in regard to those qualities supplying the key to the good life, that gaudy but evanescent illusion proffered daily by the imagery of fantasy beaming out from the various media. There is further the tendency to assume that somehow many people, perhaps people in general, are living more happily and effectively than oneself: they make more money, enjoy more popularity, have better sex, achieve greater career success, manage a better psychological adjustment, and on and on. This free-floating envy stems directly from the unrealistic expectations of the inflated ideal self, which in turn are constantly fed, literally force-fed, by the omnipresent imagery of fantasy. It is natural for a person oriented toward and wishing for spectacular success to attribute it to other people who, in various ways, appear to reflect its trappings. Like the images from the media, however, these people are generally perceived only transitorily and at a distance. In truth, most of them commonly lead much more pedestrian and troubled lives than an individual ever suspects; nearly everyone does. But the envious assumptions endure, and they tend to deepen the perceiver's feeling of personal inadequacy.

Related to both the sense of personal inadequacy and the envious assumptions concerning others' successes is the tendency to pervasive self-dissatisfaction. This is the conscious manifestation of the deeper-lying guilt characteristic of the complex. People tend to be dissatisfied with themselves, and as a result they are dissatisfied with their lives—their achievements, salaries, spouses, homes, appearance, skills, and what not. Because of their unrealistic expectations and unconscious self-devaluation, what they are and have is apt to appear shabby and mediocre in comparison with the accomplishments and possessions and essences of many other people. Even though they can point to many individuals and groups who are clearly less well-off and less accomplished than themselves, they have the distinct impression that "successful" people in general are definitely outstripping them. A manifestation of the unconscious arrogance associated with this demoralization and inadequacy feeling is the fact that people suffering it are far more concerned with those above them on the totem pole than with those below them. This grinding dissatisfaction can be seen as a major determinant of the psychopathic narcissism that appears to be running wild in America today. Because of their inner discontent, many Americans are caught up in a cynical, greedy quest for more and more of the trappings of success, of the "good life."

While similar to feelings of inferiority, the inadequacy feeling in question has a different innuendo and implication. Rather than a distinct feeling of inferiority, it entails a noisome sense of insufficient *apparent normalcy*. People suffering the inadequacy complex do not necessarily feel ugly, weak, stupid, and socially offensive, particularly in comparison with their friends, intimates, and everyday associates. But they do tend to feel insufficiently attractive, strong, intelligent, charming, and educated in connection with a distant, but hypnotic, set of images and illusions that can be best subsumed under the terms "success" or "the good life." It is as if they do not have enough talent and power to achieve real success, to gain entry into the good life that is so continuously dangled before their eyes, and that is surely being enjoyed, so it seems, by so many others in society. Thus, they feel shortchanged, left out, ripped off; and because of these persistent disappointments and disillusionments, they fall prey to their own unconscious self-devaluation.

It needs to be stressed that these attitudes toward the self, as well as the assumptions regarding others, are typically not up in the front of consciousness. Like the elements in other psychological complexes, they tend to hang on the fringes of awareness in either a preconscious or unconscious state. Further, when confronted by circumstance that stimulate such thoughts and feelings, people tend to ward them off with denial, rationalization, projection, and other ego-defense mechanisms. But they are apparent to the careful observer, and they can be seen to underlie much guilt, narcissism, anxiety, hostility, and depression, as well as a virtually endless array of secondary symptoms that mar the lives of too many people in modern America.

I have suggested that the inadequacy complex differs from other well-known psychological complexes in regard to the problem of etiology. While other complexes typically have their origins in early infantile experiences deriving from an idiosyncratic family context, the inadequacy complex has its essential cause in pervasive, here-and-now experiences deriving from a much broader societal context. As a corollary to this, the psychodynamic nucleus of the complex is seen to consist of an aggregate of self-evaluative thoughts and images, with a variety of the more primitive emotional and motivational factors having secondary, reactive significance. Employing psychoanalytic terms, it is viewed primarily as an ego-superego complex. By drawing further on psychoanalytic theory and momentarily adopting the topographical point of view—delineating the conscious, preconscious, and unconscious layers of the psyche—one gains the impression that as the complex develops in the individual case, it spreads downward into the psyche, moving from the more conscious, cognitive-perceptual surface to the less conscious, emotional-motivational depths. In accordance with the general developmental model of personality, psychological complexes are usually viewed as spreading upward in the character structure, with early emotional-motivational disturbances ultimately effecting cognitive-perceptual processes. There is thus the impression of something like a reversal of the usual developmental sequence.

   The dynamics of the inadequacy complex revolve around the concept
of chronically irritated self-ideal discrepancy. Although this particular formulation is associated with Rogerian theory, the idea concerning the
potential for dissonance between the two aspects of the self is integral
to most traditional psychodynamic theories of emotional disorder and
mental illness.
   Rogerians see the basic source of emotional maladjustment as stemming from internally perceived discrepancies that threaten the integrity
of the self, and thus generate anxieties and growth-restrictive defensive
reactions. These discrepancies occur primarily between the self and experience on the one hand and between the actual self and ideal self on
the other. According to Rogerian theory, in successful psychotherapy
modifications of both the actual and ideal components are achieved that
permit greater harmony between expectations and experience, thus
facilitating both reduction of anxiety and the maintenance of positive self-
regard. On this particular point Rogers states, "As a consequence of the
increased congruence of self and ideal self and the greater congruence
of self and experience, tension of all types is reduced . . . physiological
tension, psychological tension, and the specific type of psychological tension defined as anxiety."[45]
   Other theories employ the same basic concept, albeit in different terms.
Freudians speak of a pathological tension between the ego and an unrealistically demanding ego-ideal in explaining various states of maladjustment
in which the symptoms and subjective distress focus on depression and
insistent feelings of failure. In cases of this type, the analyst's principal
therapeutic objective is to help bring about a modification of the analysand's
ego-ideal, so that it is in better accord with his/her real capacities and with
reality in general. Similarly, Horneyians emphasize the therapeutic importance of diminishing the punitive influence of an arrogant idealized self upon
the real self in counteracting the widespread neurotic tendencies to self-
contempt and self-hate. Writers of the existentialist school extol a kind of
intrepid self-affirmation, accepting oneself as accepted in spite of being unacceptable, in maintaining what Paul Tillich called the courage to be, an attitude that is basic to the existential model of mental health and one that
tends to be lost or severely weakened in various states of maladjustment.
The implication here is that pathological proneness to debilitating anxiety
is intimately bound up with chronic, morbid self-devaluation, an inability
to accept oneself in spite of personally perceived limitations.
   While perusal of other theories—Jungian, Frommian, and Adlerian, for
example—would produce similar formulations, the above is sufficient to
illustrate the well-known connection between an irritated self-ideal
discrepancy and various forms of frank psychopathology.
   I have emphasized the point that inflation of the ideal self is the principal influence of the experiential bind upon individual personalities. The

reader might well raise a question concerning the relationship between an inflated ideal self and chronic feelings of inadequacy. He/she might ask, ''If a people expect a lot of themselves, have exalted images of what they could or should be, why not assume a related sense of potency or personal significance in such cases?'' The answer lies in the fact that more often than not such an inflated ideal self is discrepant from the actual self, and as a consequence it sets up a dangerous disharmony within the personality. In terms of concrete experience, such persons' sense of what they are falls painfully short of what they feel they ought to be, and it is this inner discord that feeds both a sense of inadequacy and an unconscious process of self-devaluation.

As mentioned earlier, an underlying self-ideal discrepancy is translated moment by moment into consciousness as a sense of personal inadequacy in regard to the actual self: what people feel they really are, here and now. The ideal self is the less conscious aspect of the total self, and persons suffering self-ideal discrepancy are usually unaware that the performance standards deriving from their ideals are apt to be unrealistically high, and hence part of the problem. Put differently, the emphasis within the subjective stream of consciousness is invariably on a sense of actual personal sufficiency and almost never, barring rare flashes of insight, on the opposite sense of exorbitant expectations. As a matter of fact, most people are only vaguely aware of their ideal selves, and useful insights concerning the unreality of many of the preconscious and unconscious expectations embedded therein are commonly achieved only in effective psychotherapy or in other kinds of deeply revelatory personal experience.

A general typology of self-ideal relationships displays three essential categories, only one of which entails the troublesome discrepancy lying at the heart of the inadequacy complex. It is possible to conceptualize a class of people whose images of themselves are modest, even humble, and who at the same time do not aspire to much in life. In the typology they would be classified as LSLI (low self–low ideal), and by the logic involved they would appear to enjoy a certain measure of self-ideal congruity. Perhaps we are thinking of shallow persons, even simpletons, or maybe people tucked away in remote areas and thus relatively shielded from the imagery of fantasy. But theoretically, they are immune to the complex.

On the other extreme, one can imagine a class of people whose ideals and standards are typically high, but who, because of exceptional endowment and the acquisition of special skills, have realistically high images of themselves. In the typology they would be HSHI (high self–high ideal), and they, too, would theoretically be self-ideal congruent and thus insulated from the complex. While admittedly rare, this type is by no means an impossibility; it is exemplified by leaders and significant contributors in all walks of life. This is not to suggest that leaders and singularly creative people are necessarily immune to the complex, merely that they are more likely to enjoy a healthy and durable self-ideal congruity. However, when one thinks about it, it does make sense that people of exceptional endowment and achievement are probably better able than most to parry and resist the double-edged assault of the experiential bind.

It is a third type, coded LSHI (low self–high ideal), whose sense of what they actually are falls painfully short of what they aspire to be, who demonstrate the pathogenic discrepancy predisposing them to the complex. This type is characterized by the average citizens in America whose social positions, natural gifts, and worldly achievements fall into some broad middle range, but who, massaged constantly by the imagery of fantasy, expect and demand much more of themselves and life. They are the subject of this book, and in America their numbers are legion.

Since the ideal self, by definition, normally eclipses the actual self, a fourth type manifesting a backward discrepancy and coded HSLI (high self–low ideal) is really something of a theoretical contradiction and difficult to characterize. One thinks of the schizophrenics who are ostensibly content to sit in the mental institutions indulging their delusions of grandeur, while aspiring to nothing in the real world, as possible illustating this reverse discrepancy. But it is generally accepted within the psychiatric community that such persons are in fact so extremely LSHI that the associated intrapsychic tensions have caused them to break with reality and fabricate fictitious identities and life spaces. Perhaps the generalization holds, given the centrality of the self-construct within the personality, that such a reverse discrepancy can occur only under conditions of severe psychotic or psychopathic disturbance.

THE DISCREPANCY IN DETAIL

In order to gain a clear understanding of the inadequacy complex, it is necessary to examine the underlying self-ideal discrepancy in some detail. I have suggested that the principal intrapsychic influence of the experiential bind is the inflation, or aggrandizement, of the ideal self. The intrapsychic tensions inherent in the complex seem to be due more to a rise in expected performance than a decline in perceived personal capacity, although the latter is a very real aspect of the discrepancy and cannot be discounted. Admittedly, this assignment of greater importance to the inflation of the ideal self, in contrast to the deflation of the actual self, in the dynamics of the complex is based on a judgment that cannot be proven at this point. However, in my mind, it is the realm of vicarious experience, superheated by the media, that is causing the more significant dislocation within the self-construct of the average American today. Certainly, it is this realm of experience that has grown the more rapidly in modern postindustrial societies in the past forty years or so. Further, this kind of experience exerts a special pull on the ideal self, which naturally seeks to idealize, internalize, and emulate heroic models perceived at a distance.

Assuming for the moment that the internal psychological stress produced by the discrepancy is due relatively more to inflation of the ideal self, it is important to examine both the structure and dynamics of this part of the total self. In order to do so, it will be helpful to allude momentarily to psychoanalytic theory and its conceptualization of the superego, the seat of the ego-ideal. In a detailed analysis of the Freudian superego Elliot Turiell states:

In many of his writings Freud used conscience and ego-ideal interchangeably. However, in "On Narcissism" they were used as two different, though related, concepts. The ego-ideal represents those cultural standards the ego is striving to achieve, and which have been derived from parents, education and other influences in the environment. The conscience, on the other hand, is that faculty of the mind which watches over the ego and compares it to the ego ideal. Therefore, the conscience observes the self, and criticizes when there are discrepancies between ego and ego-ideal. Conscience is obtained through internalization of the parental function of criticizing the child. . . . While Freud mainly discussed the hostile criticizing aspect of the conscience, he also viewed it as a faculty that bestows love on the self. He referred to conscience as a ". . . special institution in the mind which performs the task of seeing that narcissistic gratification is secured from the ego-ideal and that, with this end in view, it constantly watches the real ego and measures it by that ideal." When the ego does measure up to the ideal then it is the function of the conscience to bestow love and praise to the ego. Fulfillment of the ideal results in an increase of self-esteem, while a failure to meet the standards of the ideal results in a decrease of self-esteem.[46]

This whole formulation is readily applicable to the Rogerian concept of self-ideal discrepancy. Very simply, the greater the congruity between the actual and ideal selves, the greater the bestowal of love and praise by the conscience upon the actual self; and the greater the discrepancy between these two components, the greater the criticism of the actual self by the conscience. In the case of chronic, irritated self-ideal discrepancy, this can only result in a pernicious self-devaluation, which is, in the final analysis, the root danger of the inadequacy complex. Such a process of self-devaluation accomplishes the work of morbid, corrosive guilt, which is, in my mind, the very keystone of functional psychopathology, in all of its troublesome diversity.

The ego-ideal, which spurs the conscience into its surveillant function, is an aggregate of images, standards, and values that are ultimately derived from the society in which the individual lives. In the public mind the superego of psychoanalytic parlance has a distinctly moralistic flavor, serving mainly to warn against and inhibit behaviors of an immoral or criminal nature. While this is partially true, psychoanalytic research has also shown that the ego-ideal, which is the real repository of values within the superego, has other dimensions in addition to the moral-ethical one, just as society, in all its complexity, embodies much more than the moral-ethical acts of human beings. As Henry Murray and Clyde Kluckhohn put it,

One of the important establishments of the personality is the ego ideal, an aggregate of images which portrays the person "at his future best," realizing all of his ambitions. More specifically, it is a set of serial programs, each of which has a different level of aspiration. Ego ideals run all the way from the Master Criminal to the Serene Sage. They are imaginatively created and recreated in the course of development in response to patterns offered by the environment—mythological, historical, or living exemplars. Thus the history of the ideal self may be depicted as a series of imaginative identifications, of heroes and their worship.[47]

Again, while I have consulted psychoanalytic theory in this discussion of the ego-ideal, all of this can be directly translated into self theory and the concept of the ideal self.

It is my contention that the pathological inflation of the ideal selves of millions of Americans, occurring in the face of the experiential bind, has overwhelmingly to do with aspirations pertinent to the achievement of worldly success and preeminence. The imagery of fantasy preponderating in the vicarious experiential realm is contributing to a secularization of those ideal selves at the same time that it is feeding their exaggerated development. Consequently, the subjective distress of the inadequacy complex derives overwhelmingly from a sense of social-physical-intellectual insufficiency, and almost never from a complementary sense of moral-ethical laxity. In fact, moral-ethical considerations promoting self-denial and behavioral restraint are apt to be perceived by the individual sufferer as part of the problem, and tacitly evaluated as personal weaknesses or impediments.

An awareness of the secularization of the ideal self that is taking place in modern postindustrial society is critical to an understanding of the inadequacy complex, particularly in its tendency to generate behaviors and symptoms of an antisocial stripe. The alarming increase in this kind of behavior in America is not due to a generalized diminution in the capacity to feel guilt among the populace, as asserted by some writers, but rather to an insidious transformation of the models, and hence the values, of the collective ideal self. I believe that rather than feeling less guilt, people in America are literally feeling more. However, it is not traditional moral-ethical guilt as much as it is the guilt of worldly insufficiency. The atrophy of traditional religious values in America has resulted in a profound transformation of personal ideals, as well as the guilts such ideals have always engendered. These changes have had an equally profound impact on both the inner life and overt behavior of many people.

In considering the self-ideal discrepancy lying at the root of the inadequacy complex, it is critical to bear in mind the harshness and urgency that is apt to characterize the ideal self. This agency of the mind defines not only what people would like to be, but in many instances what they *must* be, if they are to enjoy any measure of self-esteem and inner peace. Psychoanalytic writing is full of references to the pathological influence of a sadistic, punitive superego, and it is regularly invoked in explaining the acute suffering associated with various neurotic and psychotic disorders. In such cases the conscience denounces the ego incessantly, and we can assume from Turiell's account of superego dynamics that it is driven to this action by an unfulfilled ego-ideal. People caught up in the inadequacy complex endure a great deal of anxiety and depression that arises out of an identical process of self-denunciation.

So far, in examining the dynamics of the complex, I have emphasized cognitive factors, implicit ideas, and images constituting the two principal parts of the self-construct. This has been done by design since these self-evaluative cognitions are seen to be the nucleus of the complex. Further, I think of these attitudes as deeper dynamics in the sense that they frequently operate outside awareness in a preconscious or unconscious manner. However, the complex also involves a number of related phenomena, both affective and motivational, that can be seen as natural reactions to a chronic sense of personal inadequacy. These primary reactions involve hostility, anxiety, depression, guilt, and pathological narcissism. It is not particularly clear in my mind whether to think of these reactions as dynamics or symptoms, and perhaps a rigid differentiation is superfluous. Of importance is the fact that they are dependable concomitants of irritated self-ideal discrepancy, either in toto or in various combinations.

HOSTILITY

The key to understanding the hostility and aggression generated by the complex comes from the "frustration-aggression" hypothesis developed by John Dollard et al.[48] While subsequent research required modification of the original hypothesis, the idea that some form of hostility-aggression is a natural, if not inevitable, response to frustration is generally held as valid. The inadequacy complex is intimately associated with hostility-aggression because it is a constant and profuse breeder of both anticipated and actual frustration. In regard to the former, anticipation of frustration prior to actual experience is a highly probable reaction in persons suffering from irritated self-ideal discrepancy. This anticipation is caused primarily by unconscious projection of negative self-regard forward in time, with the result that situations and involvements, particularly novel ones, are approached in an attitude of wary, cynical self-consciousness. Free-floating hostility is a natural concomitant of irritated self-ideal discrepancy. It is safe to say that people with this intrapsychic dynamic will literally ooze with defensive hostility over the anticipated reactions of other people, as well as the outcomes of many personal involvements.

The actual frustrations associated with the complex also stem directly from the underlying self-devaluation. And again, unconscious projection is the mechanism whereby momentary negative self-regard is simultaneously beamed out to other people, so that their reactions are perceived as being congruent with the self-assessment. As with perceptual reactions in general, this misinterpretation is fostered in transitory and ambiguous situations. It tends to wash out under scrutiny. However, in the course of the average workday in our busy, fast-paced society, many interpersonal interactions are basically transitory, thus providing fertile soil for the occurrence of such distortions.

It is relatively easy to illustrate this projection, which is similar to, though not identical with, the familiar Freudian ego-defense mechanism by the same name. Readers will recall one of those "bad days" during which they felt psychologically down and generally unready to face the world. More than likely the memory will include the experience that on such a day it is typically hard to relate to other people, that in some vague way they seem cold and indifferent rather than warm and friendly. If readers pursue their reminiscence, they will probably also recall that on such a day efforts at dealing with normal tasks and projects seem ineffective, even fumbling and futile. As a consequence, something like an attitude of defensive hostility, coupled with a desire to withdraw, begins to creep into one's mood. This generalized feeling of rejection mixed with a sense of functional impotence is maintained largely by unconscious projection of negative self-regard outward into the interpersonal environment, the net result being a kind of objective confirmation of one's subjective sense of self. The point here is that persons who are filled with self-contempt and self-doubt tend, on the basis of unconscious projection, to perceive others as regarding them in the same way, and the subjective experience is very compelling. Further, such unconscious projection of self-doubt sets the stage for interpersonal withdrawal and defensiveness, both of which tend to sink these people more deeply into a sense of alienation, incompetence, and frustration. Hence, the generation of a troublesome vicious cycle.

The opposite to this illustration also applies. Readers will, more happily, recall a typical "good day" during which other people characteristically seem warmly responsive, and regular projects appear to be handled with relative dispatch. On this kind of a day the generalized feeling of interpersonal harmony mixed with functional competence is also due in large measure to projection of immediate self-regard, except that in this latter instance the self-regard is much more apt to be warm and positive. This more benign projection also tends to facilitate behaviors and attitudes that serve to perpetuate the day's happier tone, namely, interpersonal participation and inner confidence. Hence, the initiation of a virtuous cycle. Of course, it goes without saying that the condition of chronically irritated self-ideal discrepancy predisposes people to a larger number of bad days over good days within any time frame, taken randomly.

The level of unsatisfied craving and hence the level of general frustration that people suffer is as much a function of their self-constructs as it is a result of the actual scarcity or abundance of their life situations. It is particularly the inflated ideal self within the total self that predisposes so many people in contemporary America to excessive yearning. People tend to want those things and experiences that either directly or symbolically complement their ideal selves and bolster their sense of personal significance. In America these things have a distinctly hedonistic-materialistic form; they may be money, prestige, celebrity status, sensual-sexual pleasure, excitement, and the like.

It is interesting that two central precepts of Buddhism have to do with the necessity of suppressing sentient desire and eliminating the individual sense of self as distinct from the surrounding cosmos. Buddhism has long taught that the sense of self invariably results in cravings that are doomed to endless frustration in an impersonal world. If this is so, then contemporary Americans are in deep trouble on two counts, psychologically speaking. Not only is the sense of "self-versus-the-world" basic to the Western psyche; but because of the daily influence of the experiential bind, the American strain of the competing Western self-ego, is being rent internally by an inner structural discrepancy. Assuming the truth of this ancient Buddhist precept, both factors can be seen as combining to breed interminable frustration and its natural emotional concomitant, hostility. The escalating index of violent crime in America looms as a grim supporting statistic in connection with this discussion of hostility.

DEPRESSION

Depression is another common emotional concomitant of the nuclear dynamics of the inadequacy complex. Further, depression frequently feeds many of the more overt and destructive secondary symptoms associated with the complex, such as alcohol and drug abuse, suicidal impulses, aimless drifting, and dropping out. While other factors enter in, psychoanalytic explanations of functional depression typically emphasize the presence of severe ego-superego conflict, in which the superego rebukes the ego in a cruel and unrelenting manner, thereby causing the individual insistent feelings of guilt and worthlessness. And again we can assume, from Turiell's analysis of superego dynamics, that this ruinous self-deprecation is ultimately caused by an unsolvable tension between the ego and the ego-ideal, by an irritated and intractable self-ideal discrepancy, in self theory terms.

However, a factor differentiating the self-ideal discrepancy of the complex from that of functional depression has to do with temporal origins. In accordance with the developmental model of mental illness and emotional disorder, the self-ideal discrepancy underlying functional depression is commonly thought of as having its root in infantile experiences. Following this general model, the discrepancy initiated in childhood tends to lie dormant until a precipitating stress, occurring in adolescence or adulthood, exacerbates it sufficiently to produce manifest symptoms. In the case of the inadequacy complex, the root source of the discrepancy is both contemporary and pervasive, and it consists of a pathogenic mixture of actual and vicarious experience that is ubiquitous in modern America.

In terms of central dynamics, then, the complex exhibits clear parallels with functional depression. Further, the suggestion arises that while in the past most depressive reactions have had their origins primarily in the restricted sphere of the family, many are now being caused by conditions in society at large. The well-known prevalence of depression in contemporary America supports this conclusion and also provides tangential evidence for the extent and reality of the complex.

ANXIETY

The susceptibility to anxiety inherent in the complex has its roots in depleted self-esteem, which, as we have seen, is an axiomatic consequence of self-ideal discrepancy. The relationship between anxiety and self-esteem is basic in depth psychology. It is inverse in nature: the higher the self-esteem, the lower the proneness to pathological anxiety. Anxiety, though it is known to have survival value in many instances, is always painful subjectively. People never want to experience one more instant of it than they have to. Psychoanalysis has shown that an enormous amount of human energy is devoted to intrapsychic defense against anxiety. According to Becker, who saw self-esteem as lying at the very core of human psychical adaptation, "Self-esteem . . . is an inner self-righteousness that arms the individual against anxiety. We must understand it, then, as a *natural systemic continuation* of the early ego efforts to handle anxiety; it is the durational extension of an effective anxiety buffer."[49]

In a psychoanalytically oriented discussion of anxiety, Gaylin illustrates the connection between decrements in immediate self-regard and this distressing emotional reaction.

More often than not, anxiety is generated from a change in our sense of self, rather than a change in our environment. . . . We need not see any actual danger, then, but can feel anxious simply by recognizing certain shifts in the power balances in the world in which we operate. Anything which weakens us, which threatens our sense of our own strength, which attacks our pride, our self-confidence, and our self-esteem, can be seen as making us more helpless and more vulnerable.[50]

In fact, Gaylin attributes "castration anxiety," one of the most basic forms of anxiety as conceived by psychoanalysts, to an essentially limitless gamut of symbolic threats to the individual's sense of potency and power. In his words, "Anything that seems to diminish us—our strength, our intelligence, our security—will produce anxiety."[51]

Thus, a vulnerability to all manner of interpersonal and situational anxieties can be seen as basic to the inadequacy complex. And it is a universally accepted fact in the fields of abnormal and developmental psychology that persistent anxiety, that implacable nemesis of inner peace and well-being, is a primary cause of mental illness, emotional maladjustment, and disturbed patterns of behavior. For that matter, Freud and his disciples have viewed it over the years as the cornerstone of neurosis and related disorders.

GUILT

The guilt associated with the complex is not moral-ethical guilt resulting from transgression of a religious code of behavior, but rather something akin to the guilt of being described by the existentialists. If my understanding of this guilt is correct, it is a more basic form of guilt than the other, and it stems less from people's acts than their life situations, the overarching set of circumstances into which each is "thrown," to use an existentialist term. As Becker put it, "Guilt is the bind that man experiences when he is humbled and stopped in ways he does not understand, when he is overshadowed in his energies by the world."[52]

The guilt peculiar to the complex is the guilt of worldly insufficiency. It arises out of the sense that one has not done enough or does not possess enough compared to other people, and this sense is greatly amplified by the media-produced illusions that work constantly on the average American's consciousness. This notion of electronic-technological amplification is useful because it says something about the dimensions of the life situations into which people are thrown in modern America. One hundred years ago and less, the actual and vicarious experiences molding the two components of the total self sprang from the relatively limited spheres of firsthand experience, direct human interaction, literature, and journalism. Today, because of accelerating technology, the experiential realms of each person are vastly expanded in terms of scope, complexity, and psychological impact. It is this expansion of personal experience, particularly media-induced vicarious experience, that is irreparably estranging the two components of the total self and thus fostering the inadequacy complex and the widespread demoralization.

It is important to understand clearly the relationship between the ideal self and the painful emotion of guilt. Not only does the ideal self elicit guilt, but it also dictates the tone, the very nature, of the guilt itself. Casual observers of the contemporary American scene might well conclude that people are rapidly losing the capacity to feel guilt, a characteristic commonly attributed to psychopaths. Widespread attitudes of cynicism, callous competitiveness, incivility, and narcissism, as well as the flagrant increase in delinquency and crime in all sectors of society, would certainly appear to support this conclusion. However, paradoxical though it may seem, it is my contention that people in modern America endure epidemic guilt, particularly those suffering the inadequacy complex. This malignant guilt is an inescapable product of the inflated ideal self, which is in turn a frequent, if not inevitable, intrapsychic structure resulting from daily exposure to the omnipresent imagery of fantasy. But because of the predominantly materialistic-hedonistic character that the collective American ideal self is assuming, it is not moral-ethical guilt as much as it is the guilt of worldly insufficiency. That is, where this secularized guilt holds sway, people do not experience anguished self-disappointment because they are aware of having wronged other people or society but because they labor under the noisome sense that they have not achieved or accumulated as much as other, successful people have. Their guilt, in accordance with the predominant values within their ideal selves, is essentially in response to a sense of competitive-acquisitive insufficiency rather than one of moral-ethical laxity. This reaction can be seen, ironically, to be a powerful determinant of just those kinds of behaviors—narcissism, callous competitiveness, indifference—that appear to signal the diminished capacity for guilt in the modal American personality of our time.

Arnold Rogow, in *The Dying of the Light*, which is a detailed account of the problem of generalized sociocultural deterioration in contemporary America, devotes an entire chapter to the decline of the superego. He argues that the superego is a questionable, if extant, part of today's American psyche. I would suggest that, rather than declining, the superego (ideal self) is in reality undergoing a transformation. The real change is in the nature of the behavior that elicits guilt and diminished self-esteem, and this in turn is a direct reflection of the values dominant in the wider society. But if the guilt still exists, it indicates that the principal components of the superego, the ego-ideal and the conscience, still operate intrapsychically. It is the degree of tension between the ego and the ego-ideal that determines the intensity of the guilt, and the valuative bias of the ego-ideal that determines the tone of the guilt.

The societal significance of all of this lies in the exhortative, directive nature of the superego. It is largely this agency within the personality that gives human behavior its compulsive, driven aspect, that causes it to exceed, in many circumstances, the bounds of reason and natural requirement. Consider, for purposes of contrast, the African lion, a ferocious beast that in terms of the structural point of view of Freudian theory consists of an id and perhaps the tiniest slither of rudimentary ego, but no superego at all. Motivated only by the id, its killing activity is limited to periodic hunger. When satisfied, it retires to the shade to lick its chops and enjoy its natural repose. And, so far as I know, there is no danger that the lion in Africa is going to denude its native environment of beauty and lion-life-sustaining resources. It is only humans, driven by an inflated and hence insatiable ego-ideal, who accumulate more riches than they can ever personally enjoy, pursue ever-tighter rings of social exclusivity, and ruthlessly kill other people they have never even met who constitute a symbolic threat to some facet of this ideal.

Barring congenital defects and some forms of mental retardation, humans appear to have evolved to a point where it is impossible for them not to have an ego-ideal. They necessarily form ideals, pursue them energetically, and experience guilt when they fall short. Hence, it is not the decline of the superego, as suggested by Rogow, but rather it is secular transformation that poses the real threat to American society.

An appreciation of this paradoxical guilt is important in understanding the inadequacy complex because rather than simply being a possible or probable reaction to irritated self-ideal discrepancy, its presence is inevitable. In this sense it has primacy over the other basic emotional reactions and the mantel of secondary symptoms. It is as central to the dynamics as the discrepancy itself, and its intensity, as mentioned above, varies with the momentary degree of discrepancy. It is the pain intrinsic to the discrepancy; it is what ultimately necessitates defensive and/or compensatory efforts.

In a secular society such as America, where worldly success is the summum bonum of life—as opposed to spiritual salvation guaranteeing one's passage into an eternal afterlife in paradise—the sense of intractable inadequacy, of inescapable worldly insufficiency, is equivalent to the sense of utter damnation in the earlier religious phase of Western society. Each, in its respective time and place, constitutes the nadir of personal failure, and because of this, each sets the intrapsychic stage for the emergence of chronic, morbid guilt, which is, after all, a form of self-hate. Gaylin characterizes the experience of guilt as a deeply personal inner turmoil that threatens to tear apart our inner structure. His description is particularly apposite to this analysis, where guilt is viewed as the primary emotional reaction to the tearing apart of the two aspects of the total self. It is so painful and disruptive because it signals a dire threat to the structure of the personality. In this sense it is analogous to fever, which, in the case of physical illness, signals potentially serious pathology and demands that something be done.

NARCISSISM

This secular guilt provides a convenient link to the problem of narcissism, which is another basic component of the complex and a natural compensatory reaction to the underlying self-ideal discrepancy. The specter of rampant narcissism in contemporary America is very much on the minds of serious thinkers and social observers. Titles such as *Me: The Narcissistic American*, *The Culture of Narcissism*, and *The Narcissistic Condition: A Fact of Our Lives and Times*, to cite but three, represent recent books written on the subject. In regard to the values and behavior of youth and young adults, it is common knowledge that the "now generation" of the 1960s has been replaced by the "me generation" of the 1970s and 1980s. Among serious observers there is consensus concerning a morbid, burgeoning self-preoccupation in Americans that is often associated with an aggressive, cynical, grossly inconsiderate pursuit of immediate materialistic and hedonistic ends. The implicit social message emanating from this behavior could be summarized in the sentiment, "Me first. Screw you, buddy!"

The dictionary meaning of narcissism is self-love. The term, introduced to psychoanalysis by Freud, is based on the Greek myth of Narcissus, who was content, so the story goes, to spend his days languishing beside a quiet pool and staring lovingly at his own reflected image. In psychoanalytical theory narcissists tend to be preoccupied with themselves, and have an overidealized self-image. However, in my mind we are witnessing something that is similar to, but at the same time essentially different from, narcissism as it is popularly understood. It is true, narcissism is apt to breed inconsiderateness and insensitivity to others. But I do not believe that people in the United States are brimming with self-love, particularly a languid, untroubled self-love. What we are seeing around us on a disturbingly broad scale is a kind of uneasy, pressured narcissism that is a compensatory reaction to deeper feelings of guilt, inadequacy, and general demoralization. In this sense, the narcissism in question can be seen as analogous to the pressured, artificial euphoria that tends to characterize various states of mania. It is generally accepted among psychotherapists that manic reactions are defenses against underlying depression, and that the forced euphoria often seen in the presenting symptomatology is part of desperate compensatory effort. In a similar manner, the narcissism and callous self-striving under consideration can also be viewed as efforts to defend the self against deeper underlying threats.

But in fact, this formulation is congruent with psychological theory in connection with pathological narcissism. It is well-documented in the psychological literature that pathological narcissism is a common compensatory reaction to deeper feelings of inferiority and self-loathing. Persons with a paucity or absence of healthy self-esteem are apt to become self-absorbed, selfish, and grandiose. The extreme example is the delusional grandiosity of schizophrenia, which is invariably superimposed over abysmal feelings of personal worthlessness. In the case of the schizophrenic, this delusional transformation of the self is necessary because the real self-estimate is too painful to bear; life simply cannot support it. And because of this dire need, the resulting grandiosity is impervious to reason and clung to with iron tenacity. Otto Kernberg, in his psychoanalytic studies of pathological narcissism, has typically found a cluster of dysphoric feelings and negative self-images underlying the more obvious self-absorption. Thus, in describing the surface traits of narcissistic personalities, he states, "The main characteristics of these narcissistic personalities are grandiosity, extreme self-centeredness and a remarkable absence of interest in and empathy for others in spite of the fact that they are so very eager to obtain admiration and approval from other people."[53] But in regard to deeper dynamics he remarks, "The available remnants of such self-images reveal a picture of a worthless, poverty stricken, empty person who feels always left 'outside,' devoured by envy of those who have food, happiness and fame."[54]

This is not to suggest that the narcissism of the inadequacy complex is identical with the pathological narcissism studied by Kernberg, or the even more disturbed form associated with schizophrenia. But surely there are parallels. One of the most basic factors in all degrees of excessive narcissism is the presence of some measure of morbid guilt and chronic self-devaluation in the deeper levels of the personality. When one stops to think about it, this connection is altogether natural. Any animal with a wound retires to a quiet place to attend to its injury and in the process manifests a sort of atypical preoccupation with itself. If we think of the guilt and self-devaluation produced by self-ideal discrepancy as a kind of psychical wound, then the narcissism and self-striving appear as natural attempts to erase the discrepancy and the guilt, and thus heal the wound. In the cases of many unsuspecting people the experiential bind, by feeding this self-ideal discrepancy, is constantly reopening a psychical wound that naturally requires some healing effort. It may not work very well for the afflicted individual, and it may contribute to the growing array of societal problems besieging this troubled nation, but I believe that the narcissism of the inadequacy complex can be understood in this light.

Christopher Lasch speaks of life in modern America as being characterized by diminishing expectations. He also refers to an attitude of "survivalism." According to him, this attitude feeds narcissism because it fosters concern with immediate pleasure, as well as pessimism toward institutional involvements that have traditionally taken individuals outside themselves. The notion of diminishing expectations appears to be at odds with my concept of inflated expectations as a basic dynamic of the inadequacy complex. This apparent contradiction is resolved when the dual structure of the total self is considered. If one concentrates on the actual self, then the notion of diminishing expectations holds. The realm of firsthand daily experience tends to deflate the actual self, and as a consequence contributes to diminished expectations with respect to real performance and achievement. On the other hand, the realm of vicarious experience, which tends to inflate the ideal self, contributes to exaggerated expectations in regard to desired, or idealized, performance. These ideal expectations operate powerfully in human psychology, and they lend their special weight to the development of the inadequacy complex.

PSYCHOPATHIC NARCISSISM

The narcissism so widespread in America appears, as time goes by, to have an increasingly psychopathic cast to it. Consulting, once again, Goldenson's *Encyclopedia of Human Behavior*, we find the following commentary under Sociopathic Personality Disturbance (The term "psychopath" has been replaced by "sociopath" in psychiatric nomenclature. However, for reasons of familiarity I will use "psychopath" in my discussion.): "A group of personality or character disorders marked primarily by failure to adapt to prevailing ethical and social standards and by lack of social responsibility."[55]

There is a very definite interlarding of callous exploitiveness with the narcissistic self-preoccupation, suggesting the above-noted lack of social responsibility. It seems that this growing psychopathic tinge can be traced, to a significant degree, to the violence that saturates the imagery beaming out from the media. As Siegel suggests, television gives an impression of the world that makes aggressive behavior more justifiable. This conclusion is apt to be drawn by all age groups, but especially by young people who are less able to discern the unreality that riddles so much of media programming. Not only is this psychopathic aspect fostered by the growing materialistic-hedonistic bias of the ideal self, but it receives further impetus from the media figures who capture the popular imagination and seem to reflect the essential quality of life in the surrounding community. When one ponders the case of a juvenile or preadolescent of average intelligence watching twenty to twenty-five hours of television and movies a week—with their endless parade of fistfights, shootouts, wild car chases, conflagrations, screaming victims, torture scenes—it is not hard to imagine, within that impressionable young psyche, the budding preconscious assumption that life is basically one big frenetic brawl, in which it is clear that looking out after old number one is the first priority. When one considers the very real possibility that this evolving assumption may coexist with the unconscious processes of identification and idealization directed at the protagonists of such fantasy dramas, the thought becomes legitimately upsetting.

Educators and mental health specialists working with adolescents today refer to the growing tendencies among their young charges to coping by blaming and coping by violence. Both of these behavior patterns can be seen, in part at least, as reactions to this battleground image of society. Further, with perhaps even more serious implications, each reflects the possible weakening of basically healthier, and more adaptive, coping skills. Blaming others, after all, is the primary defense of the paranoid character. When carried to its pathological extreme, it becomes the delusional projection of hostility that locks the paranoid schizophrenic into his grim, menacing world of persecution and bizarre murderous plots. In the case of most clinical paranoids, we know that lying at the core of the disturbance is a deep sense of personal worthlessness, together with a gross inability to assume responsibility for one's decisions, mistakes, and commitments, that is to say, for one's life. In this context, the tendency to constantly externalize blame signals a profound arrest of normal development. And while there are vast differences between this youthful ''blaming'' syndrome and clinical paranoia, there are also some unsettling parallels.

The more dangerous penchant for responding with violence is suggestive of both loss of impulse control and a flagging of the capacity to seek more reasonable solutions to problems through the use of complex verbal-analytical skills. While there is research evidence suggesting that excessive television watching can predispose young people to aggressive and/or violent behavior by virtue of program content, there is also evidence that it tends to undermine the development of verbal-analytical skills by virtue of the form of the presentation, that is, television's rapid pace and use of concrete images as opposed to abstract symbols. Ironically, these are the very skills that have traditionally facilitated the more peaceful solutions to life's inevitable problems, and they are becoming increasingly vital to successful adjustment in our technetronic society.

I believe that the growing tendencies to coping through blaming and/or violence seen among young Americans today can be understood, in many instances at least, as maladaptive derivatives of a sense of helplessness or insufficiency, and thus be viewed as manifestations of the inadequacy complex. It stands to reason that persons who feel confused, overwhelmed, or badly frustrated in a situation will tend either to retreat from the situation or to react to it with blind hostility, especially when they have little confidence in their ability to solve the problem at hand by understanding its complexities and fashioning a reasonable plan or compromise. Blaming is a form of retreat, and violence is commonly associated with confusion and fear. But whether we attempt to explain these escalating patterns of behavior in terms of feelings of inadequacy, undeveloped verbal-analytical skills, simple imitation, or all three, there is evidence that the electronic media are powerful stimulants to them on the basis of content *and* form of presentation.

SYMPTOMS

The symptoms of the demoralization are varied and diffuse, but all of them suggest a deep sense of inadequacy relative to other people and to the demands of various situations. However, as mentioned earlier, the basic nuance of this inner set is that of deficient normalcy, of falling short of the life-style that symbolizes success in American society, a life-style that many other people *appear* to be enjoying. The implicit question lingering in the person's mind would be, if raised to conscious focus, something along the line of, "Why can't I get my self together? Why can't I make it?" It cannot be overemphasized that this disquieting concern is constantly stimulated by the illusion-saturated atmosphere in which average people live, or perhaps better, exist, in contemporary America. their sense of inadequacy is in connection with how they feel they *should* be able to function and perform, and this inflated inner criterion is largely a product of that atmosphere. To repeat, the essence of inadequacy feeling in this context is not that of being no good, but of not being good enough. However, despite this variation on the feeling of inferiority, the guilt and self-devaluation that necessarily follows is typically unhealthy, and potentially catastrophic.

The spectrum of overt, clinical symptoms associated with the inadequacy complex is theoretically limitless. It may well include anxiety states, clinical depression, chronic aimlessness, social isolation, drug and alcohol abuse, vandalism, adult crime, social-interpersonal tensions, work and study blocks, and even the more serious delusions, hallucinations, thought disorders, and homicidal and suicidal impulses that indicate borderline or full psychotic states. In brief, the manifest symptomatology can be anything traceable to the process of unconscious self-devaluation and its probable consequence, chronically depleted self-esteem. Because positive self-esteem is so central to healthy personality dynamics, its depletion can give rise to a potentially boundless array of symptoms, any one of which may be serious and difficult to treat.

SELF-IDEAL CONGRUITY

According to theories of personality and psychological development, a certain discrepancy between the actual and ideal selves is normal and unavoidable. The very terms actual and ideal imply a difference wherein the ideal is higher and more perfect than the actual. However, in the normal case the discrepancy is such that, from time to time, depending upon the nature of the activity at hand, it can momentarily be replaced by the contrasting condition of self-ideal congruity. Under this condition the guilt and self-devaluation are supplanted by pride and self-affirmation. Subjectively, it is among the most gratifying of all human experiences. Hitting a timely home run, delivering a public address with verve and a touch of humor, winning the local art contest, and achieving the desired promotion at work, are more dramatic examples of self-ideal congruent experience available to average people in America. Along a less extravagant vein, such things as a good conversation, standing back and viewing a completed project, and noticing one's healthy child happily at play, are examples of this same benign phenomenon. Experiences all across this spectrum enable people, to one degree or another, to feel good about themselves, to briefly love and affirm themselves and their lives, to say yes! Not only is such experience gratifying, it is also deeply therapeutic. And like clean, fresh, invigorating air, humans cannot get too much of it.

As mentioned earlier, psychological theories in general assert that the condition of chronic and severe self-ideal discrepancy is commonly associated with a wide variety of clinical psychopathologies. In fact, it is safe to say that, like conflicted hostility, sexuality, and dependency, it is invariably part of the underlying dynamics of severe maladjustment. Where it exists, people enjoy little or none of the above self-affirmation, with its invigorating and therapeutic effects. Because of the degree and fixity of the discrepancy, few achievements permit even the briefest coalescence of the actual and ideal selves, and there is an unremitting sense of personal failure and self-disappointment. In a word, there is chronic, corrosive guilt. Caught in the grips of this unfortunate, but well-known, dynamic, it is difficult for the sufferer to perceive good in much of anything, and in extreme cases, when the discrepancy results in depressive psychosis, the world may loom to the person as the "material of overwhelming horror . . . without opening or end" that William James described in discussing the ravages of insane melancholy.[56]

Serious self-ideal discrepancy of this nature is typically thought of as having its origins in early childhood experience, particularly in the infant's relationship with its parents. On the other hand, the self-ideal discrepancy of the inadequacy complex has its origins in the experiential bind and, hence, will not begin to take root until the wider societal backdrop begins to make significant impress, usually in the juvenile and early adolescent years. This distinction is critical because the bind interacts with earlier developmental experience and will thus have widely varying influence across individual cases, depending on the kind and quality of that experience. Further, because experience in the infant years has undisputed primacy in the formation of basic personality dynamics, the influence of the bind is, except in rare cases, necessarily subordinate to the former. In cases where severe self-ideal discrepancy goes back to infancy the inadequacy complex may be embedded in more serious psychopathology, or it may serve to trigger the onset of same. In cases where the infantile years have resulted in an exceptionally healthy capacity to experience self-ideal congruity the bind may not leave a discernible mark. But in the far more common case where a certain normal discrepancy exists, it can and frequently does irritate this discrepancy into the symptoms and suffering of the complex and its attendant demoralization.

The experiential bind confronts the individual in modern America with societal double bind that is not unlike the schizophrenogenic double bind described by John Weakland.[57] According to Weakland's formulation, a schizophrenic tendency is apt to be fostered in the growing infant by a parent, or parent surrogate, who confronts it repeatedly with multilevel verbal and nonverbal communications that are internally dissonant or incongruous. Examples are the mother who infantilizes her little boy while simultaneously praising him for being her "great big man"; or the mother who verbally expresses love for her child in a cold, rejecting tone of voice. Such communication, experienced regularly, confuses the child in a subtle way, severely undermining the development of ego strength and the capacity for reality testing. The experiential bind does something similar to millions of average Americans struggling day by day to maintain their self-esteem. In the firsthand experiential realm the multiplicity of repeated messages emphasize their insignificance and impotence. In the juxtaposed vicarious realm, however, a dissonant swarm of messages emphasize the heady possibility of becoming a winner, one of the beautiful people, and thereby gaining entrance into the illusory good life. As in the case of the child of the schizophrenogenic mother, the intrapsychic result is very likely to be a buildup of confusion and despondency, that is, demoralization. In both instances, powerful divergent forces are tearing at the self, rending its internal organization rather than solidifying it.

NOTES

1. Arthur Combs and Donald Snygg, *Individual Behavior: A Perceptual Approach*, rev. ed. (New York: Harper & Row, 1959), 122.

2. Ibid., 141.

3. G. H. Mead, *Mind, Self, and Society* (Chicago: University of Chicago Press, 1934), 140.

4. Ibid., 144.

5. Sigmund Freud, *A General Introduction to Psychoanalysis* (New York: Permabooks, 1935), 435.

6. Percival Symonds, *The Ego and the Self* (New York: Appleton-Century-Crofts, 1951), 87.

7. Robert Goldenson, *The Encyclopedia of Human Behavior: Psychology, Psychiatry, and Human Behavior* (New York: Dell, 1975), 391.

8. Willard Gaylin, *Feelings, Our Vital Signs* (New York: Harper & Row, 1979), 51–52.

9. Calvin Hall and Gardiner Lindzey. *Theories of Personality* (New York: John Wiley & Sons, 1970), 45–46.

10. Goldenson, *Encyclopedia of Human Behavior*, 391.

11. Robert Havighurst, Myra Robinson, and Mildred Dorr, "The Development of the Ideal Self in Childhood and Adolescence," in *The Self in Growth, Teaching, and Learning*, ed. Don Hamachek (Englewood Cliffs, N.J.: Prentice-Hall, 1965), 226–39.

12. Albert Bandura, "Vicarious Processes: A Case of No-Trial Learning," in *Advances in Experimental Social Psychology*, vol. 2, ed. Leonard Berkowitz (New York: Academic, 1965), 1–55.

13. Albert Bandura, "Social-Learning Theory of the Identification Processes," in *Handbook of Socialization Theory and Research*, ed. David Goslin (Chicago: Rand McNally, 1969), 213–62.

14. Albert Bandura, "Social Learning Through Imitation," in *Nebraska Symposium on Motivation*, ed. Marshall Jones (Lincoln: University of Nebraska Press, 1962), 211–74.

15. Ernest Becker, *The Birth and Death of Meaning* (New York: Free Press, 1962), 67.

16. Ibid., 87.

17. Erich Fromm, *The Art of Loving* (New York: Harper & Row, 1956), 58.

18. Ibid., 60.

19. Albert Adler, *The Individual Psychology of Alfred Adler*, ed. Heinz Ansbacher and Rowena Ansbacher (New York: Harper & Row, 1956), 124.

20. William James, *The Principles of Psychology* (Chicago: Encyclopedia Britannica, 1952), 199–203.

21. Combs and Snygg, *Individual Behavior: A Perceptual Approach*, 122.

22. Ernest Becker, *The Denial of Death* (New York: Free Press, 1973), 1–8.

23. Symonds, *The Ego and the Self*, 90.

24. Becker, *The Denial of Death*, 3.

25. Hall and Lindzey, *Theories of Personality*, 45.

26. Symonds, *The Ego and the Self*, 77.

27. Becker, *The Birth and Death of Meaning*, 69.

28. Ibid.

29. Surgeon General's Scientific Advisory Committee on Television and Social Behavior, *Television and Growing Up: The Impact of Television Violence*. Report to the Surgeon General, United States Public Health Service. Washington, D.C.: Government Printing Office, 1972. In George Comstock et al., *Television and Human Behavior: The Key Studies* (Santa Monica: RAND Corporation, 1975), 230–31.

30. D. T. Suzuki, Erich Fromm, and Richard DeMartino, *Zen Buddhism and Psychoanalysis* (New York: Grove Press, 1960), 146–47.

31. Ibid., 148.

32. Esther Menaker, "The Ego-Ideal: An Aspect of Narcissism," in *The Narcissistic Condition: A Fact of Our Times*, ed. Marie Nelson (New York: Human Sciences Press, 1977), 254.

33. Ibid., 257.

34. Ibid.

35. Report to the Surgeon General in Comstock et al., *Television and Human Behavior*, 230–31.

36. P. H. Tannenbaum and B. S. Greenberg, in Comstock et al., *Television and Human Behavior*, 232.

37. W. Weiss, in Comstock et al., *Television and Human Behavior*, 242.

38. Report to the Surgeon General in Comstock et al., *Television and Human Behavior*, 230.

39. Menaker, *The Narcissistic Condition*, 263.

40. Adler, *The Individual Psychology of Alfred Adler*, 101. Adler, like most of the early depth psychologists, used the masculine form in referring to members of both sexes. In contemporary parlance it would be more fitting to say "wanting to become a real person." Adler's masculine protest really denoted a compensatory striving for general superiority. However, this was conceptualized, then, along masculine lines of social power, as perhaps it is today as well.

41. Ibid., 154.

42. Ibid., 155.

43. Becker, *The Birth and Death of Meaning*, 100.

44. Goldenson, *Encyclopedia of Human Behavior*, 171.

45. Carl Rogers, "A Theory of Therapy, Personality, and Interpersonal Relationships as Developed in the Client-Centered Framework," in *Psychology: A Study of a Science*, vol. 3 of *Formulations of the Person and the Social Context*, ed. Sigmund Koch (New York: McGraw-Hill, 1960), 218.

46. Elliott Turiell, "An Historical Analysis of the Freudian Concepts of the Superego," *Psychoanalytic Review* 54 (1967); 123–24.

47. Henry Murray and Clyde Kluckhohn, "Outline of a Conception of Personality,"in *Personality in Nature, Society, and Culture*, ed. Clyde Kluckhohn, Henry Murray, and David Schneider (New York: Alfred A. Knopf, 1956), 40.

48. John Dollard, Leonard Doob, Neal Miller, O. Hobart Mowrer, and Robert Sears, *Frustration and Aggression* (New Haven: Yale University Press, 1939).

49. Becker, *The Birth and Death of Meaning*, 67.

50. Gaylin, *Feelings: Our Vital Signs*, 27.

51. Ibid., 28.

52. Becker, *The Denial of Death*, 179.

53. Otto Kernberg, *Borderline Conditions and Pathological Narcissism* (New York: Jason Aronson, 1975), 228.

54. Ibid., 234.

55. Goldenson, *Encyclopedia of Human Behavior*, 790.

56. William James, *The Varieties of Religious Experience* (New York: Mentor Books, 1958), 136.

57. John Weakland, "The Double-Bind Hypothesis of Schizophrenia," in *The Etiology of Schizophrenia*, ed. Don Jackson (New York: Basic Books, 1960), 373–88.

3

Societal Reverberations

A number of problematic trends in contemporary America reflect the influence of the experiential bind and the pervasive demoralization. This is not to suggest that these two phenomena are the sole causes, but rather that they are significant elements within a wider network of contributing forces, some of which undoubtedly go back much further in history. I believe that all of the issues to be discussed receive powerful impetus from the imageries of both fantasy and doom.

HYPERCYNICISM AND THE LOSS OF COMMUNITY INVOLVEMENT

While the twentieth century has been labeled the age of anxiety, it would be entirely fitting to describe this particular time in American history as a period of hypercynicism. As mentioned, terms such as "rip-off" and "scam" have found well-worn niches in the contemporary American vernacular, and it is not uncommon to hear, or see in seriously written articles and essays, America referred to as the throw-away society or the land of the rip-off.

Objectively, the term "rip-off" refers to some form of perceived illegal or immoral activity—theft, deception, the charging of unfair prices, and so on. But subjectively, it carries the implication of disappointment or disillusionment, that somehow the person in being ripped off has experienced a painful and frustrating letdown. Thus one hears such comments as, "Stay away from that place, it's a rip off"; "What a rip off"; and "The so-and-so ripped me off," angrily delivered in reaction to a great variety of experiences, and not restricted only to clear-cut instances of theft, deception, or exploitation. Further, the term itself implies a quality of brutality to the experience. Things ripped off, in whatever context, are typically not handled carefully and gently. Although this is but one of a multitude of signs, the frequency of usage of this slang term in everyday conversation suggests that the experience of jarring emotional letdown is a very common one in our society.

Cynicism, a form of muted rage, is a natural reaction to repeated disappointment, especially when the disappointments seem unnecessary or are difficult to understand. The imagery of fantasy, with its unique capacity for fomenting unrealistic expectations, can be seen as a constant and powerful stimulus to this widespread and problematic personal reaction. Regaling the public incessantly with images of glamour, material abundance, and excitement, it stimulates expectations that real situations rarely, if ever, can gratify. People unconsciously anticipating perfection encounter the limitations of real life, and they come away from all manner of experience frustrated, angry, and disillusioned. In many cases, an element of paranoia is frequently interlarded with this cynicism. Not only is life perceived as endlessly disappointing, but the problem is often attributed, vaguely and casually, to corruption and malevolence on the part of others, particularly those higher on the socioeconomic ladder. That the daily installment of the imagery of doom, beaming out from the TV on the evening city news programs or the headlines in the city tabloids, provides constant and powerful reinforcement to this quasi-paranoid interpretation of events in the minds of millions of Americans goes without saying.

This reaction seems especially strong among adolescents and young adults. As a group they appear to be exceedingly vulnerable to disillusionment, and they tend to perceive corruption and malevolence virtually anywhere and everywhere. Of course, young people have always been prone to a kind of ready, superficial cynicism, it being the flip side of naive idealism. But complicating this is the fact that today's young people are relatively more immersed in the imagery of fantasy than are older adults, and simultaneously less able to see through it and hence defuse it. Regarding the former, much more of the imagery of fantasy—movies, television dramas and spectaculars, pop-music programs and recordings, clothing and entertainment advertisements—is contrived for, and targeted on, them. Regarding the latter, they are simply less worldly-wise, and thus fundamentally less aware of life's inherent limitations and tragic side. Put differently, the young don't know what they don't know, and a certain amount of mature wisdom can only be achieved by living through the inevitable blows of life. Thus, the omnipotence of youth keeps asserting that the sky's the limit, and the imagery of fantasy keeps on reinforcing this tenuous, time-limited assumption.

It certainly can be argued that there is much else in contemporary American society serving to fuel hypercynicism on a broad scale, and ample portions of the national gallimaufry of trouble-cum-tragedy are wearyingly served up to the public on a daily basis within the imagery of doom. But the imagery of fantasy works to intensify this attitude in a unique manner. As stated above, it creates expectations that are doomed to failure, while at the same time, it fosters the illusion that many other people are actually living out these expectations. Thus, by a subtle double action, by a kind of psychological one-two punch, it leads people into continual disappointment *and* self-dissatisfaction. It is this second, narcissistic frustration that is critical. The imagery of fantasy insidiously breeds both cynicism about society and cynicism about the self, and it is the latter that helps lock the person into the former. As Fromm said, people who cannot respect (love) themselves are usually unable to respect others.

The danger to society stemming from hypercynicism lies in the fact that it erodes cooperation, as well as effort that is not immediately and personally gainful. People who chronically feel disappointed—ripped off— tend to be wary of social involvements and unwilling to extend themselves at productive communal efforts. Where an element of paranoia is interlarded with the cynicism, the withdrawal is apt to be more unforgiving, and it may even motivate frankly destructive behavior, an intent to exploit before one is exploited. But in either case, cooperation and hard work for the sake of quality and/or service to others tends to be regarded as irrelevant, even stupid.

Some research done by Julian Rotter and his students, describing attitudinal and behavioral differences of people high and low in general trust, lends empirical support to these statements. Although Rotter's research does not explicitly mention cynicism, it seems safe to assume that in most instances this attitude exists in inverse relationship to trust. Where cynicism is high, general trust will be proportionately low, and vice versa.

Differentiating experimental subjects into groups of high and low trusters—based on their responses to a questionnaire called the Interpersonal Trust Scale—Rotter et al. then observed their behaviors in a variety of situations. The relationships between high and low trust, on the one hand, and, on the other, such phenomena as behavior in a stock-market game, sexual guilt, actual theft, general adjustment, popularity, as perceived by others, general intelligence, and gullibility were investigated. In regard to broad social effects, Rotter concludes, ''We can make a strong statement about the consequences to society of people's being more trusting. People who trust more are less likely to cheat or steal. They are more likely to give others a second chance and to respect the rights of others."[1] In addition, in regard to more personal effects, he states,

The personal consequences for high trusters also seem beneficial. High trusters are less likely to be unhappy, conflicted and maladjusted, are liked more and sought out more often as friends, both by low-trusting and high-trusting people. . . . High trusters are no less capable of determining who should be trusted and who should not be trusted, although in novel situations the high truster may be more likely to trust others than the low truster. It may be true that high trusters are fooled more often by crooks, but low trusters are probably fooled just as often by distrusting honest people; they thereby forfeit the benefits that trusting others might bring. As Samuel Johnson wrote, "It's happier to be sometimes cheated than not to trust."[2]

Assuming a consistent, though inverse relationship between trust and cynicism, what Rotter's data imply about low trusters can also be applied to chronic cynics.

RAMPANT CONSUMERISM: FIRST GLANCE

There is reason for concern that this hypercynicism, together with its close cousin, psychopathic narcissism, are contributing to an alarming societal problem of a higher order, so to speak. One gets the impression, as time goes by, that somehow the quality of life in America is steadily deteriorating, that the sleaze quotient is advancing inexorably. And while this state of affairs appears to be pervasive, it is most apparent in the large cities of America. Despite accelerating technological progress, things in general seem to work less well with each passing year, and interpersonal relationships grow tenser and colder. One gets the added impression that more and more people want to take things from the socioeconomic system but do not consider putting much of anything back into it. Listening to young Americans speak of the future, one frequently hears of the desire to make a lot of money in order to live in a grand style, but expressions of desire regarding the achievement of excellence in science, art, or the skilled trades, particularly in order to contribute something of value, are conspicuous by their absence. Although this is not to denigrate business administration as a college curriculum, at the university where I was employed from 1968 to 1987, enrollments in the college of business administration began to boom in 1975 while the colleges of education and liberal arts either shrank or barely hung on, a student population trend which, to the best of my knowledge, still holds. One clear reason for this trend: business is, purportedly, where the jobs and the big money are.

But this galloping consumerism is by no means limited to young Americans. People of all ages are preoccupied with acquisition rather than contribution, and they are willing to cut corners and step on each other's toes in order to serve their ends. The continuously escalating incidence of street crime is the most blatant index of this sinister trend, although the news media regale us daily with shocking reports of greed and corruption at all echelons of society. And while it is clear that most media news coverage has a distinctly negative skew, there is also little question that the emphasis on crime and corruption therein reflects something gravely wrong in modern America.

Postindustrial society is enormously complex in its organization and function. But at bottom, it is still an aggregate of individual human beings, interacting and communicating. To the extent that each is motivated to take rather than give, the superimposed social structure is weakened and imperiled. This consumerism, together with its associated atrophy of the productive orientation, can be seen as a logical outgrowth of the cynicism under discussion, much of which can be traced to the experiential bind and the demoralization. Indeed, cynicism is one pose, as it were, of the front region of chronic demoralization.

RAMPANT CONSUMERISM: ECONOMIC SYMPTOMS

In discussing rampant consumerism as a societal reverberation of the bind and the demoralization, it is impossible to ignore two related issues of huge proportions and potentially catastrophic consequences. Both are straightforward economic issues that have serious implications concerning the quality of life for millions of Americans in the coming double decade, and perhaps, as well, for America's status on the international sphere, over the same time frame.

The most pressing and ominous of these two issues is the mountain of debt America has incurred in the past ten or fifteen years. Alfred Malabre, economics editor and columnist for the *Wall Street Journal*, has treated this issue in succinct, hair-raising terms in his book entitled *Beyond Our Means*. Published in 1985, the statistics he cites are already obsolete by a half-decade. Nevertheless, they put this issue in dire perspective, particularly when one considers that they must be extrapolated upward if an accurate picture of our national indebtedness in 1990 is to be achieved.

Right off the bat, halfway down the first page of Chapter 1, Malabre tells the essence of his disturbing tale.

The profusion of goods and services that most Americans enjoy in this century's closing years reflects a very different sort of tendency: to live beyond our means. Primarily this, and not some rare ability to deliver, underlies the seemingly boundless increase in American prosperity through much of the post–World War II era. . . . Debt is at the root of this tendency to live beyond our means. Massively, debt permeates our economy at all levels—personal, corporate, and governmental. The magnitudes are awesome. In all, as a nation, we are more than $7 trillion in debt—it's impossible to say the precise amount—and the total keeps soaring. It has nearly quadrupled since the mid-1970s. It now approximates $35,000 for each man, woman, and child in the nation. It comes to more than double the nation's yearly output of goods and services.[3]

Malabre's theme throughout his analysis of this economic predicament is that there is no easy way out now. It is simply too late; the heedless extravagance has gone on too long; sooner or later the bills will have to be paid; and the paying will be painful to most Americans. In this regard he states,

For a very long time, we've been living beyond our means—for so long, in fact, that now, sadly, it's beyond our means to put things right, at least in an orderly, reasonably painless manner. . . . No amount of governmental, or for that matter private, maneuvering will avert a very nasty time ahead.[4]

Comparing the economic troubles lying ahead to the hurricane of 1938 in terms of disaster-related consequences—(economic in this case; physical in that one) he adds, "It's my conviction that the next economic hurricane—the first to strike this nation since the Great Depression arrived in 1929—cannot be prevented."[5]

Malabre envisions three scenarios, all painful, that depict the probable consequences to Americans after forty years of living beyond our means. He gives a 20 percent probability to the development of a period of hyperinflation, not unlike the one that occurred in Germany in the early 1920s. Faced with this debt, the federal government could vastly increase the money supply in order to make payment of the full obligation (personal, corporate and public) possible purely in terms of matching the dollars owed with those available. This is called monetizing the debt. However, doing this results in a proportionate devaluation of the currency. According to Malabre, in Germany, at the peak of the hyperinflation, prices changed, literally, by the hour. At the outset of 1922, the wholesale price index was 4,626 times its average in 1913; by December of the same year, it was 374,563,426,600 times the 1913 level.[6] While Malabre does not envision a total collapse of the currency such as that which occurred in Germany, just five years of 20 percent inflation would result in a doubling of the consumer price index. Inflation of this magnitude quickly erodes the buying power and the life savings of the average middle-class worker. In time, such erosion of financial security tends to erode faith in the existing political system, thus opening the doors of political power to all manner of demagogue and potential despot, and hence to a variety of possible forms of dictatorship and tyranny. If this seems dubious, recall that the German hyperinflation commenced in 1921, and in 1933 Adolf Hitler assumed total power within the Third Reich. Further, a reading of history shows that Hitler traded on the economic chaos enshrouding Germany during the 1920s in his political machinations.

Malabre gives a 30 percent likelihood to his second scenario: deflation. Under deflation, prices fall rapidly; it is what happened in the 1930s in America. This price collapse is due mainly to a marked decrease in the money supply. According to Malabre, a sharply contracting money supply would lead to mounting unemployment and, ultimately, to an economic environment similar to that of the 1930s. The deflationary scenario is possible if the Federal Reserve Bank's capacity to maintain an adequate money supply is overwhelmed by a series of bank failures resulting, in turn, from widespread debt defaults by corporations and countries holding huge bank loans. In light of the ballooning debt structure in America, such a rash of defaults is a distinct possibility.

Malabre's third scenario, to which he gives a probability of 50 percent, centers around increased governmental regulation of the economy. Nationalization of the banking system, including control of the now-independent Federal Reserve Board; government management of foreign trade and capital transactions; government setting of wages and prices; rigid governmental supervision of corporate management; and stricter enforcement of far higher tax rates are all probable developments under Malabre's third scenario. In reaction to this spreading of governmental control over the nation's financial affairs, there would, according to this third scenario, be a burgeoning of illegal practices involving black markets and the underground economy. A major cost to Americans, in addition to paying higher taxes, will be a general curtailment of personal independence in the world of work. Malabre's final assessment is not reassuring. "The best investment, under such circumstances, will be in one's affiliations. Individuals employed by large, powerful organizations with government ties and clout will surely fare better than the self-employed person who hopes to build enduring financial independence through hard work and ingenuity."[7] This scenario, Malabre's most probable, has a ring of Orwell's predicted ultra-totalitarian state, wherein the watchful eye of Big Brother will be as omnipresent as that of the "tube" in contemporary America. However, the roles of viewers and viewees will be reversed.

Related to this vertiginous debt is another economic issue that also signals Americans' penchant for living beyond their means. Although this issue has receded somewhat in the past eight or so years, it is waiting in the wings, ever ready to pull down the average American's real standard of living. Further, it was the nation's number one internal problem throughout the 1970s. I am referring to chronic, mounting inflation. Make no mistake: The optimistic pronouncements of the Reagan administration to the effect that inflation had finally been conquered sprang more from political braggadocio than a realistic understanding of the inherent tenacity of this problem within capitalism.

It was popular during the 1970s to think of inflation as the federal government's problem. Each time a new president went to the White House the public began to wonder, albeit skeptically, what he and his administration would do about inflation. This expectation was reinforced from all sides. Campaign promises always involved schemes for abolishing the menace. The press would prate endlessly on each candidate's proposals during the campaign and then begin a sustained drumfire of criticism as each administration's efforts failed, as they invariably did, to effectively reduce the telltale statistics. The academic establishment also joined the chorus. From the conservative side, the accepted doctrine blames inflation on excessive government spending followed by an irresponsible printing of money in order to balance accounts. According to economists of this stripe, the government produces inflation by flooding the economy with money, a circumstance that in turn, causes aggregate demand to run steadily ahead of supply, thus automatically creating the problem.

Although inflation has diminished significantly since the early 1980s, this phenomenon had little to do with supply-side Reaganomics. The central idea behind Reaganomics was passage of a tax cut in order to put more money into the public's pockets. The assumption legitimizing this tax cut was that the extra quantum of money would, in general, go straight into savings accounts and investments, thereby increasing the pool of affordable credit necessary for healthy expansion in the private sector. This ultimate chimera was, at the outset of the Reagan administration, a many-splendored prospect. It would (1) make for a painlessly balanced budget, because the growth in the private sector would automatically produce more federal revenues, despite the reduced tax rates; (2) foster stable prices by bringing aggregate supply into essential parity with aggregate demand, thereby meliorating chronic inflation; and (3) sharply increase the number of jobs by virtue of the investment-spurred business expansion, thereby dispatching the unemployment problem, the other side of the stagflation issue that besmirched the 1970s in America.

The truth of the matter is that inflation was temporarily wrung out of the American economy during the last eight years of the 1980s by three relatively independent factors. First, the recession of 1981–82, which was partly induced by chronic inflation, diminished aggregate demand sufficiently to start a disinflationary price trend. Second, during the same period the Federal Reserve Board, under the determined leadership of Paul Volker, kept the money supply tight enough to discourage excessive spending by individuals and corporations, this also serving to temper aggregate demand. And third, the price of OPEC crude oil decreased sharply because the OPEC nations could not get together and agree on production quotas that would keep the price of crude up, and because of new oil-field discoveries in the North Sea, Prudhoe Bay, and Mexico, which made relatively cheap crude available to American consumers. The drop in the cost of crude oil from approximately $34 a barrel in 1980 to $15 a barrel by the middle 1980s accounted for approximately six points of inflation. This is so because of the centrality of crude oil to the American economy, constituting, as it does, the principal raw material for the huge petrochemical industry, as well as the primary fuel for all forms of private and public transportation and home heating.

The upshot of this is that the plan to rejuvenate the economy, coming out of the Reagan White House in 1980, had little to do with curbing the chronic and mounting inflation of the previous decade, although this was always presented as an essential element within the triumph of Reaganomics. It was, largely, two independent and unrelated developments—one serving to reduce aggregate demand; the other serving to reduce the price of the economy's main power source—that brought inflation down from 12 percent a year in 1980 to 4 percent a year since 1985. Unfortunately, there are signs that this problem is returning already in the early 1990s.

In my view, there is a basic fallacy in this thinking that attempts to lay the problem of inflation at the government's feet. Inflation is a societal problem, not merely a governmental one. Its deep roots go back, on the one hand, to the expectations and buying habits of tens of millions of individual consumers and, on the other hand, to the attitudes and work habits of equally large numbers of employees in the work force, many of them the same individuals. Put differently, the real engine of inflation is a deeply embedded sociocultural dynamism that is reflected in the day-to-day behaviors of millions of Americans. While this is oversimplified, and while there are undoubtedly many exceptions, this dynamism is translated, in the individual case, into a relative preoccupation with acquisition and consumption over productivity and conservation. Again, Americans in general want to take from the system, but they are not equally concerned with conserving and replenishing it.

Pitted against this sociocultural dynamism, the federal government appears as a weak reed. Further, it seems patently naive to think that any administration, playing with its various economic control mechanisms—fiscal policy, monetary policy, tax-rate changes—can really banish inflation. And the record seems to bear me out. Except for one or two brief intervals, the American economy has been subject to chronic inflation since 1945. Most people, however, have been concerned with it only since 1973, when the first Arab oil embargo helped propel us into the double-digit level.

I am convinced that as long as the American public is able to shove the problem of inflation into the government's lap, and thereby escape any real responsibility for it, the issue will continue to plague the country. Thus, this societal problem bears certain parallels with the predicament of clinical paranoids. Persons suffering this condition constantly externalize blame, and, largely because of this tenacious, but pathological, defense, nothing ever improves their sad, embattled lives. As long as millions of Americans continue to emphasize consumption and acquisition over productivity and conservation in their daily habits, all the while anticipating government-sponsored deliverance from inflation, the problem will worsen and the system will be pushed closer and closer to the brink.

A number of books predicting imminent economic collapse have appeared in the past year or two. In *The Great Depression of 1990*, Ravi Batra, professor of economics at Southern Methodist University, predicted another severe depression like that of the 1930s. The Batra thesis draws on a theory of social cycles propounded by an Indian philosopher named Sarkar. From this theoretical standpoint Batra bases his prediction on the uncanny similarities between the 1920s and 1980s in terms of a number of pertinent economic indicators reflecting the consumptive and investing habits of Americans. During both decades rampant consumerism and wild speculation in the stock market on the part of the affluent existed in a society characterized by extreme wealth disparity. One basic difference between these two decades does obtain, however. The affluent in the 1920s were not lured into their consumptive and speculative frenzy by imagery of fantasy resembling, in the remotest degree, the mind-bending influence that this media-spawned phenomenon exerts in contemporary America.

If we accept the hedonistic-acquisitive societal dynamism as a real factor contributing to both chronic inflation and the mountainous run-up of debt, the question arises as to why this phenomenon operates as it does in America. In my mind, of course, it is intimately linked to the imagery of unreality, the experiential bind, and the pervasive demoralization. It is significant that the coming of television dates back very closely in time to the onset of the creeping inflation that began after the end of World War II. Not only did television arrive in America in the late 1940s, but at the same time, aided largely by television, the imagery of fantasy really shifted into high gear, particularly that aspect of it created by the advertising industry. This intensification of the imagery of fantasy undoubtedly heightened the perceived incongruity between the firsthand and vicarious experiential realm and paved the way for the gradual development of the experiential bind. Over the forty years since 1950, a quantum increment in the presence of this imagery in the lives of millions of average Americans is uniquely contiguous with the problem of chronic inflation. We have not had massive federal budget deficits every year since 1950, nor an energy crunch over this entire time span, nor forty years of federal stop-and-go economic control policies. But we have had this imagery impinging steadily and increasingly on the collective psyche of Americans over this whole period.

It is clearly fallacious to relegate responsibility for the tendency of Americans to live beyond their means, as manifested economically either in terms of forty years of inflation or the more recent reckless accumulation of debt, to any one societal agency or institution; the problem is simply too complex. However, in searching realistically for partial contributors, it seems to me that we can weight the input of the advertising and entertainment industries more heavily than that of the federal government. These two industries, via their constant use of the mass media, have much more influence on the day-to-day thinking, feeling, and behavior of the public than does the government. It is, above all else in modern America, the unending flow of advertisements and glamorous, exciting dramatic scenes that stimulates and nurtures the acquisitive-hedonistic societal dynamism under discussion. Christopher Lasch puts it this way:

The mass media, with their cult of celebrity and their attempt to surround it with glamour and excitement, have made America a nation of fans and moviegoers. The media give substance to and thus intensify narcissistic dreams of fame and glory, encourage the common man to identify himself with the stars and to hate the 'herd,' and make it more difficult for him to accept the banality of everyday experience.[8]

This penetrating statement by Lasch beautifully encapsulates what I have been laboring to analyze and illumine thus far in these pages. In the vicarious experiential realm the imagery of fantasy lures millions of average Americans into thinking—unconsciously, unrealistically, wishfully—of themselves as stars, or potential stars, or at least more like the stars than the faceless types with whom they rub shoulders daily in the firsthand experiential realm. In the process it makes the time and effort spent in this realm seem increasingly empty, pointless, banal, even loathsome. As part of this beguiling phantasmagoria, the advertising media operating within the mass of imagery incessantly pressure these average citizens to buy their way out of that banality, to spend money they don't really have as they attempt to scramble up the stairway to the stars. When, as a consequence of the internalization of this experiential bind, the inadequacy complex exists in clinical form, this compensatory acquisitiveness is given powerful inner impetus by the guilt integral to the complex. In this case, the consuming can become truly compulsive, hence uncontrollable.

Further, the imagery of doom can be seen to impart an element of callous indifference to this widespread narcissistic quest, an attitude that might be paraphrased, "I want it, and I'll do what I have to to get it, with no holds barred." While this latter may seem a bit harsh, I would argue that social conditioning is known to be an extremely powerful shaper of human behavior. The imagery of doom portrays modern America in a way that reflects the barbarity that we associate with ancient societies such as the Roman Empire. With imagery of this nature tugging regularly at their consciousness, it is not hard to see why many persons in our media-oriented society might well be led to adopt a "when in Rome . . ." approach in their narcissistic modus vivendi.

I would not for an instant suggest that we are now, or are in danger of becoming, a nation of psychopathic narcissists. But I do believe that daily exposure to the combined influence of the imageries of fantasy and doom has the potential for tipping the behavior patterns of too many Americans into this diagnostic category, particularly the young, impressionable viewers who naturally prefer the most lurid of the programs. Once this pattern has been launched and the cynical and exclusive self-seeking behavior has been reinforced, it becomes exceedingly difficult to change and rehabilitate. Past a certain point in this process individuals, their families and friends, as well as society at large, may begin to suffer the consequences. Regarding the tendency of many Americans to live beyond their means, Malabre's analysis and data suggest that some form of painful economic consequence is now a fait accompli for America as a nation.

Sidney Weintraub, a professor of economics, touches upon the acquisitive-hedonistic dynamism in an article entitled "The Human Factor in Inflation." The opening abstract of the article reads, "Everyone from shopworkers to company presidents wants a big raise—even if he produces less. That, not OPEC or government policy, is the major cause of American inflation."[9] Further on Weintraub states, "The income-productivity tug-of-war is the inexorable fact blithely ignored as we castigate the Arabs, the Ayatollah, Government largesse, Government regulation, lax money policy, rapacious business firms or aggressive labor unions. It is a mad assault on the laws of arithmetic to grab 8, 10, 25 percent more while productivity inches by slight 1 percent doses, as it has done throughout most of the 1970s in this country."[10] Elsewhere, Weintraub brings up a point that directly reflects the subtle, but powerful, influence of the imagery of unreality upon the public. In explaining the universal demand for higher pay, he remarks, "People want raises for two reasons . . . they think they need more money to keep up with the higher prices; second, there's the feeling that, if prices are higher, someone must be making more money, and it's unfair if they don't too."[11] It is the second reason to which I refer. The imagery definitely contributes to the perception that many others are enjoying glamorous success, thus intensifying people's sense of personal inadequacy and their need to catch up. On the practical level this need is translated into a preoccupation with more pay because money is the key that unlocks the door to this presumed paradise. For the average citizen the statistics regarding constant price increases together with the presumption that others are able to pay can serve as a kind of circumstantial, yet more graphic, index of the media-driven illusion. In this sense, the one reinforces the other.

If we take the human factor in inflation seriously, we can anticipate that the present mode of dealing with this problem will more than likely continue to be ineffective. As long as Washington formally assumes responsibility for the whole issue, this economic battle will be limited, at best, to a rear guard action. Millions of people in America are concerned about the high cost of living, but they are not *doing* anything about it. On the contrary, lured on by the imagery of unreality, they are promoting it. In some degree, however, this is also due to public ignorance. People think inflation *is* the government's problem. They think the next president—if he is a strong leader or if he is surrounded by the right advisers—will somehow manipulate those mystifying control mechanisms and make the problem go away.

This fallacy is not unlike a common misunderstanding in psychotherapy. Most clients coming for psychotherapy unconsciously desire magical deliverance from their symptoms. On the other hand, all psychotherapists know that in order to help clients overcome their symptoms, they must somehow enlist each client's active cooperation and willingness to struggle. If a working relationship is not established, the therapy will go nowhere, and eventually the client will drop out of treatment, poorer, older, and disillusioned. Psychotherapists do not cure their clients. They work with them to help them achieve a measure of change and personal growth. If we momentarily think of the federal government as roughly analogous to the therapist, and the public concerned about the high cost of living, as roughly analogous to the patient, then we can see that effective treatment of the problem must at least begin with the establishment of a realistic working relationship, one in which *mutual* effort and responsibility are regarded as crucial. In the last analysis, only the public can modify the acquisitive-hedonistic dynamism because, ultimately, it is the public that is responsible for it. Weintraub appears to reach a similar conclusion in that he feels that the answer to inflation must somehow entail a widespread balancing of the income-productivity relationship. He ends his article on the following note: "Monetary policy to fight inflation and tax cuts to combat the induced recession are dogs chasing their tails. A serious, sensitive, across-the-board incomes policy must be adopted and must ultimately prevail, if the United States is to restore its economic stability and assert its strength."[12]

A few final thoughts on the economic symptoms of rampant consumerism in contemporary America. The reader might object to all of this material on the problem of inflation, arguing that at roughly 4 percent it can be lived with, and that 4 percent is way down from the 12 percent prevailing at the outset of the 1980s. Further, he/she might also argue that the 1 or 2 percent a year rates characteristic of the late 1940s and the 1950s and the escalation up to roughly 4 percent occurring during the 1960s were negligible and that from this perspective I am making mountains out of molehills. It is true, in light of such hyperinflation as that occurring presently in Argentina these are pragmatically defensible arguments.

My answer and my larger concern are based on the following. The law of supply and demand tells us that when aggregate demand exceeds supply, rising prices are the invariable result. That much, all practitioners of economics, the so-called dismal science, agree on. One and 2 percent yearly cost-of-living increments, escalating to 4 percent, over a period of twenty-five years are, admittedly, not indicative of serious inflation. But why twenty-five years of official statistics indicating that aggregate demand was in excess of aggregate supply? I am unaware of any other period of similar length in our national history showing a trend like this. Economists frequently use the term "rising expectations" to account for the steady growth of aggregate demand. What accounts for twenty-five straight years of rising expectations in the period following the end of World War II? My answer is, of course, that it was caused primarily by the slow but steady increase in the imagery of fantasy impinging constantly on the collective American psyche, a phenomenon ultimately facilitated by the coming of television.

Sometime between 1970 and 1980, as a result of the burgeoning of this imagery, the incongruity between the vicarious and firsthand experiential realms worsened sufficiently to bring on the experiential bind. Recall Weintraub's account of the 1970s, which described frequent demands for pay hikes running anywhere from 5 to 25 percent while productivity inched along at 1 percent increments. The work force in America was clearly represented increasingly by people wanting more pay, but refusing to produce proportionately more goods and services. And it was during this decade that stagflation, an unheard-of combination of chronic inflation and rising unemployment, reared its ugly head and became Public Enemy # 1. It is my belief that contiguous with the loudly heralded onset of double-digit inflation, and having distinct causal significance in connection with it, was a national surge in galloping consumerism that arose as a natural reaction to the swelling tide of imagery. Despite the alarming economic statistics and predictions, the consumption went on, even gathering intensity, as we entered the 1980s under Ronald Reagan's soothing, optimistic, theatrical leadership.

During the greed- and vanity-ridden 1980s the consumerism fulminated, not unaffected, I would submit, by Reagan's repeated and official pronouncements concerning the surety of an abundant future for all Americans. And, despite the full-throttle consumerism, inflation appeared to have been vanquished. This state of affairs verged on the miraculous, and it seemed to prove the validity of supply-side theory.

What really happened to excessive chronic inflation? It is accepted among financial circles that inflation, as an index of the American tendency to live beyond one's means, has been replaced by the specter of mountainous indebtedness that experts like Alfred Malabre write about. This substitution of debt for runaway prices occurs by virtue of our growing preference for foreign products and our tendency to indirectly use foreign credit to finance our purchases. We buy Japanese cars, TV sets, VCRs, Walkmen, and cameras by the boatload; we buy German cars and cameras in nearly equal volume; we buy Taiwanese shirts, slacks, and undercloth-ing by the closet-full; we buy Italian shoes and suits by the trunk-full; we buy French perfume by the atomizer-full, and so on; and we travel to exotic places by the plane-full. Much of this buying is made possible by heedless use of credit cards. Yuppies by the city-full are up to their eyeballs in debt; yet they still have pockets-full of walking-around money. Why? Because the banker, when called upon to do so, will gladly rear-range accounts to allow postponements of full payments if a borrower (credit card holder) is willing to pay more interest down the line. The accepted practice in America today is to mortgage the future in order to live up to the imagery of fantasy now.

This expansion of credit is indirectly supported by foreign investment in U.S. securities, land, companies, and banks, the Japanese being the principal buyers currently. Financiers and economists know that interest rates—the cost of credit—would have gone through the roof a long time ago if it were not for regular sales of treasury bonds to foreign govern-ments, as well as periodic private sales of firms and real estate to foreigners in the private sector, part of the proceeds of which ultimately provide banks with more money, for more credit, for more rampant consumerism by individual Americans. The older index of the tendency to live beyond our means was inflation; the more current index is that of excessive per-sonal debt. Although both are troublesome, the latter appears to be more dangerous because control of it does not lie completely in our hands. What if the Japanese or the Germans or the English decide to cut their rate of investment in U.S. treasury bonds sold at regular auctions, or worse, stop their investment altogether? I am pretty sure that economists and per-sons in high positions in government worry about this dire prospect because if and when it does happen, the credit bubble will constrict or shrivel away to nothingness, depending on the degree to which foreign investors restrict the inflow of funds. Or, what if higher inflation returns as foreign funds become less available for postponement, via credit, of the costs of galloping American consumerism?

In either scenario, life within the firsthand experiential realm will become more stressful and hence more deflating to the actual selves of millions of Americans. On the other hand, life within the vicarious realm will undoubtedly go on as if nothing had happened. The imagery of unreality will beam out unabated, massaging the public with a fundamentally unrealistic mix of fantasy and skewed information, thereby maintaining its disharmonizing pressure within the total selves of these same citizens. Put differently, the experiential bind can be expected to worsen for them if the means to their habits of rampant consumerism are restricted or cut off. As the bind worsens *for* them, so will its internalized psychical imprint—irritated self-ideal discrepancy—worsen *in* them. Which brings us to the next topic of discussion.

CRIME AND VIOLENCE

I believe that poverty is the fundamental cause of most crime in America and that most crimes begin at least as crimes against property committed by unfortunate Americans in dire need. To be sure, in absolute terms the instances of white-collar crime are many, even the more unnecessary and hence newsworthy ones such as those committed by Ivan Boesky and Leona Helmsley. But in relative terms, crimes committed by the affluent comprise an extremely small percentage of the total yearly crime in America. Most of it is perpetrated by persons who find themselves outside the economic system but who need and want much more than they have.

A second purely economic factor contributing to America's bloated crime rate is wealth disparity. Despite its being the world's richest nation, the per capita standard of living in America ranks approximately eleventh among the 165 or so countries in the world. Ravi Batra, cited earlier, sees glaring wealth disparity as the principal failing of American capitalism. In a sequel to his book predicting a great depression of 1990 entitled *Surviving the Great Depression of 1990*, he provides statistics illustrating the egregious maldistribution of wealth in this, the richest of modern nations. His figures apply to the year 1986.

America is fast becoming a nation of two classes, with the haves growing richer, the have-nots growing poorer, and the middle class slowly sinking into oblivion. The minimum wage in America is $3.35 [now $4.25] an hour, and an unskilled worker working the normal 40 hours a week and 2080 hours a year would earn $6968. This is what hundreds and thousands of Americans make per year. . . . Do you know what the maximum wage was in 1986? $125 million—17,940 times the minimum wage and 11,363 times the poverty figure [$11,000 a year for a family of four]. . . . The average American annually makes about $29,000, which is only 1/4,310th of the maximum salary in 1986.[13]

At another point in the book he returns to this topic stating, "According to revised estimates of the Joint Economic Committee, 420,000 households or 0.5 percent of the population owned 27.3 percent of the wealth in 1983. . . . With $15 trillion in total wealth, the top wealth owners owned $4.2 trillion, or an average of $10 million per family."[14] In developing this theme, Batra observes that since the nation's total wealth does not change rapidly over time, such a concentration of wealth in the pockets of a tiny minority of the population necessarily means that millions of other Americans are simultaneously faced with living in continuous want and deprivation. In support of this generalization are statistics indicating that today some forty million Americans live below the poverty figure published periodically by the federal government.

Most crime in America occurs in large cities, where sybaritic wealth existing cheek by jowl with the most squalid poverty illustrates this cruel disparity with revolting and stupefying impact to anyone who cares to look. Given the killing conditions that the urban homeless and ghetto dwellers invariably endure in the firsthand experiential realm, it is no wonder that many of them lose faith in the system and themselves, become brutalized, and turn to a life of crime. But, ironically, even most of the homeless and the inner-city residents own or have regular access to a TV, and by naturally tuning into the programs that their inherited lack of opportunity would demand, they unwittingly open themselves to the experiential bind at its psychotoxic worst. In the case of the male adolescent and young-adult ghetto dwellers, this daily exposure to the imageries of fantasy and doom is tantamount to lighting the fuse on a keg of dynamite; sooner or later the explosion will come. Probably because of a combination of genetic differences and the conservative perspectives of age—female ghetto dwellers of all ages and older males—betoken both a diminished relative certitude of the explosion and a somewhat lower intensity of response, not absolutely but at least by degrees. But wherever poverty and dire need exist in America the crime rate continues to escalate. As Batra puts it, "crime soars amid poverty."[15]

Further, it is my contention that the experiential bind is also feeding a particularly disturbing recent aspect of this phenomenon. I speak here of the fulmination of violent crime. America is by far the most violent of all the developed nations in the world. In addition to this scourge, we are witnessing an alarming increase in grisly, seemingly intentional, violence: rape, isolated murder without apparent materialistic motive, bias attack and murder, cult murder, casual shooting of helpless robbery victims, and the like. Virtually all of this violence is perpetuated by men. And it is perpetuated by losers, or men who regard themselves as losers.

Human existence has always been fraught with struggle; the tragic side of life is basic and inescapable. However, much in America, now and in the past, has tended to obscure this existential truth. As a result, its psychological ramifications have, likewise, become twisted and increasingly morbid. Rather than assuming failure, average Americans assume (unconsciously, in the back of their minds) success, even extravagant success, of a materialistic nature. And this assumption is necessarily interpreted relatively. Success in this society means accumulating or achieving more than others have. The historicocultural factors contributing to this mental set are complex and interwoven, but among them are Western science, technology, capitalism, the Protestant ethic, the myth of rugged individualism, and pragmatism. However, to me the mass media, particularly the electronic media, as the culmination of this long evolution of forces, are the prepotent stimulants to this unrealistic and dangerous assumption operating today in the minds of millions of Americans.

Molded by the wider society and massaged continually by the imagery of fantasy, they assume too much, and this basic unconscious assumption predisposes them to feelings of failure and hence to insidious self-devaluation. Much of the burgeoning violence can be seen as a direct result. More and more people in contemporary America feel like failures in life. What is worse, they feel like failures surrounded by more successful people who somehow, by treachery or special advantage, have essentially stolen or fallen into their success. This latter malevolent, quasi-paranoid nuance to their thinking receives continuous reinforcement in the imagery of doom. In both men and women this sense of themselves vis-à-vis the world feeds a poisonous psychological mixture: frustration, rage, guilt, and chronically depleted self-esteem. Although this formulation is oversimplified, it holds in general that women tend to turn this mixture inward into depression, whereas men tend to turn it outward into overt aggression.

Paradoxically, this aggression has its source in deep, unsalvable feelings of insignificance and inadequacy. It does not come from a sense of strength, but rather from that of weakness. And in Western culture this is pure anathema to males. The most horrifying and senseless acts of violence are committed, more often than not, by individuals who are trying to make their mark, make their presence felt, and who are unable to do so in socially acceptable ways. They are driven by their guilt to these acts in much the same way that more successful men and women in hedonistic and materialistic America are driven to accumulate wealth, obtain position, wield power, and even to work productively and creatively. In the latter cases, however, the buildup of socially accepted success curbs the potential for this paradoxical destructiveness. Certainly, in such acts of wanton violence there is also an inchoate impulse to revenge for perceived wrongs suffered; but intrinsic to the basic motive is the need to assert the self. There is a twisted and pathetic groping for a sense of potency and relevance for feelings of personal adequacy.

Within a culture the difference between normal and pathological guilt, psychodynamically speaking, is quantitative, essentially a matter of degree. Structurally, this can also be phrased in terms of the degree of self-ideal discrepancy existing in the personality. In each individual case there is some unpredictable stress point, past which the tensions emanating from this discrepancy have the potential for fomenting overt pathological behavior. In the barren environments of poverty, particularly the urban ghettos, the probabilities of this individual stress point being exceeded are the highest because it is here that the experiential bind exerts its most malignantly demoralizing influence, endlessly and insidiously, day in and day out. But even people in the highly insulated upper classes, not to speak of those in the great middle class, are not totally immune to its influence. Witness the Boeskys, Helmsleys, and Milkens. While lawyers regularly lock horns in legal and semantic battles over the punishable culpability of such apprehended felons, we all, I think, sense the irrational, narcissistic greed and the potential societal damage inherent in their acts. The reader may doubt the relevance of the experiential bind to any of this antisocial behavior, especially that perpetrated by the highly affluent. However, I believe that it has central, though not necessarily sole, causal relevance for most criminal as well as noncriminal goal-oriented behavior in America. Such is the power of the modern mass media, the second god, as Tony Schwartz calls them collectively.

In *The Denial of Death*, Ernest Becker posited the necessity of subjectively perceived heroic acts, large or small, as a means of denying the ultimate failure of all human life. Whether the form of the act is commonplace or exceptional—going to work or going to the moon—its achievement helps the individual momentarily repress awareness of our universal destiny. He argued that this is absolutely critical to the maintenance of sanity, because the threat of death is intolerable to most humans. Becker, an existentialist, saw the attempt to deny our ultimate personal fate as the deepest wellspring of productive and creative human effort. From such an elemental existential perspective, we would appear to be awash in the paradoxes of life in this troubled land. People killing to minimize their sense of deadness—or perhaps, perpetrating madness to stave off the threat of insanity. Spiritual poverty epidemic in the richest of nations. Issues of this magnitude have everything to do with a society's basic values and how they are disseminated to its individual members, especially the young.

AMERICA'S TROUBLED CHILDREN

It is reasonable to state that many, if not most, parents in contemporary America are worried to distraction about their children, either in connection with helping them out of actual life-threatening predicaments or in helping them avoid same in the future. Drug and alcohol abuse, fatal or permanently disabling automobile accidents, sexual promiscuity resulting in incurable venereal disease or the birth of unwanted children, serious and formally punishable crime and gross failure to equip themselves for meaningful and independent adult lives because of implacable obtuseness to the value of a solid formal education: these are some of the more intractable child problems that plague the consciousness of responsible American parents today. Although good parents have always fretted periodically through the vicissitudes of their children's development, in past eras these stages of trial and tribulation were, or at least seemed to be, generally of a more manageable sort and scale. Consequently, fathers and mothers felt more equal to their traditional parental roles, and for the most part they adequately fulfilled their obligations to their maturing-but-needy offspring though a combination of grit, wit, and practical wisdom. Today, in reaction to their growing sense of perplexity and helplessness, many parents in America appear to be either retreating from or frankly abdicating their child-rearing responsibilities. In the first instance, which occurs more commonly in the relatively affluent classes, parents are sending their troubled and troubling children in droves to mental health specialists, physicians, clergy, special services teams within the public school system, in-treatment programs in hospitals, and the like, all in an urgent quest for professional rehabilitative help. In the case of more or less total abdication of parental control and authority, which occurs more commonly in the less-affluent social strata, children are, literally and with increasing incidence, running wild. Contemporary American children confront the nation with one of its thorniest problems. They are the most troubled age group in the population, while simultaneously they constitute the country's most valuable resource, its best hope for a secure and abundant future.

Why are the children of this richest, and, as yet, most powerful of nations so beset by, so awash in, trouble-cum-tragedy? In a book entitled *The Disappearance of Childhood*, Neil Postman, with his typical lucidity and insight, approaches this nettling issue from the standpoint of media ecology. Postman is well aware of the power of the electronic media to vastly alter our entire intellectual environment, and in the process to alter our ways of thinking, our behavior patterns, and over time, to gradually alter some of our most basic societal institutions and mores.

One of Postman's premises in this book is that childhood is a social invention, not a biological necessity. According to him, childhood as we have come to know it was introduced in Western culture as a consequence of the invention of the Gutenberg printing press, which, in turn, issued in "print culture". Historically, this critically important phase in the evolution of Western culture can be dated roughly from the year 1500. With the birth of print culture, written words and numbers contained in pamphlets and books and made available to the public by virtue of the new printing technology became the principal vessels of information, the principal means by which new knowledge was both distributed and recorded. The invention of childhood was necessitated by the fact that print culture required complex skills for the efficient and meaningful use of written words and numbers in conducting society's business, skills such as reading, writing, and arithmetic. The proper learning of such skills required a relatively long, quiet, stable, and protected apprenticeship prior to attaining adulthood with its manifold freedoms and responsibilities. Postman illustrates how this whole process made possible the existence of adult secrets, essentially things about being an adult that children didn't know, and that had to be gradually achieved during the apprenticeship of childhood. Having largely to do with manners and morals, these secrets could be used to control and guide children's behavior through the use of shame until the apprentices had graduated. Such secrets provided adults with two basic advantages: (1) adults could, as mentioned, control their children to some extent by virtue of the secrets; and (2) these elements of arcana contributed to the respectability of adulthood. Adults know more than the children did, and knowledge is power.

Culminating with television, the evolution of the "electronic" environment or culture—its roots go back to the invention of the telegraph, and it includes the rotary press, camera, telephone, phonograph, movies, and radio—has opened the flow of the daily information stream to all who can sit up and watch the ever-flickering, mesmeric screen. This includes children as well as adults because of two basic factors. First, watching television requires no special skills. As Postman writes, "To say it as simply as one can, *people watch television*. They do not read it. Nor do they much listen to it. They watch it. . . . Watching television not only requires no skills but develops no skills."[16] On this note, Postman quotes another author, Reginald Damerall, who observes that no adult or child becomes better at watching TV by doing more of it. The required skills are so elemental that we are yet to hear of a TV-viewing disability.[17] All age groups are able to grasp much of the fundamental meaning in most television programming because the text consists of a rapid flux of "watched" pictures. Again, Postman provides illumination. He argues that words and pictures are different universes of discourse. Pictures show things. On the other hand, words reflect ideas, the work of human reason and imagination. Postman illustrates this point with the words "cat," "work," and "wine," arguing that such things do not occur in nature. These words are concepts about the regularities we observe in nature. They are essentially acts of human creativity, occurring in reaction to the immanent press of experience that is always coagulating about us. And they arise out of complex mental skills, which require considerable study and disciplined apprenticeship for their proper development. In connection with this last point Postman remarks, "It cannot be said often enough that, unlike sentences, a picture is irrefutable. It does not put forward a proposition, it implies no opposite or negation of itself, there are no rules of evidence or logic to which it must conform."[18] Simply stated, the *form* of information on television makes differential levels of cognitive ability largely irrelevant in grasping its essential meaning. As Postman puts it, "Pictures . . . call on our emotions, not our reason."[19]

The second factor contributing to television's undifferentiated accessibility has to do with its round-the-clock operation. This twenty-four-hour-a-day broadcast schedule occurs in response to an insatiable need in its audience for novelty and news, and this appetite can be seen as a spin-off of the pictorial nature of the medium. By employing a form of communication that demands little or nothing by way of skill in order to use and/or enjoy it, TV automatically creates, over time, an undiscriminating audience that requires constant titillation to hold its attention. Borrowing terms from Postman, it is accurate to suggest that TV's form tends to shape a mass clientele consisting of "adultified" children and "childified" adults, relatively speaking. Knowing this, and being profit oriented, television executives make sure that their tubes are poised to glow continuously wherever they exist. This means, of course, in virtually every dwelling, private and public, in America. Postman provides statistics illustrating American children's use of TV at times when most responsible parents would want them in bed asleep. According to his figures, approximately 3 million children, age two to eleven, are watching television every night of the year between 11:00 P.M. and 11:30 P.M.; 2.1 million are watching between 11:30 P.M. and midnight; 1.1 million between 12:30 A.M. and 1:00 A.M.; and just under 750,000 between 1:00 A.M. and 1:30 A.M. He adds the point that this happens not only because the pictorial form of the TV message poses no cognitive mysteries, but also because a television set cannot be hidden in a drawer or placed on a high shelf, out of the reach of children. As he puts it, television's "physical form, no less than its symbolic form, does not lend itself to exclusivity."[20] His stated reason for presenting these statistics is to counter suspicions among readers that he is exaggerating this point.

Postman concludes his remarks in this section of his book with a somber thought to the effect that, given its fundamental nature, television, as the spearhead of the electric media, finds it difficult or impossible to withhold any secrets, and without secrets there can be no such thing as childhood.[21] Even more dire from the standpoint of the present discussion is his comment that in order to supply its audience with a continuous flow of novel and interesting information, television must use every existing taboo in the culture.

I think that Postman's analysis of television's contribution to the disappearance of childhood in America hits the nail squarely on the head.

Further, in terms of television's insidiously negative influence on the developing intelligence of American children, I know that I could not improve on his analysis, and I recommend this brilliant and entertaining book to anyone interested or concerned about this issue. Perhaps I can add something from the standpoint of depth psychology, however.

The Experiential Bind in Today's Child Development

The influence of the experiential bind upon the individual is dependent on many factors, especially that of early experience within the nuclear family. It is an axiom among the various theories of psychological development that this early experience has undisputed primacy in the formation of basic personality dynamics and structure. Whatever effect the bind has on the individual will be a function of the deeper integrity of the personality as it has been molded during infancy and childhood.

But there are various lines of evidence suggesting that conditions within the nuclear family in contemporary America may well be predisposing children to the adverse influence of the bind, and hence to the inadequacy complex and the demoralization. Narcissism, as a growing problem, has been a common theme in the writings of social observers and critics in the past ten or fifteen years. In addition, narcissistic disorder, or pathological narcissism, is one of the most frequent diagnoses being made by psychoanalysts and other mental health specialists in the context of formal psychotherapy and related treatments. Whereas at the turn of the century and well into the 1950s, the classical psychoneuroses—conversion hysteria, obsessive-compulsive neurosis, phobia, and anxiety neurosis—were the dominant diagnoses made in the context of outpatient treatment, as times have changed, pathological narcissism and borderline psychosis have displaced the relatively healthier structural neuroses as modal diagnoses among this class of patient. Further, there is the even greater, quasi-epidemic, incidence of depression, a symptom that is commonly associated with pathological narcissism and borderline psychosis.

Heinz Kohut, like Otto Kernberg, has done extensive research on pathological narcissism from the deeper vantage point of the practicing psychoanalyst. He posits the need for a comprehensive theory of the self within the larger edifice of traditional psychoanalytic theory in order to understand and effectively treat this syndrome. For Kohut, a weakly developed self, together with a relative inability to regulate and maintain healthy self-esteem, lies at the heart of pathological narcissism. In discussing the syndrome he states,

The principal source of discomfort is the result of the psyche's inability to regulate self-esteem and maintain it at normal levels; and the specific (pathogenic) experiences of the personality which are correlated to this central psychological defect lie within the narcissistic realm and fall into a spectrum which extends from anxious grandiosity and excitement, on the one hand, to mild embarrassment and self-consciousness, or severe shame, hypochondria, and depression on the other.[22]

Although he writes and theorizes in psychoanalytic terms, Kohut feels that in order to build a cohesive self the child needs three rather basic experiences during its early developmental years. One, "mirroring," is essentially warm, abundant love together with appropriate empathic sensitivity to the child's various needs. Coming primarily from the mother or mother surrogate, mirroring provides the infant with security and a basic sense of personal value. It is the opposite of maternal indifference and rejection. It comes ultimately from the mother's own healthy self-esteem, as well as her abundant desire to nurture *this* baby. It conveys to the newborn infant an unwavering sentiment of love, and joy in his/her existence, purring in effect, "You're here and you're fantastic." "Idealization" is the opportunity to make early positive identifications with strong, protecting parents, and in the process, to "merge our anxious selves with their tranquility . . . their calm voices . . . their relaxed bodies," as Kohut and Ernest S. Wolf put it.[23] They believe that this early idealizing experience will be retained by the child as the nucleus of the strength it feels as it lives its life under the guidance of its inner goals. It is the root of self-confidence, which in turn is the social-interpersonal face of healthy self-esteem. Typically directed more toward the like-sexed parent, it provides the child with realistic models for future growth. "Twinship," or the "alter-ego," is essentially the supportive company of other similarly aged children. This latter, while less critical to the development of a cohesive self than mirroring and idealization, enables the child to learn, early on, adaptive attitudes and skills in connection with competition and cooperation. According to Kohut, to the extent that these experiential factors are lacking, the chances that the child will develop a healthy narcissism, or positive self-esteem, are diminished or extinguished.

Assuming Kohut's formulations are valid, and reasoning, so to speak, in a backward direction, from effect to cause, one might interpret the increasing incidence of disturbed narcissism, as reported both by social critics and psychotherapists, as an indication that in some general sense Kohut's three basic conditions for the development of a cohesive self are becoming less and less available to American children in the context of the nuclear family. Switching our attention to a number of contemporary trends more directly reflecting conditions within the family provides further reason for suspecting this state of affairs. Such disturbing issues as the escalating rate of divorce; single-parent families; two working spouses, necessitating the shift of much of the burden of early child rearing to strangers; the increasing tensions and alienation between the generations;

the increased potential for interpersonal conflict produced by the new extended, or blended, family (resulting when divorcees with children remarry); sharply increasing rates of child abuse, alcohol and drug abuse, to name but some of the issues, can all be seen as potential obstacles to the child's successful development of a cohesive self, as this process is conceptualized by Kohut.

All of this has implications concerning the influence of the experiential bind upon growing children, particularly adolescents, who are known to be passing through one of life's most difficult stages, psychologically speaking. Based on Kohut's researches and theorems, it is logical to assume that to the extent that a cohesive self has not been formed in childhood within the nuclear family the weakened, or fragmented, self will be more susceptible to the insidious disintegrating influence of the bind. Returning to our model of the total self—actual plus ideal self—will help clarify things. If mirroring is insufficient to meet children's *subjective* needs—always an important consideration in depth psychology— and as a result they emerge from childhood low in security and feelings of personal worth, that is, guilty and low in self-esteem, they will be more vulnerable to the (actual) self-deflating pressures of the firsthand experiential realm. The inevitable hardships of life will have a more demoralizing effect. Insufficient twinship will also predispose them to the downward press of the firsthand realm. Lacking adaptive attitudes and skills in connection with competition and cooperation, they will be less able to thwart the frustrations and countervailing pressures and to hammer out real accomplishments that might serve to heighten their self-esteem, by bolstering their actual selves.

Regarding the ideal dimension of the total self, insufficient idealization in childhood will sensitize them to the self-inflating pressures of the vicarious experiential realm, to the hypnotic lure of the imagery of fantasy. In this unfortunate circumstance, the garishly overdrawn supermen and superwomen who make up much of the imagery of fantasy are all too often the substitute heroes to whom American youth turn today. Drawn into this web of imaginary heroes, they will more than likely begin to develop expectations for themselves that they cannot live up to; and this is the psychodynamic key to the demoralization under focus here.

Contrarily, it follows that strong early identifications with real parents and human figures will naturally serve as a crucial buffer against the influence of this omnipresent imagery. Absorbed in and gratified by activities reflecting such realistic and attainable identifications, individuals in all phases of their lives will be less intrigued with the imagery of fantasy and pay less attention to it, will cathect it less powerfully. Where these early healthy identifications are lacking, or are less well established, there will be an abnormally strong tendency to replace them with figures in the wider society. The study by Havighurst, Robinson, and Dorr, mentioned in the previous chapter, empirically demonstrates the outward-ranging tendency of the identification process. Further, this centrifugal thrust will be intensified by the preexisting lack of appropriate internalized models because they are intrinsic to, and thus necessary within, our psychological makeup as a species.

If mirroring, idealization, and twinship are all seriously lacking to children within their nuclear families, then theoretically they are pathologically predisposed to the full effect of the experiential bind: simultaneous deflation of the actual self and inflation of the ideal self. In this case, chronically irritated self-ideal discrepancy, onset of the inadequacy complex, serious demoralization, and clinical patterns of aberrant and/or antisocial behavior are highly probable consequences.

In discussing psychopathogenic experiential deficits in childhood, such as those conceptualized by Kohut, we are dealing with intangibles that are exceedingly difficult to demonstrate and measure. Almost never can we predict, in the individual case, that the developmental process will go seriously awry. Further, such deficits are always partially defined by the child's subjective needs, which vary widely from case to case. But theoretical generalizations based on related strands of evidence are legitimate and potentially useful. The increase in clinical cases of disturbed narcissism and the well-known divisive pressures operating within the nuclear family, taken together, suggest that in contemporary America conditions for the establishment of a cohesive self are becoming less available to growing children, who, because of this, are being rendered more susceptible to the influence of the experiential bind. Postman's analysis suggests, even more worrisomely, that this pathogenic experiential mix is occurring increasingly in the lives of younger and younger children. The upshot of this maleficent conjunction of forces may well be, to use Postman's terms again, a nation of "adultified" children giving rise, later on, to a population consisting largely of "childified" adults or worse.

The Double Bind–Experiential Bind Negative Synergy

Earlier I have suggested that the electronic media are lending something of a schizophrenogenic nuance to American society. In that vein I likened the experiential bind to the concept of the schizophrenogenic double bind described by Weakland. Limited to the family setting in Weakland's theory, the double bind involves, among other things, a mode of communication recurring in vitally important parent-child interactions, wherein

The individual [child] is caught in a situation in which the other person [parent] is expressing two orders of messages and one of these denies the other [such that] . . . . the individual is unable to comment on the messages being expressed to correct his discrimination of what order of message to respond to, i.e., he cannot make a metacommunicative statement.[24]

According to Weakland, this mode of communication on the part of parents is schizophrenogenic with respect in children because by continually confusing them and throwing them into emotional turmoil, it tends to undermine their capacity to test reality. Reality testing is a fundamental characteristic of a healthy ego, and its absence or relative absence may indicate a formal thought disorder, which, when present, is pathognomonic of schizophrenia.

Metacommunication is a concept that is also familiar to most psychotherapists. In the therapeutic context, it refers to such things as body language, emotional accompaniments to the flow of associations, things left unsaid, fluctuations in the speed of verbalization with changes in topic, to all those aspects of clients' productions distinct from their specific verbalizations. It is useful in gaining insights into clients' deeper motives and conflicts. Pathological examples are the quality of belle indifference accompanying a hysteric's account of an existing serious illness or, more sinisterly, a preschizophrenic's smirking as he or she relates the accidental death of a parent or sibling. Both indicate to the therapist that the deeper emotional meaning of the incident to the client deviates from its commonly accepted, consensual meaning. In the context of intensive psychotherapy such examples of internal dissonance signal conflicts that require more insight and, if possible, resolution. In the context of interpersonal relations they can be a source of confusion to intimates of the communicator, particularly to children. Within the family double bind described by Weakland, they tend to be commonplace.

Also, as stated earlier, I believe that the experiential bind operating on a societal basis is doing something similar to all Americans, particularly American children. The glitz, glamour, excitement, savagery, and easy success constantly portrayed in the vicarious experiential realm denies the toil, hardship, struggle, and modest, essentially peaceful, achievements of the firsthand experiential realm. Most adult Americans don't take the trouble to deny or thoughtfully controvert the imagery of fantasy, that is, make their metacommunicative statements with respect to it. They are too busy, or they enjoy it too much and passively accept it. But most children from infancy to early adolescence can't make a denial or controversion. They simply do not have the necessary education or realistic perspectives on life yet. The combined effects of (1) the omnipresent, endless flow of images, (2) their attention-riveting, hedonistic content, (3) their rapid, mesmeric pace, and (4) the naively gullible perspectives of children prior to midadolescence, all serve to suppress effective viewer denial of this reality-denying flood of imagery. Recall, too, Postman's statement that pictures, unlike sentences, are irrefutable.

Thus, in terms of its power to confuse children and undermine their emerging capacity to test reality, the societal experiential bind can be seen to affect children in ways analogous to the familial double bind of formal psychological theory.

The general psychoanalytic theory of the psychogenesis of schizophrenia goes something like this. Excessive frustrations and stresses occurring in infancy lead to early repression of essentially normal feelings and drive impulses in the growing child. Later on in adolescence or adulthood, either because of the physiological strengthening of the drive impulses—primarily sex and aggression—and/or living stresses that tax the ego's capacity to maintain adequate repression, the formerly banished material erupts into consciousness, inundating the ego with primitive feelings and impulses. Because of the climate of stress within the family and the archaic nature of these feelings and drive impulses, they are freighted with primal guilt and anxiety. Harry Stack Sullivan, the great American psychiatrist who pioneered early attempts at psychoanalytic therapy with schizophrenics, spoke of the uncanny quality of consciousness experienced by persons undergoing an acute schizophrenic psychosis. Under this assault from within, the ego is momentarily, or in some cases permanently, overthrown or put out of commission. Since the ego is the seat of reason, as well as the executive agency in the normal adult personality, its overthrow results in the bizarre, unpredictable, regressive patterns of behavior characterizing schizophrenic states.

Integral to this whole morbid process is the fact that psychic components under repression—impulses, feelings, memories, thoughts—are not obliterated or jettisoned. They are merely withheld from consciousness behind a repressive barrier. Because of this, they remain in the primitive state characterizing the mentality of the infant at the time the repression was necessitated. They are not assimilated into the rest of the developing psyche and thus are not tamed and molded by the socializing process. Further, in their state of exclusion from consciousness they constantly strive for expression. Consequently, they require a constant outlay of mental energy to ward them off, to keep them under repressive wraps. Although this formulation applies to neurotic conditions as well, the added energic requirement is much greater in prepsychotic and borderline states because of the archaic nature of the repressed drive impulses, which makes them more sharply egodystonic. This abnormal intrapsychic burden explains the typically tense, withdrawn, anergic, demeanor of preschizophrenic people. They are daily faced with a predicament not unlike that of a person attempting to deal with the complexities and stresses of delivering a speech, while at the same time keeping a steady pressure with one hand against a nearby swinging door in order to keep out a band of loud, determined hecklers. For preschizophrenics, ordinary interpersonal interactions have this quality of hassle-cum-trauma. Acute schizophrenia, to continue with this metaphor, occurs when the hecklers break through the speaker's restraint, and in the ensuing commotion the speaker's general composure and ability to continue are swept away, to be replaced by a miscellany of bizarre rantings, grimaces, manneristic gestures, and withdrawal into tormented, self-absorbed isolation. Central to this discussion is the idea that the healthy human psyche is a balance of forces in dynamic equilibrium, a "vital balance," to use Karl Menninger's term. Weakland's conception of the double bind is a refinement, from the standpoint of communications theory, serving to illumine schizophrenogenic ego-weakening stresses in the context of parent-child interactions.

The healthy ego, one characterized by reason, the capacity to delay gratification, and the ability to integrate the demands of the id, the superego, and external reality, is really an aggregate of learned habits that tend to be implanted over time by the manifold influences of the socializing process. Although, like most habits, healthy ego habits are tenacious, they can be overthrown either partially or completely when extraneous pathogenic pressures destroy or weaken the vital balance of psychical forces mortaring the healthy human psyche. Whether such pathogenic pressures come from within in the form of pent-up archaic sexual, aggressive, and narcissistic feelings and impulses that have burst through the intrapsychic repressive barrier or from without in the form of the luridly sexual, aggressive, and narcissistic images from the omnipresent imagery of fantasy, they carry a serious atrophic potential in connection with the development of normal ego habits among children. In fact, in the second case, ego integrity is often threatened on both the external and internal fronts, as it were, because the endless stream of irrefutable pictures and images tends to inflame the naturally strong sexual, aggressive, and narcissistic urges of preadolescents and adolescents.

While I am not for a moment suggesting that regular viewing of television and movies causes schizophrenia among children and adolescents, I do believe that it can have a subtle ego-weakening potential by virtue of its powerful and inescapable contribution to the experiential bind. In this sense, the electronic media can be seen to be lending a schizophrenogenic nuance to American society, especially as it impinges on the minds of these younger viewers. If average American children could fully deny the relevance of the imagery of fantasy to experience in the firsthand realm, as thoughtful adults can, then it would not have this insidious potential for them. But there is growing evidence on all sides suggesting that they can't, that the endless flow of images is fomenting unrealistic expectations in their minds and feeding their pervasive demoralization, as well as "disappearing" their childhood in the process, to borrow again from Postman's text.

Kohut's referring to the self as "the core of our personality" makes the following comments regarding its central intrapsychic role.

Once the self has crystallized in the interplay of inherited and environmental factors, it aims towards the realization of its own specific programme of action—a programme that is determined by the intrinsic pattern of its constituent ambitions, goals, skills, and talents, and by the tensions that arise between these constituents. . . . [this is] the self, an independent center of initiative, an independent recipient of impressions.[25]

In discussing various syndromes of self-pathology, Kohut describes the "understimulated self" as one of a number of frequently occurring clusters of disturbed self-experience. He states,

This is a chronic or recurrent condition of the self, the propensity to which arises in consequence of prolonged lack of stimulating responsiveness from the side of the self-objects [parents or parent-surrogates] in childhood. Such personalities are lacking in vitality. They experience themselves as boring and apathetic, and they are experienced by others in the same way. Individuals whose nascent selves have been insufficiently responded to will use any available stimuli to create a pseudo-excitement in order to ward off the painful feeling of deadness that tends to overtake them. . . . If the analyst is able to penetrate beneath the defensive facade . . . he will invariably find empty depression."[26]

It is my hunch, in light of the evidence for the decline of adequate child rearing performed by caring biological parents, that the understimulated self is the modal syndrome of self-pathology in America today. These children are deeply predisposed by their inner feelings of deadness to turn to the ever-present, ever-beguiling tube to find the excitement that they crave. These are the individuals who, scarred early in life by the double bind and host of other well-known forms of family pathology, and later drawn into pathological degrees of self-ideal discrepancy by the experiential bind, are predisposed to serious, perhaps incapacitating, emotional disturbance and mental illness when they finally are called on to face life as adults.

While mental health specialists such as Heinz Kohut tell us that they are treating more and more self-pathology in the form of clinical cases of pathological narcissism, they are obviously reaching only the most affluent tip of the iceberg. It is a certainty that there are hundreds of thousands more adult cases that never get any formal treatment at all. And it is highly probable that millions of American children and adolescents being reared in the teeth of the experiential bind will commence their adult years under the handicap of equally severe, possibly intensified, emotional disturbance.

Early in his thinking, Freud differentiated between the psychoneuroses and the narcissistic disorders on a crucial point. He believed that the latter could not be treated psychoanalytically because they could not be reached emotionally in the treatment. Because of the early onset of their psychopathology and the impenetrability of their ego defenses, they could not develop a stable positive transference to the analyst, and the positive transference is the motive force, as it were, behind a successful analysis. As a boat cannot move without wind in its sails, so an analysis cannot progress fruitfully without the emergence of a stable positive transference on the part of the patient toward the analyst. Positive transference of this type resembles the "working alliance" of modern psychoanalytic technical theory. It has to do with trust and respect, the kind of emotional bond existing between a normal young adult and his/her caring parent. In Freud's view, this critical emotional deficiency qualitatively differentiated the psychoneuroses from the more severe narcissistic disorders. Schizophrenia has always been viewed as the severest form of narcissistic disorder, the functional psychosis with the poorest prognosis in general. Pathological narcissism, on any mental health specialist's scale of severity, is seen to lie somewhere between the less serious neurotic conditions and the more serious functional psychoses.

Mental health specialists also know that there is a relationship between modal forms of individual psychopathology and the sociocultural backdrop at any point in history. Put differently, the societal manifold as it changes over time dictates what passes for emotional and mental health or ill health among its constituent members. The most familiar example of this concerns the disappearance of conversion hysterias so common in the late nineteenth century. As society's sexual norms have liberalized, the unconscious conflicts over sexual impulses and feelings that lay at the roots of conversion hysteria have also largely vanished.

To me, it is clear that the experiential bind is a critical factor in the emergence of pathological narcissism as an increasing, if not the modal, form of individual psychopathology in America today. Largely because of the burgeoning presence of the electronic media in the vicarious experiential realm, people are endlessly inundated by images of the unattainable that they are irresistibly drawn to and that tend to deny the relevance and value of their efforts and achievements in their own experiential realm. This beguiling, illusory backdrop is contributing to the formation of serious obstacles in connection with the development of a cohesive self early in life within the nuclear family, and virtually insuperable ones to its extended maturation as children, over time, inevitably move into the embrace of the wider society. Chronically irritated self-ideal discrepancy is the very antithesis of the cohesive self, as depicted in Kohut's theory. The documented increase in the frequency of pathological narcissism—as a more schizophreniform degree of self-pathology than the structural neuroses of yesteryear—is an unsettling sign of the schizophrenogenic influence of the experiential bind. Not only are children becoming prematurely "adultified," as Postman clearly sees, but they are being drawn into a maelstrom of psychological pressures that may direct many of them toward spending their mature years as handicapped, "childified" adults. Thus, many of them may have to suffer both the disappearance of their childhood *and* their adulthood as well.

Structured social phenomena such as the experiential bind have an added problematic dimension: the self-perpetuating and cumulative tendencies that typify their pathogenic fallout. If the bind is contributing to difficulties on the part of children in the formation of a cohesive self within their nuclear families, then when they become parents, the chances are that their children will be confronted with similar, perhaps even more formidable, obstacles in their own early maturational struggles. We know that child abusers and sexual molesters have more often than not been subject to abuse and molestation in their own childhoods, that children of alcoholics are predisposed to alcoholism, that children of psychotics are predisposed to psychotic episodes during their own lives, and so on. Such patterns of maladaptive behavior can be expected to perpetuate themselves in tainted families, as well as radiating cumulatively when members of these families forge new relationships and social bonds with members of untainted families. All of this will contribute to the stresses inhering in the firsthand experiential realm. With TV ordained to glow ever more luridly, tastelessly, and ubiquitously in the vicarious realm, the bind, for millions of Americans, can be expected to intensify its malign psychopathogenic influence on the American public in the future.

This same momentum will, more than likely, also infect the less clinically disturbed behavior patterns of American children as they acquire the means to economic independence and move into the status of adulthood. The erosion of the secrets of adulthood implicit in the electronic media's basic need to move information rapidly and superficially, its ineluctable penchant for total disclosure will tend to undermine youth's natural drive to acquire its ultimate status and identity via emulation of adulthood traditionally defined, that is, via the accumulation of education, technical knowledge, and some form of wisdom. With no secrets to pursue competitively, the quest for differential status via the accumulation of money for rampant consumerism can be expected to intensify. Americans will compete in the manner comfortable and familiar to them. As the contemporary Adam Smith averred in one of his trenchant books on the subject, money is the way you keep score. Together with the American tendency to lackluster performance on the work and production side of economic reality, this habit of self-actualization through consumption, coupled with the heedless sale of existing tangible assets—businesses, real estate—in order to obtain quick credit, is well calculated to lead us, as a citizenry, to the status of indentured servants to the Japanese sometime during the twenty-first century.

There will, of course, always be secrets to uncover in the areas of science, art, history, philosophy, and the like. But trying to seriously interest the

average TV-saturated American adolescent of 15 in such intellectual subject matter would only be a bit less difficult than attempting to do so with
a cocker spaniel. In the latter instance, you would have to make, say,
the binomial theorem or Kant's categorical imperative smell like meat—
and I don't mean the paper on which it is printed, but rather, its intrinsic
symbolic meaning. In the case of the American adolescent, you would
have to give it super sex appeal or the promise of orgastic pleasure, two
rather formidable problems in epistemological presentation and educational marketing. But the need would spring from TV's use of images
rather than sentences and, to go back to Neil Postman's analysis, analogic
symbols rather than digital ones. By the fact of their being irrefutable in
form, and hence requiring no rules of logic or evidence for their valid
cognitive assimilation, the medium's use of pictures as its principal vessels
of information is gradually removing the traditional academic disciplines
from the realm of possibility for many American children who have sucked
on it from infancy. In order to be interested in and capable of ferreting
out the infinite number of secrets waiting to be divulged in the worlds
of science, art, history, and philosophy, children need the long apprenticeship of childhood, the principal involvement of which for the past 300
years or so in America has been the achievement of literacy and basic
numerical competence through formal education, Postman's "second curriculum." It is here that the basic left-brain competencies are systematically
formed and developed, those involving skill in actively manipulating
alphabetic and numerical symbols according to the rules of logic. It is here
that the mentality responsible for the creation and maintenance of Western
culture since the Renaissance has, generation by generation, been carefully
cultivated. It is this basic mentality that the electronic media are, ter-
mitelike, slowly and insidiously undermining through the undifferentiated
availability of Postman's "first curriculum" and the imagery of unreality
that I survey. It is a well-known fact in educational psychology that interest hinges significantly on competence. As daily, excessive TV viewing, emphasizing passive registration of fleeting pictures, undermines
quantitative and linguistic competencies, so does it simultaneously erode
interest or potential interest in the universe of intellectual secrets. But
strong interest, combined with the requisite skills, in intellectual secret
hunting among the young are what we as a nation need if we are to maintain our relative position in the future-shocked, technetronic world of
today.

Postman concludes his discussion on an admonitory, but encouraging,
note directed at responsible, concerned parents. He urges them to become
actively involved in controlling the electronic media's access to, and hence
curbing its influence on, their growing children. He stipulates the two
necessary phases involved: (1) limiting the amount of exposure children
have to the media and (2) providing them with a continuously running

critique of the themes and values of the media's contents. He warns parents that this vital media-buffering function will be difficult to sustain, and it will require a level of attention that most parents are not prepared to give to child rearing. On the other hand, he reminds the reader of the rewards to be reaped. The first, having immediate implications, involves helping their children to have their childhood. The second, having more delayed consequences, involves the creation of a sort of intellectual elite who will be much favored when, down the line, they themselves begin to seek career employment. In concluding, he states "that it is not conceivable that our culture will forget that it needs children. But it is halfway to forgetting that children need childhood. Those who persist in remembering shall perform a noble service."[27] I would simply add the thought that children don't know what they don't know, and children in contemporary America don't know that they need childhood. The electronic media are inadvertently working to prevent them from having their childhood, the most critical of all developmental phases in humans. Those parents who are aware and care ought to heed Postman's advice. Many of the children who lose their childhood are, for the reasons I have developed above, predisposed to lose their adulthood as well.

THE HECTIC PACE OF LIFE

Related to the various societal reverberations already discussed is yet another issue that appears to be hooked to the bind, the inadequacy complex, and the demoralization. Much has been written over the past fifteen years or so about the changing, churning quality of life in contemporary America, its overwhelming pace. Toffler's *Future Shock* is the most detailed account of this phenomenon that I am aware of. He argues that accelerating change causes all relationships that people enter into now to be characterized by increasing transcience and impermanence. In his account he refers to the "throw-away society," stating, "In their lives, things, places, people, ideas and organizational structures all get 'used up' more quickly. This affects immensely the way they experience reality, their sense of commitment and their ability—or inability—to cope."[28]

Again, the imagery of unreality can be seen as a constant stimulus to this quality of transience in people's lives, much of which is a direct result of their own unconscious reaction to the imagery. By creating unattainable expectations, the imagery of fantasy sets up related attitudes of dissatisfaction, impatience, and restlessness and, of course, serious guilt where the inadequacy complex has taken root. The imagery of doom, on the other hand, stokes the fires of paranoid mistrust, which tends to throttle affiliation with and commitment to larger social agencies and institutions, as well as devotion to time-consuming excellence in connection with work projects. Millions of people in America are in a hurry to get somewhere—to realize their inner expectations, to catch up with the apparently successful people, using whatever tactic is available—and much of the impermanence under focus can be ultimately traced, in large part, to these widespread and urgent inner proddings.

The overt indications of this restless dissatisfaction are abundantly obvious. Escalating divorce, the increasing incidence of job and career change, experimentation with different life-styles, and rampant consumerism are some of the better-documented trends exemplifying it. Among the young, there is evidence of a growing disdain for steady, determined self-application in preparing for careers and jobs, for serving as apprentices and journeymen before they become masters at the top of the pay scale. They want instant gratification, instant success, and their general modus operandi is more and more one of switching from involvement to involvement, hunting for ripe opportunity, than that of staying put and laboring toward carefully planned goals. Today it is not uncommon for college students to transfer to four and five schools during their undergraduate years, and to change their majors as many times. In my nineteen years of experience working in a college counseling center, my longitudinal impression has been that, over this span of time, students' spoken reasons for transferring have increasingly reflected the desire to find better-connected colleges, that is, colleges offering more career-related pull or clout in the "real" world of remunerative work. On a subtler level, however, there are myriad signs of this restlessness in routine, everyday behavior. The TGIF (Thank God It's Friday) sentiment, the frequency of dreamy talk about vacation trips and alternate life-styles at lunch and coffee breaks, an underlying quality of impatience and indifference in conversations and casual social relationships, the ubiquitous foot swinging under the table during meetings and serious discussions, all suggest a pervasive attitude of search, a desire to get through the present situation and move on to something better. Where serious emotional disorder enters the picture, we may see such problems as alcohol and drug abuse, autistic thinking, or prolonged withdrawal from normal work and interpersonal relationships. In cases such as these, individuals are more apt to be oriented toward fantasies, utopian situations that exist only in their heads.

Toffler attributes future shock primarily to unbridled technology, and I believe he is right. I am suggesting that a certain amount of the transcience that he describes can be traced to the influence of the experiential bind, particularly that aspect of it created by the imagery of fantasy. However, my thesis is in complete accord with his. The imagery of fantasy beaming out from the collective media is a product of advanced technology. This imagery fosters expectations that for most people are unattainable. As part of the broader experiential bind, it feeds noisome feelings of inadequacy, a sense that one lacks certain traits and abilities necessary for real success. In many cases this feeling of inadequacy may develop into a distinct psychological complex, with varied symptomatology and underlying dynamics. The restlessness and searching orientation under discussion is reflective of the inner turmoil associated with this negative self-estimate. The fact of the matter is that millions of Americans today are running from themselves, as much as they are running after (toward) success.

It seems to me that there is a discernible common denominator underlying the societal reverberations under focus here. Phenomenologically, we have a picture of millions of people in America, restless, dissatisfied, constantly searching for something better, compulsively consuming goods and services of every conceivable kind, and in the process radiating a hypercynicism that is tied to chronic demoralization. What is common to these disparate behaviors, in much the same way that an unconscious dynamic conflict may be common to a variety of different psychological symptoms, is a progressive weakening of the sense of limitation and restraint. When one considers the possible consequences of this trend, it can be regarded as a kind of societal loss of reality testing with serious self-destructive, perhaps suicidal, implications. Speaking on the problem of the exhaustion of valuable natural resources, B. F. Skinner, the noted psychologist, remarked not long before his death, "It's fantastic how we are consuming irreplaceable goods. If everybody in the world were living as we do, there wouldn't be enough energy in the world to last the rest of this century."[29]

Of course, it is my belief that the principal stimulus to this loss of healthy restraint is the imagery of unreality in both of its forms. To me, it cannot be overemphasized how important this imagery is in the lives of people in America. Writing on the decline of quality in contemporary America, historian, Barbara Tuchman, appeared to reach similar conclusions regarding the power of modern advertising.

Advertising augments the condition [loss of quality]. From infancy to adulthood, advertising is the air Americans breathe, the information we absorb, almost without knowing it. It floods our minds with pictures of perfection and goals of happiness easy to attain. Face cream will banish age, decaffeinated coffee will banish nerves. . . . almost anything from deodorants to cigarettes, toothpaste, hair shampoo and lately even antacids will bring on love affairs, usually on horseback on a beach.[30]

Advertising, however, is but one main source of the imagery of fantasy. In addition, it is constantly proffered by both the printed and electronic entertainment media. Further, as I have repeatedly suggested, the imagery of doom reinforces, with equal constancy, cynical doubts about the reality of extending oneself for the sake of quality and/or service as ends in their own right, doubts that might be paraphrased as "Why kill myself when everyone else is cheating at, or lucking into, success?" As Tuchman suggests, and as I have attempted to show throughout this discussion, this imagery creates the illusion that paradise, or its earthly facsimile, success, is possible, is available, is being enjoyed by many others who are shrewder or luckier than oneself. In the face of this grand illusion there is little wonder that both realistic perspective and the sense of limitation are atrophying on a broad scale in the minds of millions of Americans today. It should be borne in mind that people suffering the inadequacy complex are, in the vast majority of cases, entirely adequate human beings. Only in contrast to the expectations engendered by the grand illusion could they be judged, by themselves or by others, as inadequate.

In a more philosophical vein, we might think of this loss of perspective and personal restraint in terms of a growing obtuseness concerning the tragic side of life. Perhaps, too, this apparent obtuseness has its roots in denial, given the very real possibility of thermonuclear world holocaust. However, while no one wants to consider this aspect of human existence, it is also undeniable that all really serious human religious, philosophical, and artistic deliberations on life recognize the tragic and give it ontic significance. Early in the development of his philosophical thought William James concluded that "tragedy is at the heart of us."[31] In his discussion of the "sick-soul" in *The Varieties of Religious Experience* he remarked,

There is no doubt that healthy-mindedness is inadequate as a philosophical doctrine, because the evil facts which it refuses positively to account for are a genuine portion of reality; and they may after all be the best key to life's significance, and possibly the only openers of our eyes to the deepest levels of truth.[32]

Treating the problem of human failure at another point in the discussion, James asserted,

Failure, then, failure! so the world stamps us at every turn. We strew it with our blunders, our misdeeds, our lost opportunities, with all the memorials of our inadequacy to our vocation. And with what a damning emphasis does it then blot us out. . . . The subtlest forms of suffering known to man are connected with the poisonous humiliations incidental to these results.[33]

And on the same note he quoted Robert Louis Stevenson, "There is indeed one element in human destiny that not blindness itself can controvert. Whatever else we intended to do, we are not intended to succeed; failure is the fate allotted."[34]

This may have a dismal ring to it, but there is an important point to be considered. While an awareness, and acceptance, of the tragic side of life has its dangers, and morbid preoccupation with it might well lead to nihilism, depression, even suicide, if handled maturely, it can serve to protect people against the pain and stress of chronic disillusionment and disappointment. As James wrote, this is a poisonous kind of pain. Internalized, it can become pathological guilt, the anguished self-disappointment that typically drives the sufferer to some form of avoidance or expiation. We know that guilt operates widely in serious psychopathology. As I have tried to show, a secularized form of it is basic to the inadequacy complex and the pervasive demoralization, which, in turn, are the affective soil feeding the various behaviors symptomatic of the need for expiation and/or avoidance of this morbid guilt. Taken en masse, these behaviors are contributing daily to the dehumanizing of America.

A mature acceptance of the tragic side of life—its dangers, its limitations, and above all, its incompleteness—is no small personal accomplishment. It is difficult to acquire, and it takes a certain measure of courage to maintain it. It is fostered by proper guidance and education, in the home, in formal schooling, and in the wider society. It is invaluable because it underlies realism, perspective, and good judgment. These attitudes will benefit people in their passage through life. But through the individual, they will also redound to the benefit of society at large.

I believe that today in America people are being systematically miseducated, literally deceived, by the imagery of unreality and/or the first curriculum. Day by day they are being subtly indoctrinated with the ideas that there are no limits, no necessary frustrations, no end to new and titillating pleasures, especially if one is hard-nosed enough to go out and take them or lucky enough to fall into them. The societal reverberations discussed here are some structured collective symptoms of this indoctrination. The youth of America are bearing the brunt of this endlessly beguiling communications phenomenon. A fantastic, illusory carrot is being dangled in front of them, day in and day out.

NOTES

1. Julian Rotter, "Trust and Gullibility," *Psychology Today*, October 1980, 102.
2. Ibid.
3. Alfred Malabre, *Beyond Our Means* (New York: Random House, 1987), 3.
4. Ibid., xii.
5. Ibid., xv.
6. For a more detailed, and fascinating, account of the German hyperinflation of 1920–23, read John Kenneth Galbraith, *Money: Whence It Came, Where It Went* (Boston: Houghton Mifflin, 1975), 146–63.
7. Malabre, *Beyond Our Means*, 162.
8. Christopher Lasch, *The Culture of Narcissism*, (New York: W. W. Norton, 1978), 21.

9. Sidney Weintraub, "The Human Factor in Inflation," *New York Times Magazine*, November 25, 1979, 116.

10. Ibid., 119.

11. Ibid.

12. Ibid., 164.

13. Ravi Batra, *Surviving the Great Depression of 1990* (New York: Simon & Schuster, 1988), 17.

14. Ibid., 273.

15. Ibid., 69.

16. Neil Postman, *The Disappearance of Childhood* (New York: Delacorte Press, 1982), 78–79.

17. Ibid.

18. Ibid., 73.

19. Ibid.

20. Ibid., 79–80.

21. Ibid., 80.

22. Heinz Kohut, *The Analysis of the Self* (New York: International Universities Press, 1971), 20.

23. Heinz Kohut and Ernest S. Wolf, "The Disorders of the Self and Their Treatment: An Outline," *International Journal of Psychoanalysis* 59 (1978): 417.

24. John Weakland, "The Double-Bind Hypothesis of Schizophrenia," in *The Etiology of Schizophrenia*, ed. Don Jackson (New York: Basic Books, 1970), 374–75.

25. Kohut and Wolf, "The Disorders of the Self," 414.

26. Ibid., 418.

27. Postman, *The Disappearance of Childhood*, 153.

28. Alvin Toffler, *Future Shock* (New York: Random House,1970), 41.

29. "B. F. Skinner," *U.S. News and World Report*, November 3, 1980, 80.

30. Barbara Tuchman, *New York Times Magazine*, November 12, 1980, 41.

31. Gay Allen, *William James* (New York: Viking Press, 1968),   .

32. William James, *The Varieties of Religious Experience* (New York: Mentor Books, 1958), 137–38.

33. Ibid., 119.

34. Ibid., 119–20.

4

Rehabilitation and Prevention

All of the following measures are oriented toward mitigating an existing irritated self-ideal discrepancy in adolescents and adults, or counteracting the development of a potential dynamic structure of this kind in the personality of growing children.

The concept of self-ideal discrepancy/congruity in psychology is not unlike that of supply-demand disparity/parity in economics. In both conceptual abstractions it is the relationship between the two end factors that is critical. Relative balance between these two factors is the relationship making for a cohesive, viable, functional system. Within the individual personality this balance tends to keep the threat of morbid guilt at bay; within a capitalist economic system it tends to hold back the threat of chronic inflation. In both cases, it is exorbitant demand that appears as the likeliest direction of skew away from this tenuous balance, at least in contemporary America. In both cases, the imagery of fantasy can be seen as a powerful proximate stimulus to this tendency to exorbitance. In the economic sphere the very purpose of advertising is to create artificial wants among the consuming public, whose spending habits, when properly fanned by the endless ads, contribute to the assumed economic growth. Robert Heilbroner, professor of economics, addressing the role of advertising within capitalism, puts it thus.

A second, equally fraught consequence of the ideology of economics concerns the widely recognized phenomenon of the "commercialization" of life." . . . the self-determination of life patterns, the most private of all activities, is everywhere deliberately subjected to the influence of "advertising," the purpose of which is to induce individuals, without knowing anything of them, to change their mode of living. These instances of a relentless commercialization, perhaps the single most self-destructive process of modern capitalist civilization, could be multiplied manifold.[1]

In a discussion of the ego-ideal and its origins, Norman Cameron states,

The ego-ideal is an unrealistic part of the superego which has its origin in a narcissistic over-valuation of the self and an idealization of parental power and perfection. During the infantile period when the self and others are still imperfectly distinguished, the ego-ideal is probably experienced as a participation in some kind of imaginary omnipotence. For some reason, the ego-ideal escapes the less optimistic modifications which mold the ego in accordance with the reality principle. It evolves with the aid of more abstract ideals and values into an unattainable standard within the superego, which the rest of the superego uses as a measure of what the ego actually achieves.[2]

Oriented to unreality and omnipotence from the very start, the ideal self is being overstimulated by the imagery of fantasy through the juvenile, adolescent, and adult years. Here, too, in the psychological sphere, is the proximal source of the exorbitant demand. Although we naturally tend to assume that the wider societal experience will encourage the reality principle and strengthen the developing ego, we can see, on the contrary, that certain exceedingly powerful and pervasive elements of that experience are constantly reinforcing expectations, longings, and identifications of a distinctly omnipotent, unrealistic character. In this respect, people in contemporary America are being infantilized throughout the life cycle by powerful societal institutions rather than merely during childhood by concerned parents and doting grandparents. But as is true of all infantile yearnings, in the greatest majority of cases these media-cultivated hybrids must undergo extensive frustration or brute denial in the real world. This sets the stage for continuous inner turmoil. The outcome in the individual case is all but impossible to predict. In many cases there is no discernible living problem; in many we find periods of demoralization interspersed with more benign phases; in others there is multiform psychopathology in all degrees of severity.

As implied in the above, the fundamental aim of all of the rehabilitative and preventive measures to be discussed is to help people counteract this tendency to make exorbitant demands on themselves, to help them find the key to that vital intrapsychic balance that is invigorating and life enhancing because it facilitates fairly regular moments of self-ideal congruent experience. Since we are all, in the final analysis, singular as human beings, this point of balance differs for each one of us.

REHABILITATION: PSYCHOTHERAPY

Although this objective is easy to outline, it is not necessarily easy to accomplish, nor does formal therapy proceed neatly and efficiently when it is accomplished. As with most psychotherapy that addresses basic living problems, effective treatment of chronically irritated self-ideal discrepancy does not produce quick, permanent relief from the attendant symptomatology. Rather, when the vital balance is realistically achieved, it is more often than not the result of a slow, incremental, often painful, process of self-discovery and self-mastery. This point bears on a major deception of many of the newer pseudotherapies that are springing up in great profusion all around us. They offer quick cure rather than gradual change, adjustment rather than improved coping skills, happiness and fulfillment rather than increased personal resilience and resourcefulness. Like the imagery of fantasy, they frequently cause their clients dillusionment and a sense of having been ripped off. Freud once remarked that in psychoanalysis the patient exchanges neurotic misery for normal unhappiness. While this may have a pessimistic ring to it, it is closer to the truth in regard to *all* forms of psychotherapy than the glowing promises of many modern therapy brochures and advertisements. But it doesn't sell very well in America.

Effective treatment of the inadequacy complex entails alteration of a great deal of persistent bad feeling, particularly guilt, depression, anxiety and hostility. In order to accomplish this on any permanent basis, the tension between the two aspects of the self-construct must be revealed and diminished. The key to the treatment is thus the modification of certain cognitive structures within the personality that have crystallized over time. In my opinion this applies to all serious psychotherapeutic work. Although there is a complicated interplay between cognitions and emotions in any psychological complex or symptom, the keystone is invariably an aggregate of related cognitions—thoughts, assumptions, and beliefs, often unconscious—regarding the self, the world, and the relationship between the two. In this sense cognitions are seen to be the primary elements of the psyche, the superstructure, so to speak. Emotions have a secondary reactive significance, even though they acquire energizing and directive influence on cognitions in the course of development. This helps explain why many of the recent short-term therapies that emphasize mere mobilization of feelings (for example, encounter weekends) produce superficial, short-lived, results. Where serious symptoms and significant psychopathology are involved, they simply do not get at the kernel of the problem.

This discussion of treatment will be general. It is essentially a statement of therapeutic goals and philosophy pertinent to the complex, rather than a detailed description of specific techniques. Effective treatment can be accomplished by therapists from a variety of theoretical schools and persuasions. The objectives discussed are really not at all esoteric, but I believe that they are critical to helping the client resolve the complex and its attendant demoralization. If I were to classify this treatment approach, it would be best described as a form of reconstructive reality therapy.

Persons with the inadequacy complex who find their way into formal therapy come with the implicit hope that the therapist, who is assumed to have special knowledge, will cure them of their inadequacies by helping them to become more perfect, more accomplished, and more successful in their daily lives. Their basic negative self-regard has led them to look for a means to compensatory self-perfection. However, the essential antidote to the complex is not self-perfection, particularly as this is understood by persons caught in the complex and under the spell of the imagery of unreality. Rather, it lies in the achievement of a healthy and durable self-acceptance, one that prevails in the face of perceived limitations and imperfections. Thus, a certain humility is integral to this most intimate of valuative attitudes. Such forgiving self-affirmation is the intrapsychic equivalent of healthy parents' generous, even unconditional, love of their infant. The nurturant, life-sustaining essence of this healthy parental reflex, which recalls Kohut's concept of mirroring, lies in the fact that it permits mistakes and failures and rarely backs the growing child into an emotional corner or impasse. In existentialist terms, it is this "acceptance-in-spite-of" that fosters the "courage to be," which in turn is crucial to creative participation in the wider society.

Self-perfection in pursuit of the imagery of fantasy does not work for a number of reasons over and above the most obvious one, which has to do with the implausibility of successfully chasing rainbows. First, most persons caught in the complex are actually quite adequate; they only feel themselves to be inadequate because of their exorbitant, media-fed goals and expectations. Second, this illusory self-perfection is unattainable because the unconscious demands of the inflated ideal self are basically insatiable. As long as an irritated self-ideal discrepancy exists, the individual will feel subjectively inadequate no matter how accomplished he/she is in real life. An inflated ideal self (ego-ideal) can be as unrelenting as the infamous sadistic superego of psychoanalytic theory. As we have seen, it is integral to this superego; it is, in fact, the motivating source of the relentless self-devaluation. Third, the preoccupation with self-perfection characteristic of the complex is ultimately rooted in self-doubt and self-contempt, attitudes that are quite the opposite of the forgiving self-affirmation just mentioned. As long as this unrealistic demand upon the self persists, one can be certain that healthy self-acceptance is lacking.

In working to help clients suffering the inadequacy complex achieve healthy self-acceptance, therapists have two essential tasks. First, they must try to show the clients that their expectations and self-dissatisfactions are based on illusions, that much of the imagery working on their consciousness is saturated with unreality. Second, they must try to help their clients achieve a greater measure of self-affirmation *despite* their felt limitations and imperfections. This second goal is approached more in the context of the interpersonal relationship than by cognitive means, although it is certainly facilitated by the accompanying orientation to reality. The essential truth to be learned by people caught up in the inadequacy complex is that personal fulfillment in work, love, and life comes more from self-acceptance and self-trust than from self-improvement in accordance with unrealistic standards. It is ultimately this self-acceptance "in-spite-of" that enables people to relax their guilt-driven, narcissistic self-engulfment and involve themselves in socially useful activities. As psychologists such as Becker, Fromm, and James have long taught, activities of this nature in which people can meaningfully lose themselves are the true sources of self-esteem. It's not unlike trying to go to sleep at night; concentrate too hard on it and you'll be awake for hours; forget it and abandon yourself to your favorite fantasy and slumber comes naturally and sweetly. Healthy self-esteem comes from losing oneself in meaningful participation with others; seeking it via concerted, planned self-improvement is a matter of shinnying a greasy pole. Don't misunderstand me here. The latter approach may well result in improved skills and talents which may in turn make for greater worldly success. But in most cases, the resulting success will be a guilty one, because, by virtue of its narcissistically idealized focus, it is always subjectively disappointing, never enough. Human quests of an essentially narcissistic nature carry this paradoxically insatiable consequence. The psychiatric textbooks are filled with case histories of anorexics who, despite their being on the brink of starvation and/or death, still "feel fat" and wealthy alcoholics who are driven to their self-destructive habits because of obsessive worries over money. Lacking the crucial "in-spite-of" nuance, their self-acceptance is always momentary, always subject to the whip of self-ideal discrepant guilt. This is what keeps them shinnying the greasy pole of narcissistic self-improvement. I believe that the experiential bind is sucking millions of Americans into fruitless quests of this kind. The therapist's task is to assist the client in replacing a vicious cycle—guilty self-devaluation and withdrawal—with a virtuous one—tolerant self-acceptance and involvement.

It is extremely important for clients to realize that their self-devaluation is unconscious, chronic, and excessive. An implication of this insight is that they are really better than they think they are in comparison with other people, especially the seemingly successful ones. However, these ideas are not always readily accepted by clients. Mesmerized by the imagery of fantasy, persons suffering the complex desperately want a more adequate person to show them the way to life-enhancing self-improvement, to fusion with their inner ideals. This desire can be the source of the most tenacious resistance, since it is fundamentally unrealistic while at the same time it is regularly and powerfully reinforced by the imagery. Consequently, the emphasis on self-acceptance and "seeing through" the subtle deceptions of the imagery often lacks therapeutic value in the client's mind.

The interpersonal encounter between therapists and clients is critical in helping clients develop healthy self-acceptance. Existentialist conceptions of psychotherapy are useful here. In discussing intensive treatment of neurotic patients, Hanna Colm argues that acceptance of the patient by the therapist and the therapist's helping the client to accept this acceptance are necessary in bringing about or restoring to the patient the courage of confidence; and it is this inner courage that enables the patient to participate meaningfully in the work of society. Borrowing from religious teaching, existential psychology makes much of the concept of courage. According to Colm, Paul Tillich, the Protestant theologian upon whose writings existential psychologists frequently draw, argued that, "The courage-to-be is the courage to accept oneself as accepted in spite of being unacceptable. . . . Accepting acceptance though being unacceptable is the basis for the courage of confidence."[3]

Although this might seem convoluted, it is, in my mind, central to both mental health in general and to resolution of the inadequacy complex. This form of courage—the acceptance and affirmation of self in spite of limitations and imperfections—indicates a willingness to face up to the element of struggle in life, its tragic dimension. It implies a readiness to take chances, to work hard, and to persevere in the face of anxiety and guilt.

Struggle is basic to the human condition, and the capacity to struggle is central to mental health. The psychoanalytic term "ego strength" can be interpreted literally. The healthy ego is a tough ego, able and willing to struggle and bounce back from adversity. However, it seems that people in modern America reject, or have lost sight of, this truth. They think of the well-adjusted person as functioning with the ease and efficiency of a finely tuned machine. When confronted with tenacious difficulties that require struggle, they all too quickly assume that something is terribly wrong and run off to an expert for help. All too often, particularly where social-interpersonal problems are at issue, the expert's services are both costly and ineffectual.

This seeking out of experts, this faith in technology, appears to apply maximally in America. Americans, more so than any other Western populace, have lived for the past fifty years under the shadow of the machine and electronic communication. As a consequence of their immersion in this technetronic environment they have come to expect, unconsciously, instant results and machinelike efficiency of themselves.

But humans are not machines. They are infinitely more complicated than any machine, and they are called upon to face tasks and exigencies of enormous complexity and ambiguity. Machines are carefully engineered to perform a precise function or series of related functions, and this limit applies to computers, the so-called thinking machines, as much as it does to mechanical pumps. Well-engineered machines typically perform efficiently and tirelessly within their preconceived spheres of operation. But humans can never be engineered for the tasks and exigencies of life, which are basically unspecifiable and in a constant state of flux. As William James stated in his famous chapter on the stream of thought. "No state once gone can recur and be identical with what it was before. . . . and that whatever was true of the river of life, of the river of elementary feeling, it would certainly be true to say, like Heraclitus, that we never descend twice into the same stream."[4] Hence, the ever-present demand for risk taking, trial and error, and consciously willed, sustained effort—in short, for struggle. But today, millions of Americans naively reject this truth. It seems to me that this naiveté is especially likely in persons born after World War II who have lived exclusively with the machine and the electronic media, and who have been massaged from infancy by the imagery of unreality. Of course, it is my contention that this river of imagery is the primary stimulus to this growing obtuseness to the reality of struggle in the human condition.

In *The Culture of Narcissism*, Christopher Lasch argues that proliferating professionalism is characteristic of modern America. A part of this development is the fact, mentioned above, that people tend to quickly consult a specialist when faced with a problem. If the market for all manner of specialists exists, then sooner or later the specialists will appear, with all of the requisite professional accoutrements and symbols. It is possible that an advanced technetronic society tends to breed feelings of inadequacy among its individual members, in part at least, by shifting responsibility for the solution of many living problems away from the person onto a so-called expert. The electronic media, by virtue of their penchant for moving information continuously and superficially, contribute to this specialist dependency by augmenting confusion within their respective audiences. thus, one promising antidote to the development of the complex lies in a renewed emphasis on personal responsibility. Taken together with the realization that much of what passes for professional expertise is vastly overrated, this emphasis has considerable preventive potential in regard to the spreading of the complex among younger Americans. As Lasch states, the waning of personal moral responsibility necessarily means a waning of the capacity for self-help. Children grow into competent, confident adults largely through participation in the activities of their peer groups, activities that require skills in both the areas of competition and cooperation. Passivity and lack of involvement are well-known correlates of insecurity and incompetence.

In their conception of psychotherapy, existential psychologists place great importance on the interpersonal encounter between therapist and patient. For existentialists, it is primarily in the context of an encounter between two people that patients gain the self-acceptance and courage they need in order to overcome their neuroses through participation in the wider sociocultural reality. Again according to Colm, Tillich wrote, "No self-acceptance is possible if one is not accepted in a person-to-person relationship."[5] Further discussing the therapeutic encounter, Hanna Colm emphasizes the importance of shared experience. She refers specifically to the creation by the therapist of a "we-feeling" between the two participants that comes from the therapist's willingness to admit to his/her own shortcomings, imperfections, and human emotions. On this point she remarks,

When the patient is overwhelmed with facing his hate or envy or competitive violence, a "we" response, such as "We tend to be hateful if we are frightened or frustrated," can be more helpful than merely a detached, unjudging "This is your defense," which only adds to the patient's agony and loneliness and self-condemnation. The "we" response gives the patient a feeling of communion in human finiteness.[6]

Continuing on this note she adds,

The analyst who says "we tend to" also counteracts an unnecessary and unrealistic buildup of himself as perfect in the eyes of the patient. This response conveys to the patient that the analyst accepts his own humanness; it is probably the most convincing way of showing the patient that he is accepted in spite of his hate. Both [Hans] Trueb and [Ludwig] Binswanger say in effect that this response conveys the feeling, "We meet as partners in our human shortcomings and inadequacies"—an experience which the patient will have more fully only at the end of analysis when the analyst allows his own emotional human reactions to come more fully into the open.[7]

While made in reference to the practice of existential analysis with neurotic patients, these points are applicable to the general psychotherapeutic treatment of the inadequacy complex. Within the interpersonal encounter, sincere acceptance of clients by therapists, particularly if they can freely admit to their own human shortcomings, can do much to help clients develop realistic self-acceptance, that is, self-acceptance "in-spite-of" limitations and imperfections. As in all psychologically healing human relationships, the principal elements are honesty, empathy, and positive regard.

Thus the therapist must work at two levels simultaneously. On the cognitive level he/she exposes or defrocks the imagery of fantasy in its various manifestations—media programing and advertising, personal ripples in the wider environment—and in the process helps clients to see how this collective phenomenon is constantly feeding expectations that neither they nor anyone else can realistically live up to. In this vein the therapist works to show clients that, judged by the facts of reality, their sense of personal inadequacy relative to other people and to most of life's demands are unfounded. On the interpersonal level, the therapist attempts to create an atmosphere in which clients can emotionally accept and affirm themselves despite their human limitations and imperfections. This treatment approach serves, theoretically at least, to counteract the twofold influence of the experiential bind on clients' total self-construct. Exposure of the imagery of fantasy, as well as clients' unrealistic expectations, can be seen as an effort at corrective deflation of the ideal self. On the other hand, the acceptance and honest sharing of experience within the interpersonal encounter can be viewed as an effort at corrective inflation of clients' actual selves. Further, if the encounter proves to be an emotionally meaningful experience to clients, it should foster identifications with the therapist, thus reinforcing at a deeper psychical level the cognitive pruning of the ideal self. The work at both levels can be seen as aimed at facilitating the establishment, by clients, of a vital intrapsychic balance, one that, through correction of the media-fed tendency to exorbitant demand, fosters the possibility of more and more self-ideal congruent experience.

My emphasis, within this outline of formal treatment, is admittedly on the realistic deflation of the ideal self. It is relevant that this same emphasis appears in papers on orthodox psychoanalytic technique in connection with the treatment of classical structural neuroses, as well as with cases of pathological narcissism. In a paper published in 1934 in the *International Journal of Psychoanalysis*, psychoanalyst James Strachey argued that in treating neurotics the essential object of the analytic process was to bring the patient's superego into closer alignment with the existing realities. According to Strachey, if this was achieved it would be likely to lead to a general improvement of the patient's condition. He described how, during the analysis, the analyst becomes an "auxiliary superego" to the patient, and then, through the action of "mutative" interpretations in the context of the transference relationship he works to both soften the patient's superego and align it with the existing realities.

The most important characteristic of the auxiliary superego is that its advice to the [patient's] ego is consistently based on *real* and *contemporary* considerations and this in itself serves to differentiate it from the greater part of the original superego. . . . If all goes well, the patient's ego will become aware of the contrast between the aggressive character of his feelings and the real nature of the analyst, who does not behave like the patient's "good" or "bad" archaic objects. The patient, that is to say, will become aware of a distinction between his archaic fantasy object [parent] and the real external object [analyst]. The interpretation has become a mutative one, since it has produced a breach in the neurotic vicious circle. For the patient, having become aware of the lack of aggressiveness in the real external object, will be able to diminish his own aggressiveness; the new object which he introjects [analyst] will be less aggressive, and consequently the aggressiveness of his superego will also be diminished.[8]

At another point in his paper Strachey made the following observation.

Thus there are two convergent lines of argument which point to the patient's superego as occupying a key position in analytic therapy: it is a part of the patient's mind in which a favorable alteration would be likely to lead to a general improvement, and it is a part of the patient's mind which is especially subject to the analyst's influence.[9]

In a more recent edition (1978) of the same journal Heinz Kohut and Ernest S. Wolf make the following remarks concerning the treatment of the noncohesive self in cases of narcissistic personality disorder.

If, however, the therapist can explain without censure the protective function of the grandiose fantasies and the social isolation and thus demonstrate that he is in tune with the patient's disintegration anxiety and shame concerning his precariously established self, then he will not interfere with the spontaneously arising transference mobilization of the old narcissistic needs. . . . And again, as in the case of the narcissistic behavior disorders, the remobilized needs will gradually—and spontaneously—be transformed into normal self-assertiveness and normal devotion to ideals.[10]

Recall that morbid guilt is the unavoidable intrapsychic resultant of irritated self-ideal discrepancy, or severe ego-superego tension in psychoanalytic terms. Whether it be a case of classical structural neurosis, more serious pathological narcissism, or a bind-induced demoralization, it is clear that melioration of this poisonous negative self-regard is critical to successful treatment and rehabilitation. Put differently, the condition of relative balance between the actual and ideal selves, making possible more frequent moments of self-affirmation via self-ideal congruent experience, appears to be the common goal toward which many depth therapists work. This is congruent with the idea that morbid guilt is the keystone of functional psychopathology, at least in Western culture. Finally, as I have repeatedly stated, I believe that in modern America the media-driven, inflated ideal self is the principal determinant of this widespread intrapsychic disharmony and the attendant guilt.

In the long run, the object is to facilitate clients' capacity for meaningful, responsible participation in the work of society, participation that will inevitably involve personal risk and struggle. But, as both Adler and

Becker so convincingly argued, this is the only way to effectively renew and maintain adult self-esteem. Basic to this whole process is the orientation to reality. Exposing the illusions that contribute to the unreality of clients' expectations of themselves and others and, hence, to clients' self-devaluation, is absolutely necessary. As long as they believe in the illusions and, hence, in the legitimacy of their expectations, their attempts to overcome their feelings of inadequacy and achieve personal fulfillment will be doomed to frustration, a matter of shinnying a greasy pole.

Although client self-improvement in pursuit of the imagery of fantasy is destined to failure and is thus not a legitimate therapeutic goal, helping clients find ways to realistic growth is a valid and vital aspect of the treatment. Theoretically, all such therapeutic efforts can be subsumed under the concept of realistically bolstering the bind-deflated actual self. Again, as with the issue of self-acceptance "in-spite-of," realism is the keyword. Because of the pervasive pull of the imagery of fantasy, orienting clients to reality is a fundamental object of the treatment, and it underlies all specific intervention.

As part of the process of promoting realistic growth, assessment of strengths and abilities in specific, concrete terms is important. Deluded by the ubiquitous imagery, clients are very apt to lose sight of many of their actual assets and talents. Related to this is the necessity of teaching them to avoid blanket self-criticism when confronted with frustrations, and along with it the temporary sense of defeat and failure. This kind of overdone, indiscriminate self-denunciation is essentially a product of the fulminating hostility and guilt characteristic of the complex. In response to the setbacks, mistakes, misguided intentions, and social faux pas to which we are all prone, persons caught in the complex are predisposed to overreact inwardly to themselves with pitiless self-excoriations—"You fool, you idiot; you never do anything right!!!" Such blanket reactions are both inaccurate and harmful, and if they are part of clients' habitual self-appraisals, they urgently need to be replaced by habits of more modulated and discerning self-criticism—"I messed that one up, but tomorrow's another day" or "Presenting information in group situations is not one of my greatest strengths."

The specific living objectives emerging from the therapy will, in all probability, have to be pursued by clients with patience and determination. This is true of all worthwhile accomplishments in life. Consequently, the importance of commitment must be emphasized throughout treatment. Developmental change and growth necessarily involve risk, hard work, and frequent setbacks. This truth is by its very nature difficult enough for humans to accept, but it is further obscured by the imagery of fantasy that beams out an endless stream of dramatic successes, instantly and painlessly achieved. Related to the need for commitment is the fact that in the last analysis, clients must accomplish real growth and their various living objectives largely by themselves. While it is true that we depend on others for support and assistance in our projects and problems, we also know that as adults this dependency cannot be overdone. Barring incurable illness or injury, adults are ultimately responsible for themselves, and they must be prepared at all times to dig down into their stores of personal resources and struggle. It is thus important to help clients understand that the need for patience and hard work in pursuit of goals and rewards is in no way a sign of personal inadequacy.

Maturity and mental health necessarily involve a moral-ethical stance toward life and the world. Religious, philosophical and educational thought systems in general, in their intellectual analyses of mature social behavior, all stress the importance of moral-ethical values as living guides. Although treatment of the complex does not and should not involve specific moral suasion or teaching, reinforcement of moral-ethical values where they already exist can facilitate realistic growth. The preoccupation with rampant consumerism, competition, and winning is growing ominously in contemporary America, and it reaches grotesque proportions in much of the imagery of fantasy. As stated earlier, people mired in the complex suffer insistent feelings of social-intellectual-physical inadequacy, but rarely those of moral-ethical laxity. In formal treatment, placing renewed value on such attitudes as compassion, cooperation, fairness, and respect—creating an atmosphere of what Martin Buber called "I-Thou," rather than "I-it," in interpersonal relations—can facilitate movement into the kind of social interests and involvements that ultimately build and maintain adult self-esteem. It is in fact easier to cooperate with people than to try to outdo them; to communicate simply and directly with them rather than trying to impress them with brilliant verbal performances; to listen and defer, when conditions indicate, rather than always seeking to have the last word; to take one's place in the group rather than compulsively striving to stand out. Consequently, deeply seated attitudes of equality and fraternity, if they actually exist within the personality, tend to lubricate the process of participation in the wider social reality.

As Adler taught, preoccupation with winning, dominance, and superiority weakens social interests and predisposes people to a narcissistic life-style. The narcissism of the inadequacy complex has a psychopathic element to it, so that social involvements are apt to have more the quality of manipulations and exploitations than will cooperative efforts. Paradoxically, the guilt of the complex is a form of guilt that often motivates people to destructive or irresponsible behavior patterns. And, again somewhat paradoxically, helping clients strengthen their moral-ethical imperatives can work to mitigate this secularized guilt.

As with all other therapeutic efforts appropriate to treatment of the complex, realism is of the essence here. In the real world of sensitive, striving human beings, traditional moral-ethical values are, in the long run, pragmatically useful guides to living and working. The imagery of fantasy, as the term suggests, is replete with glossy fictions. Its implicit narcissistic philosophy is basically fallacious.

We live in a troubled society, one that is reeling under the weight of widespread interpersonal alienation and mistrust of established institutions. My bias is of course that the double-edged imagery of unreality (fantasy and doom) is constantly contributing to this potentially catastrophic situation. Although this imagery is not the sole cause, it is certainly significant. Loss of reality testing is fundamental to all forms of serious individual psychopathology. It seems reasonable to assume that a whole society may be predisposed to a kind of collective maladjustment if its principal information system, its communications media, are saturated day to day with unreality. I believe we are actually experiencing something like this in contemporary America.

At the simplest level, a society is nothing more than a collection of individuals. To the extent that these individuals are motivated by humanitarian concerns, the society itself will be more realistic, safer, and saner. My hunch is that it will also be a society in which it is easier for average persons to maintain their self-esteem and their sense of personal adequacy.

Many existing therapeutic techniques are applicable to helping clients initiate the process of realistic growth, to facilitate realistic bolstering of their actual selves. Such things as modeling, management, construction of a detailed change plan, support, advice, judicious pressure, and career counseling come readily to mind. Career counseling, involving administration of a battery of tests, is entirely appropriate when needed. Selection of a meaningful career path is an important buffer against the complex, and the standard career consultation can help clients ascertain vocations and career paths that they are suited to in terms of aptitudes, interests, personality traits, and general values. This is particularly applicable to adolescents and young adults who are in the traditional career-planning phase of their lives, as well as to older adults who have fallen into career doldrums and who are in need of new directions.

All of these techniques focus on helping clients find ways to maintain and renew their self-esteem in the real world, in the firsthand experiential realm. However, the crux of the treatment involves exposure of the irritated self-ideal discrepancy and its attendant unconscious self-devaluation that together comprise the dynamic nucleus of the complex and the demoralization. Helping clients to self-acceptance "in-spite-of," as well as to various approaches to realistic personal growth, all hinge on exposure and melioration of this pivotal discrepancy, which is the intrapsychic equivalent of the overarching incongruity between the vicarious and experiential realms in modern America.

In the treatment situation the therapist will more than likely be confronted with an amorphous mixture of complaints and symptoms. Therapeutic practice tends to be like that. The complex may be associated with other acute symptoms—phobias, obsessions, psychosomatic ailments, severe depression, psychotic confusions—that urgently require other therapeutic approaches, chemotherapy, or hospitalization. In such instances, the complex may be the underlying cause of these symptoms or merely an additional living problem. The therapist will have to plan treatment on the merits of each case. This discussion has focused on what might be called the "simple" inadequacy complex. Whether the complex is of the simple type or embedded in other serious forms of psychopathology will become increasingly clear to the therapist as he/she works along.

PREVENTION: PARENT-TEACHER COLLABORATION

While formal treatment of symptoms of the bind-induced demoralization may fall to psychotherapists in the various mental health professions, preventive measures aimed at helping children parry the potentially demoralizing grip of the bind are the natural province, and challenge, of parents and educators.

Neil Postman ideally conceptualizes the second curriculum, the public educational curriculum, as serving a balancing, or "thermostatic," function via-à-vis the first, electronic, curriculum of media-dominated contemporary American society. According to him, as a thermostat provides balance against biologically debilitating extremes of temperature in our physical environment, so should the formal education of American citizens provide balance against the intellectually debilitating extremes proponderant in our electronic information environment. In his assessment of the electronic media's influence on the minds of American children, Postman uses the word "curriculum" deliberately. In *Teaching as a Conserving Activity* he defines a curriculum as a "course of study whose purpose is to train or cultivate both mind and character."[11] He then argues that schools not only *have* curriculums but *are* curriculums, in the sense that everything about a school has an effect, intentional or not, on the shaping of the young. Finally, he proceeds to the assertion that by this definition television also qualifies as a learning curriculum.

Many parents, as well as educators, seem to believe that television is an "entertainment medium," by which they mean to imply that little of enduring value is either taught by or learned from it. . . . But all of this can be seen in a clarifying light if we simply define a curriculum as a specially constructed information system whose purpose, *in its totality*, is to influence, teach, train, or cultivate the mind and character of our youth. By this definition, television and school not only have curriculums but are curriculums; that is, they are total learning systems. . . . Viewed in this way, television is not only a curriculum but *constitutes the major educational enterprise now being undertaken in the United States.* That is why I call it the First Curriculum. School is the second.[12]

As an educator, Postman deplores the intellectually stultifying influence of television on the nation's schoolchildren. In his analysis he criticizes the first curriculum for being attention centered, nonpunitive, affect centered, present centered, image centered, narration centered, moralistic, nonanalytical, nonhierarchical, authoritarian, contemptuous of authority, continuous in time, isolating in space, discontinuous in content, and immediately and intrinsically gratifying. As Postman carefully shows in his analysis, all of these anti-intellectual characteristics are inherent to television by virtue of it form of presentation and its pace. As he puts it,

No amount of academic complaints or "responsible" calls for TV reform can change any of the above. TV is not a school, or a book, or any curriculum other than itself. It does what its structure makes it do, and teaches as it must. The real pragmatic issue is not TV but its relationship to the other systematic teachings in the information environment. The question is, To what extent can the biases of TV be balanced by the biases of other information systems, particularly the school?[13]

Postman devotes the second half of his book to detailing his proposed second curriculum, both in terms of specific courses and their more general rationale within the thermostatic framework. At the outset he confesses to the difficulties involved in suggesting a plausible theme for a diverse, secularized population such as that comprised by contemporary American schoolchildren. He adopts "the ascent of humanity through the discovery of knowledge in the arts, humanities and sciences as part of our unending quest to gain an understanding of nature and our place in it" as a conceptual scaffolding on which to build the second curriculum.[14] In the interest of combating the mindless pressure of the wider, media-spawned, information environment, he advocates the consistent emphasis, within the curriculum, on helping children become interested in intellectual depth, as well as competent at artistic expression. As he puts it, "I am proposing, as a beginning, a curriculum in which all subjects are presented as a stage in humanity's historical development; in which the philosophies of science, of history, of language, and of religion are taught; and in which there is a strong emphasis on classical forms of artistic expression."[15]

Language education is a key element in Postman's conceptual scheme. He is well aware that people's ability to think clearly and comprehensively on a subject is intimately tied up with their relevant language skills, that "words increase our understanding, and our understanding increases our words."[16]

As might be expected, media education is also an integral aspect of his curriculum, the thrust being essentially critical-evaluative. In regard to this important aspect of the second curriculum, he states,

Media education is not. . . . the use of modern media, in or out of the classroom, to complement traditional studies. . . . modern media should be brought into the classroom principally as specimens to analyze, not as aids. The Second Curriculum must study, evaluate and criticize the First, not make alliances with it.[17]

I cite Postman's work specifically because of his use of the concept of thermostatic balance as the second curriculum's basic orientation in combatting widespread intellectual atrophy resulting from first curriculum plague, or media blight. As a psychologist, I worry about the deeper psychopathological effects of the media on the nation's school-children. In systematically countering this malign influence on our children, Postman's concept of thermostatic balancing is applicable here as well. Such a balancing influence can be seen, theoretically, as integral to the defusing of the experiential bind, and hence to the melioration of the irritated self-ideal discrepancy lying at the root of the growing public demoralization. According to what we know about the human tendency to internalize experience, an augmented environmental, or external, balance should foster, over time, an improved psychical, or internal, balance in the cases of many potential young victims. Further, parents can, and should, join hands with teachers in the systematic enactment of this balancing effort. Parents have more potential influence over their children than any other societal institution, even that of the media, in many cases at least.

As in formal psychotherapy of the inadequacy complex, the essential focus of this effort should be to expose the illusory nature of the imagery of unreality and to undermine its credibility and its idealizability. To the extent that this can be accomplished, children will have more psychic energy and more libido, which will be available for the idealizing and internalizing of attainable goals and emulable idols. In terms of our intrapsychic model, this balancing effort goes under the heading of "realistic guidance of the developing ideal self." Complementarily, and more in line with the traditional mission of public education in America, are all of those elements of the second curriculum devoted to facilitating the development of an adequate actual self.

In a recent article entitled "Crack and the Box," journalist-novelist Pete Hamill traces much of the cause of America's involvement with drugs to forty years of commercial television. Considering the extent of daily TV viewing by the average American family—seven hours, according to the last Nielsen survey—he states,

This has never happened before in history. No people has ever been entertained for seven hours *a day*. The Elizabethans didn't go to the theater seven hours a day. The pre-TV generation did not go to the movies seven hours a day. Common sense tells us that this all-pervasive diet of instant imagery, sustained now for forty years, must have changed us in profound ways.[18]

Exploring similarities between drug use and TV watching, Hamill notes that TV is a consciousness-altering instrument, is conducive to intellectual and imaginative passivity among habitual viewers, implicitly upholds hedonism as a value (life should be *easy*), and tends to foster narcissism and superficial emotionality among viewers of all ages. His conclusions reflect those of other serious observers from different disciplines: Schwartz, Postman, Lasch, Stern, to name a few cited in this book. In casting around for solutions, he also proposes a thermostatic, balancing approach featuring the efforts of parent and teachers.

What is to be done? . . . As a beginning, parents must take immediate control of the sets, teaching children to watch specific television *programs*, not "television," to get out of the house and play with the other kids. Elementary and high schools must begin teaching television as a subject, the way literature is taught, showing children how shows are made, how to distinguish between the true and the false, how to recognize cheap emotional manipulation. All Americans should spend more time reading. And thinking.[19]

Hamill's concluding statements are both consistent with his theme and dramatic in their portrayal of the uncaring vested interests against which this educational balancing effort on behalf of our children must struggle: "For years, the defenders of television have argued that the networks are only giving the people what they want. That might be true. But so is the Medellin cartel."[20]

Hamill's prescriptions are strikingly similar to Postman's regarding parents' responsibilities in protecting their children from overdoses of the first curriculum. Both involve active monitoring and control of children's TV viewing. Postman advocates continuous intellectual guidance, running critiques, by parents of the values and themes within TV programs, whereas Hamill advocates adding this as part of the second curriculum. However, both attach first importance to systematic parental efforts to help their children begin to see the imagery of unreality for what it is: a grand illusion that has, for the most part, little to do with the realities of the firsthand experiential realm. Postman, as an educator, goes into much greater detail in his book in describing the elements of his proposed second-curricular antidote to first-curricular plague. He is well aware of the attention-riveting and mind-bending power of the electronic media, and in his admonition to concerned parents he warns them of the attention and effort involved in this struggle against the plug-in drug.

Although more concerned about the debilitating influence of TV on children's intellectual development, both Postman and Hamill would appear to be writers who would agree with my emphasis on exposing this omnipresent imagery in order to realistically modify the ideal self in formal psychotherapy. Unquestioning immersion in the imagery of fantasy pathologically inflates the ideal self, and in the process undermines intellectual development. This unfortunate consequence stems from the imagery's appeal to the archaic, narcissistic overvaluation of the self discussed by Norman Cameron, from the primal grandiosity latent in all humans. Even average intellectual skills are, to some extent, arduous of achievement. On the other hand, they are necessary for effective coping with the complex stresses of the firsthand experiential realm in our technetronic age. But many children, lulled by this powerful enticement to grandiose expectations of themselves and life, react with contempt to the intellectual rigors of the classroom, to the prospect of learning how to manage their lives independently and effectively as adults. Put differently, if you anticipate achieving celebrity as a pop-music star, sports hero, or charismatic private eye, where's the relevance in acquiring the skills to be another faceless accountant, engineer, or social worker? These are all too vague, tedious, and boring. Further, children cannot anticipate the demoralization awaiting them as adults when their romantic dreams have been thoroughly punctured by the slings and arrows of outrageous fortune and they are faced with their portion of the sea of troubles that the flesh is heir to—when they harbor within themselves the condition of chronically irritated self-ideal discrepancy as they tread the hard pavements of their own firsthand experiential realms. And the children who will be at the worst disadvantage on reaching adulthood will be those presently allowed, because of parental indifference or naiveté, unlimited access to the first curriculum. As Postman suggests, concerned parents who are willing to limit and critique the first curriculum are not only allowing their children to have a childhood but are simultaneously creating an intellectual elite who will, as adults, be much favored by business, the professions, and the media themselves, in their subsequent search for the best jobs and career tracks. Again, the idea that children don't know what they don't know, applies here.

First and foremost, it is up to parents, particularly in the preschool years, to protect their pliant, trusting, naturally curious offspring from overdoses of the insidiously cumulative, beguiling first curriculum. This is the principal quarantine against the idealized internalization of the vast array of fantastic models and fallacious standards of worldly achievement infesting this virulent curriculum. It is the necessary protection against the threat of media-based stimulation of a prematurely and intractably inflated ideal self within the developing child. And I hope it goes without saying that on the other side of proper parental influence lies the more traditional responsibility for providing children with adequate amounts of love, discipline, and guidance in the interest of helping each child lay down, as early as possible, the foundation of a solid, resilient, actual self-construct.

As Postman warns, the challenge is heavy and the prospective effort considerable. However, the danger to children and to the future is real. The first curriculum is subtle in its omnipresent enticement of their attention away from the potentially taxing but ultimately growth-inducing challenges, stresses, gratifications, and triumphs of the firsthand experiential realm. I believe that such challenges cannot, in general, be met squarely by persons whose attentions and skills emanate from a psychological core rent by the condition of chronically irritated self-ideal discrepancy, from chronic, severe ego-superego tension.

Parental influence in the infantile years is critical because it cannot be effectively supplanted or corrected later on by the schools, the churches, the mental health profession, or the entire scientific community. Recent research in neurophysiology tends to be corroborative of the older concept from developmental psychology of phase-critical learnings—the idea being that once the optimal time period is past, the crucial phase-related learning can never again be fully achieved. The corroborative research indicates that in terms of neuronal circuitry, humans become hardwired for the response patterns acquired in these early developmental phases of infancy and that no amount of later corrective experience can produce completely effective compensating circuits. Long ago William James taught that while not identical with mind, brain is the organ most closely related to mind and that it imposes ineluctable limits on mind. In the light of the neurophysiology of the time, James had the following thoughts on the prepotency of early habits in the individual's behavioral repertoire at any point in time.

For, in the first place, the brain is essentially a place of currents, which run in organized paths. . . . It must never be forgotten that a current that runs has got to run out *somewhere*; and if it only once succeeds by accident in striking into its old place of exit again, the thrill of satisfaction. . . . will reinforce and fix the paths of that moment and make them more likely to be struck into again. The resultant feeling that the old habitual act is at last successfully back again, becomes itself a new stimulus which stamps all the existing currents in. It is a matter of experience that such feelings of successful achievement do tend to fix in our memory whatever processes led to them.[21]

More recent research in neuropsychology, aided by methodological improvements of a century of experience, suggest similar conclusions. Michael Gazzaniga, author of *Mind Matters*, states,

In computers, different electrical circuits produce different machines with different capacities. This same appears to be true for the brain. Most brain scientists assume that the actual pattern of connections in a particular brain is vastly important to understanding the patterns of behavior associated with that brain. While the general anatomical relations are the same for all human brains—for example, the nerves from the eyes project to specific regions of the brain—the details of projection vary from one person to another. The possibilities for variation in what is called the association cortex, the part of the human brain believed to be most active in the production of thought, are enormous. . . . To date, however, we can demonstrate only that variations in cell-to-cell organization can occur and can be produced by changing the milieu of the developing brain.[22]

In a recent book entitled *The 3-Pound Universe,* Judith Hooper and Dick Teresi, reporting on current findings and research techniques in the areas of neuroscience, make observations in close agreement with those of Gazzaniga. In a section entitled "Making our Own Brain Maps," they compare the human brain to a computer and emphasize the lack of finality in the brain's internal organization. On this particular subject they quote Michael Merzenich of the University of California at San Francisco, who states,

The brain is not a machine in which every element has a genetically assigned role; it is not a digital computer in which all the decisions have been made. Anatomy lays down a crude topographic map of the body on the surface of the cortex, which is fixed and immutable in early life. But the *fine-grained* map is not fixed. Experience sketches in all the details, altering the map continually throughout life.[23]

In this part of their book they also report a fascinating study done by Donald O. Hebb, a famous behavioral psychologist, who took some of the rats he worked on as experimental subjects home with him and raised them as pets. This group of rats, Hebb observed, were better able to solve their maze problems than other genetically identical rats that had not been treated as pets in their leisure time. Much later, in the 1960s, Mark Rosenzweig decided to elaborate on Hebb's "smart rats." He and his research colleagues at the University of California at Berkeley raised littermates in enriched environments (communal cages full of running wheels and toys, where the rats were handled and petted by their caretakers) or in an impoverished environment (individual cages with low sensory stimulation). They then took out the rats' brains, weighed and measured them, and reported that the enriched group had a thicker cerebral cortex. Despite the initial dubiety of the world of science, William Greenough at the University of Illinois decided to replicate Rosenzweig's procedure and then do a more neurologically detailed analysis. Using brain staining and microscopic techniques, he found that the individual neurons of the stimulated rats had more dendritic branches. More dendritic branches mean more synapses and more connections, because multiple synapses along a dendrite are the neuron's receiving stations. "And more information, in a very important sense!" Greenough pointed out.[24]

Using the above methodologies and their resulting data as a basis for speculating on the role of experience in changing the brain's very architecture, Hooper and Teresi conclude this part of their discussion with the comment that, "The brain does not live on glucose alone. Cultivating feeds it. Isolation kills it."[25]

All of these statements are reminiscent of Carl Jung's proposition that adults can never fully abrogate their basic psychological problems dating from infancy, and that only through long-term analytical psychotherapy followed by related efforts throughout the rest of life might they make discernible gains against their debilitating symptoms. Once the primal grooves become worn, there is no absolute altering of their essential configuration. This is why responsible parental influence is quintessentially important to the child's future and to that of society as well.

While a part of me might well be in favor of some form of responsible, discerning government censorship of the electronic media—so convinced am I of their psychopathological potential in the case of millions of young Americans—I understand that the infringement of the First Amendment poses insuperable obstacles. However, if enough concerned parents broadened their traditional roles to initiate the media-controlling and critiquing responsibilities outlined above during their children's preschool years, the protective process would begin when and where it should. And if public education, building upon and extending this early parental initiative, offered a systematic thermostatic curriculum along the lines suggested by both Postman and Hamill, many young Americans would no longer need external government protection by the time they reach adulthood. Disinterest, even disdain, based on insights into the illusory nature of the first curriculum and, one hopes, fortified by more realistic identifications, would have rendered them immune to much of the intellectual-emotional drivel therein. Protective censorship, for them at least, would be superfluous. And if their numbers were large enough, you just know the quality of the programing would improve. That is the nature of market-sensitive, profit-bent capitalism.

The concept of metacommunication, mentioned earlier, is useful in illustrating yet another extremely subtle way that the first curriculum influences its viewing audience, especially the more youthful segment. According to John Weakland, the essence of the family double bind, as a prime source of metacommunicative confusion, lies in the incongruity existing between the different levels of much human verbal interchange, most commonly between spoken words, on the surface, and in their deeper-lying emotional accompaniments. It is commonly accepted among psychotherapists that unstated emotional messages often comprise the more penetrating aspects of such interchange, particularly that occurring between parents or parent-surrogates and their typically model-hungry children. As corollary to the above is the idea, also accepted by most therapists, that growing children tend to internalize more what their parents are than what they say and do. This is so because the latter two aspects of interpersonal behavior, the words and the acts, are much more subject to momentary change than are their emotional bedrock, so to speak. While this vulnerability to metacommunicative confusion applies maximally to children, adolescents are frequently subject to it as well.

Consider the experience of the average male juvenile, preadolescent, or adolescent as he idly watches the evening TV news program in New York or in other cities across the nation while waiting for his supper. Consider, now, the likely effects on him of the metacommunicative aspects of these programs: the pageant of color and upbeat background music; the strikingly attractive anchors, commanding yet serene, even humorous, in their faultless rendering of the rapid succession of news stories; the interspersal of ads with their promises of success and pleasure in all areas of life by virtue of mere consumption; the general up-beat atmosphere of the show. Particularly with respect to crime, the staple topic of this most powerful form of the imagery of doom, the metacommunicative thrust could certainly be interpreted by such impressionable viewers as affirmative, even celebratory, stating in effect, "This is where the action is, fella! This is what the world is about!"

Given Postman's convincing arguments concerning the irrefutability of pictures, together with the omnipresence of TV in modern America, can there be any doubt about the probable potentiating influence of such shows on the criminal proclivities of young men, macho and randy as they naturally are at this age? Can there be any doubt about the connection between the availability of such shows and the startling increase in shocking youthful crime: the gang rapes of mentally defective females by middle-class high school males; the ghoulish murders of the young girls and old ladies next door, again by young men from middle-class backgrounds; the attempted immolations of neighborhood boys because of their refusal to buy drugs, perpetrated by lower-class preadolescent males? Can there be any question that such impressionable young men need parental guidance and formal educational programs designed to help them see through the metacommunicative deceptions of these and other elements of the imagery of doom? While much of it is circumstantial, I believe that the weight of the evidence is undeniable.

In light of its focus on the demoralizing effect of the omnipresent imagery of unreality, this book can be seen as a sequel to Alvin Toffler's *Future Shock*. "Future shock," as Toffler puts it, "is the human response to over-stimulation."[26] Toffler's discussion of this pervasive and potentially psychotoxic phenomenon, written over twenty years ago, is trenchantly informative, so far as it goes. Attributing the phenomenon to runaway technology, he sees it as fostering a quality of transience to every aspect of Americans' lives. In their rush to stay abreast of the endless combers of new technology, they have created the "throwaway society." Worst of all, Toffler argues that the pace of technological innovation is positively accelerated, that Americans must run ever faster to stay on the treadmill of technetronic consumerism.

I have attempted to throw light on another aspect of the very real problem of pervasive, technology-driven overstimulation in modern America, namely, its tendency to invade, through the normal process of internalization of experience, the minds of millions of unsuspecting people. Once inside the individual in the form of perduring psychical structures, and perhaps their correlated neural circuitry, it is exceedingly difficult to change. Referring to such acquired, in-built, phenomena in terms of an older, perhaps simpler model, William James characterized habit as, "The enormous fly-wheel of society, its most precious conservative agent. . . . [which] dooms us all to fight out the battle of life upon the lines of our nurture or our early choice, and to make the best of a pursuit that disagrees, because there is no other for which we are fitted, and it is too late to begin again."[27]

I believe that much of this overstimulation is contributing to the experiential bind and to the highly probable, if not inevitable, demoralization described in earlier chapters. To me, in light of James's brilliant metaphor, this lends added urgency to the need for a parent-school, thermostatic, second curriculum along the lines detailed by Postman and consonant with Hamill's suggestions.

Now, a word to those relatively healthy adults who may sense within themselves the operation of some of the demoralization under discussion here, but who do not feel the need for formal psychotherapy. In those cases a self-administered thermostatic second curriculum may help. Here too the focus should be on discreditation of the imagery of unreality, together with development of the practice of self-acceptance "in-spite-of." To the extent that these two projects are realized, the vital intrapsychic balance that permits fairly regular moments of self-ideal congruent, life-enhancing experience should also be firmed. But a necessary caveat: those attempting this process should not anticipate finding the key to entry into anything like the alluring spaces of the vicarious realm, which are, for the most part, pure fantasy, heady at first but always unsustainable. Over time, demoralization is the price for getting hooked on them.

NOTES

1. Robert Heilbroner, *The Nature and Logic of Capitalism* (New York: W. W. Norton, 1985), 117–18.

2. Norman Cameron, *Personality Development and Psychopathology: A Dynamic Approach* (Boston: Houghton Mifflin, 1963), 194.

3. Hanna Colm, *The Existentialist Approach to Psychotherapy with Adults and Children* (New York: Grune & Stratton, 1966), 141–42.

4. William James, *The Principles of Psychology* (Chicago: Encyclopedia Britannica, 1952), 149–51.

5. Colm, *The Existentialist Approach to Psychotherapy with Adults and Children*, 153.

6. Ibid., 150.

7. Ibid.

8. James Strachey, "The Nature of Therapeutic Action in Psychoanalysis," in *Psycholanalytic Clinical Interpretation*, ed. Paul Louis (London: Collier-MacMillan, 1963), 17–20. (Originally printed in *International Journal of Psychoanalysis* 15 [1934]: 127–59.

9. Ibid., 10.

10. Heinz Kohut and Ernest S. Wolf, "The Disorders of the Self and Their Treatment: An Outline," *International Journal of Psychoanalysis* 59 (1978): 424.

11. Neil Postman, *Teaching as a Conserving Activity* (New York: Delacorte Press, 1979), 49. In this section of his book Postman outlines, conceptually and philosophically, his proposed thermostatic curriculum. His presentation is lucid and thought provoking. I heartily recommend this book to all concerned persons, especially parents of school-aged children.

12. Ibid., 49–50.

13. Ibid., 70.

14. Ibid., 135.

15. Ibid., 147.

16. Ibid., 152.

17. Ibid., 188.

18. Pete Hamill, "Crack and the Box," *Esquire*, May 1990, 64.

19. Ibid., 66.

20. Ibid.

21. James, *The Principles of Psychology*, 46–47

22. Michael Gazzaniga, *Mind Matters* (Boston: Houghton Mifflin, 1988), 8–9.

23. Judith Hooper and Dick Teresi, *The 3-Pound Universe* (New York: Dell, 1986), 61.

24. Ibid., 65.

25. Ibid., 66.

26. Alvin Toffler, *Future Shock* (New York: Random House, 1970), 280.

27. James, *The Principles of Psychology* 68.

5

Technology and Contemporary American Values: The Deeper Roots

America, at this point in its history at least, is awash in materialistic hedonism. Like Toffler, I attribute this unhealthy complex of national ideals and values primarily to runaway technology. He sees this unbridled technological juggernaut as the source of an accelerating material overstimulation that is quickening the pace of life excessively, and in the process creating the "throwaway" society. According to Toffler, the lives of millions of product-hungry, "future-shocked," Americans are increasingly characterized by a heedless transience that is damaging to both individual mental health and the social fabric.

I believe that electronic communications technology, one of the more recent strains of the inexorable technological innovation, is overstimulating the American public in another, more damaging manner. By creating an incongruous, fantasy-ridden, realm of vicarious experience that is rivaling the older, firsthand realm in terms of the amount of time and attention per day spent in it, the electronic media are contributing to a growing split, or dissonance, in the overall experience of millions of unsuspecting, but mesmerized, viewers. Based on the psychological axiom regarding the human tendency to internalize experience, I believe that this external split is finding its way, increasingly, into the core psychodynamics of many of those same viewers and that it is having a seriously demoralizing effect on them. As in the case of Toffler's phenomenon, this development has sinister implications for American society at large. How has this happened?

WESTERN TECHNOLOGY: A BRIEF
HISTORICAL OVERVIEW

Jacques Ellul, a French professor of law, has written an exhaustive analysis of the influence of technology on Western society in *The Technological Society*. In his foreword to this important book Robert Merton writes:

By *technique*, for example, [Ellul] means far more than machine technology. Technique refers to any complex of standardized means for attaining a predetermined result. . . . Technical Man is fascinated by results. . . . Ours is a progressively technical civilization: by this Ellul means that the ever-expanding and irreversible rule of technique is extended to all domains of life. It is a civilization committed to the quest for continually improved means to carelessly examined ends. . . . ''Know-how'' takes on an ultimate value.[1]

Ellul states that technical activity is the oldest human activity, mentioning hunting, fishing, and food gathering among the earliest examples. In this vein he argues that magic, dealing with matters of a more spiritual nature, as it does, qualifies as an example of technical activity going back to human beings' most primitive attempts to cope with the problem of their existence. The reason that magic, as opposed to material techniques, has regressed over the course of history is that because of its spiritual focus and hence lack of measurable efficacy, there is no progression of discoveries built up, one upon the other, no evolution over time. As Ellul puts it,

The two great streams of technique. . . . have evolved in completely different ways. In manual techniques we observe an increase and later a multiplication of discoveries, each based on the other. In magic we see only endless new beginnings, as the fortunes of history and its own inefficiency call its procedures into question.[2]

According to Ellul, the Greeks spurned technique. Despite the fact that they were the first society to have a coherent scientific activity, there existed in ancient Greece an almost total separation of science and technique. This phenomenon sprang from the Greek philosophical conception of life which scorned material needs and the improvement of practical life, discredited manual labor, held contemplation to be the goal of intellectual activity, refused the use of power, and respected natural things. The Greeks were suspicious of technical activity because it represented an aspect of brute power and implied a want of moderation.

In ancient Rome, however, there was a basic impetus to the perfection of social technique, both civil and military. In Ellul's view, this emphasis on social technique arose out of the fact that everything in Roman society related to Roman law in its multiple forms, both public and private. This emphasis on technique was rooted in the more concrete, as opposed to abstract, trait of the Roman mind, which apotheosized efficiency, organization, internal social coherence, and continuity. According to Ellul, the Roman judicial system could be applied always and everywhere in the empire; it was adapted to unfailing continuity; and these were totally new social phenomena that Rome introduced.

For different reasons, the evolution of Western technique atrophied under early Christianity. The Christian devotion to the salvation of the individual soul as a precondition to entrance into a more perfect afterlife caused judicial and other technical activity to be held in total contempt, to be considered as the very enemies of the human race. This animosity toward technique also prevailed in the later phase of Christian dominance in the West. Ellul describes the society that developed from the tenth to the fourteenth century as "vital, coherent and unanimous; but it was characterized by a total absence of the technical will. It was a-capitalistic' as well as 'a-technical.'"3

Ellul argues that it was the search for justice before God, the measuring of technique by other criteria than those of technique itself, that constituted the great obstacles that Christianity opposed to technical progress during the period of Christian dominance. Later, during the Protestant Reformation, a major aspect of Christian theology in its effort to return to the most primitive conception of Christianity removed many barriers to the evolution of technique. Despite these basic changes, however, it was, in Ellul's view, not so much from the new theology of the Reformation as from the shock of the Renaissance, from humanism and the authoritarian state, that technique received a decisive impetus.

To continue with his account, in the period from the sixteenth to eighteenth century the absence of technique in all areas but the mechanical is striking. The world had to wait for the eighteenth century to see technical progress explode in every country and in every area of human endeavor. As he puts it, the industrial revolution was but one aspect of the technical revolution. And while the technical revolution had its essential detonation in the eighteenth century, it really attained full stride in the nineteenth century.

Ellul attributes this radical acceleration of technique in the nineteenth century to the conjunction in time of five distinct, but mutually synergizing factors: (1) the cumulating fruition of a long history of technical experience, of many different inventions; (2) a population explosion; (3) the suitability of the economic environment, a stable, but at the same time fluid capital supply; (4) the plasticity of the social mileu; and (5) the appearance of clear technical intention.

To Ellul, the fourth factor was the most decisive. It involved two essential sub-factors; (1) the disappearance of social taboos and (2) the disappearance of natural social groups. The taboos were also dual in substance and origin. The first set vehemently proscribed any tampering with the natural order of things, and its origins lay in Christian theology. The second set proscribed modifications of the social hierarchy, and its roots lay in the traditional sociopolitical order. The natural social groups within eighteenth-century European culture centered around closely organized families, guilds, and other groups formed by collective interests—the university, the parliament, the confraternities, and the hospitals. Such groupings provided the average man with patronage, security, and intellectual, and moral satisfactions. Further, while strong enough to meet his needs, they were not so large as to make him feel submerged or lost. The gradual disappearance of both the taboos and natural social groups resulted in an atomization of society, an isolating of individuals, which greatly facilitated the technologizing of Western society by creating an inexhaustible supply of cheap, mobile labor.

It goes without saying that the technologizing of Western society has continued with ever-increasing momentum and societal impact through the entire twentieth century. It is accelerating positively as you read this. In fact, today we can talk realistically about the technologizing of the planet Earth. Ellul, in describing the geometric expansion of technique during the twentieth century, states, "In the twentieth century [the] relationship between scientific research and technical invention resulted in the enslavement of science to technique.[4]

Ellul also touches upon the root motivations in human devotion to the development of technique over the course of history. In discussing magic he states, "In the spiritual realm, magic . . . is a mediator between man and 'the higher power,' just as other techniques mediate between man and matter. . . . It affirms human power in that it seeks to subordinate the gods to men, just as technique serves to cause nature to obey."[5]

Here he is in close concordance with systematic depth psychology, regarding the most primitive layers of motivation in the human psyche. Freud conceptualized the id, and within it the pleasure principle, as the root sources of proactive human behavior, the ego and superego being essentially epiphenomena resulting from the socialization process and existing primarily to gratify id impulses in sublimated form. The Freudian id is rapacious in its quest for immediate pleasure. It lacks any sense of limit and is unable to think in the negative in connection with its wishes and even its own existence. Freud taught that the concept "no" does not exist within the id. In the case of normally socialized adults, id derivatives take the form of steady flow of narcissistic, sexual, and aggressive impulse-wishes; with the development of psychopathology these wishes tend to become expectations or demands; and in psychopathological extremes the demands rigidify into delusions that are, at base, subjective, wishful recreations of the world. For Freud, the wellsprings of human behavior expect obedience from the world, and if this obedient providence is not forthcoming, in cases of advanced pathology, the world is changed, albeit in purely subjective, fantasized terms.

Adler spoke of the striving for a feeling of superiority, perfection, and totality as the basic dynamic force behind all human activity, the ubiquitous and compulsive striving from minus to plus in every situation. Anathematic to this basic striving is the feeling of inferiority, which, when fixed in the personality, necessitates a compensatory preoccupation with an exaggerated sense of superiority. In Adler's system this predictable reaction to the feeling of inferiority simultaneously intensifies narcissism and stunts social concern, thereby providing the basis for all forms of functional psychopathology. As in Freud's theory, a corollary to this basic human motivation is the need to change the world so that it reflects the individual's desired sense of superiority or perfection. And as in Freud's theory, with the deepening of individual psychopathology the pursuit of superiority becomes increasingly selfish and socially destructive.

Erich Fromm, representing the neo-Freudian and existential points of view, discussed the peculiar position of men and women at the peak of the evolutionary process. Alone possessed of reason and self-awareness, we are aware of ourselves as being separate from nature, aware of our end, our finitude. Simultaneously we are part of nature, embedded in biological bodies, with their impulses, cyclical needs, and inevitable vulnerability to decay and death. Human beings are thus to Fromm an anomaly, part angel and part animal, a "freak of the universe." In *The Anatomy of Human Destructiveness* Fromm remarked,

Man's life cannot be lived by repeating the pattern of his species; *he* must live. Man is the only animal who does not feel at home in nature, who can feel evicted from paradise, the only animal for whom his own existence is a problem that he has to solve and from which he cannot escape. . . . Man's existential, and hence unavoidable disequilibrium can be relatively stable when he has found, with the support of his culture, a more or less adequate way of coping with his existential problems. But this relative stability does not imply that the dichotomy has disappeared; it is merely dormant and becomes manifest as soon as the conditions for this relative stability change. . . . Every new state of disequilibrium forces man to seek for new equilibrium. Indeed, what has often been considered man's innate drive for progress is his attempt to find a new and if possible better equilibrium.[6]

It is really unnecessary to refer to more famous psychologists, living or dead, to further document the idea that interest, want, and purpose comprise the underlying dynamism within human mentality. Suffice it to draw once more on the century-old, timelessly trenchant, thoughts of William James, who averred that "no actions but such as are done for an end, and show a choice of means, can be called indubitable expressions of mind."[7]

Whether it be the endlessly cyclical desire for pleasure, the urgent and ceaseless striving for a sense of superiority in as many fields of endeavor as possible, or some larger, ontological quest for a feeling of unity with nature and inner peace in connection with the fact of their existence, humans, as individuals or in groups, have always wanted more than they have had at any point in time, and they have zealously sought the means to these remoter ends. Modern Western technology admirably serves this insatiable wanting, at least in the material realm.

Although many serious social observers applaud the advance of technology, a number of them worry about and decry its growing authority to control the destiny of humankind. Among these latter are such men as Aldous Huxley, George Orwell, Lewis Mumford, Norbert Wiener, and Jacques Ellul. Erich Fromm, exploring the anatomy of human destructiveness, made the following comment, which appears to anticipate this discussion.

The new forms of equilibrium by no means constitute a straight line of human development. Frequently in history new achievements have led to regressive developments. Many times, when forced to find a new solution, man runs into a blind alley from which he has to extricate himself; and it is indeed remarkable that thus far in history he has been able to do so.[8]

Neil Postman, who harbors even stronger doubts concerning the ultimate consequences for American society inextricably bound up with our deification of technology, voices the following thoughts in the final chapter of *The Disappearance of Childhood*: "That technology itself has been deified. . . . and that childhood is waning are woeful signs. . . . But America has not begun to *think*. . . . we are just beginning to notice the spiritual and social debris that our technology has strewn around us.[9]

TECHNOLOGY AND MATERIALISM

America's absorption with things, with "stuff," is a direct result of its absorption by technology, particularly that of the electronic media. To begin with, technology works better with things or products than it does with services. Put differently, natural-science technology is infinitely more effective than social-science technology, with biotechnology standing in the middle ground. The reasons for this are complex and do not require lengthy explanation in this discussion. It is enough to suggest that technology is the handmaiden of science, and science is better able to generate more valid cause and effect laws when the phenomena under study are inorganic, when they do not have life and, above all, volition. Where the pertinent deterministic relationships are better understood because the scientific data are less confusing and the resulting scientific laws are more precise, the related technologies are likewise more effective. Airplanes, cameras, radios, TV sets, internal combustion engines, and mechanical pumps all perform the functions for which they were designed, better and more reliably than do, say, cancer chemotherapies and psychoanalysis.

Added to this general functional superiority is the fact that products, being objects, tend to be both more visible and imperishable than services, and in their way they provide more tangible evidence of people's accomplishments in life, their scores. That conspicuous consumption is a fundamental and pervasive interpersonal dynamic in a modern, secular society devoted to the principle of individual competition goes without saying. Americans will preen and flaunt themselves as no other national populace in the world will today. Indifference on the part of others is harder to bear for most Americans even than active repugnance or hatred because it tends to kindle their lurking feelings of inadequacy and their guilt. Going around once, in anonymity, is the antithesis of doing it with gusto; and this prospect of lack of notice is, psychologically speaking, the closest parallel in modern America to the fate of damnation in the medieval period.

Third, products have always been of prime importance to homo faber by virtue of their limitless practical utility. However, Ellul puts this homely truth into an interesting light by illustrating that the modern, technology-dictated, concept of comfort emphasizes rest and physical euphoria, whereas the medieval concept emphasized a sense of moral and aesthetic order. According to Ellul, space was the primary element contributing to comfort in the Middle Ages; perfected personal goods and machines are those contributing primarily to modern comfort. But as Ellul points out, technology had not come to dominate medieval society as it has modern society; medieval humanity did not bind up its fate with technical progress as modern humans do. This again suggests that the march of technology in Western society has, thus far, been progressively and increasingly linked with materialism.

But of course it is the advertising industry that is the penultimate force behind contemporary American materialism. And it is the omnipresent tube, as a relatively recent innovation within communications technology, that gives the ad industry its immense power to persuade the American public that, with each passing day, it needs more and more stuff. Finally, this seemingly immaterial sector of modern technology maintains its mind-bending spell over its mass audience by proffering an endless stream of alluring pictures, which are essentially things.

Postman's thoughts on TV advertising are again provocative and penetrating. In brief, he argues that TV commercials can be taken as a kind of religious literature, the majority of them assuming the form of religious parables, that is, short fictitious narratives from which a moral or spiritual truth is drawn. In *The Disappearance of Childhood* he analyzes "The Parable of the Ring around the Collar" as an illustration. He notes that the structure of this TV parable is comfortably traditional; the story has a beginning (problem), a middle (solution), and an end (moral lesson). In the beginning, a couple are enjoying a meal in a restaurant. Their pleasures are abruptly transformed into shame and humiliation when their waitress notices the man's dirty collar and loudly announces his transgression to the rest of the diners. In the middle, the scene shifts to their home, where the wife, after having used the commercial's infallible detergent, proudly shows her husband his perfectly purged shirt. In the end, the couple are back in the restaurant enjoying their meal, free of the threats of chastisement and ostracism.

According to Postman, the parables in TV commercials are organized around a consistent theology, the fundamental precept of which upholds technological sophistication as the pathway to salvation (earthly success). On the other hand, technological innocence is the pathway to perdition (earthly failure, utter anonymity). This is the basic cause of unhappiness, humiliation, and discord in life. In reference to the cardinal sin of technological innocence, Postman points to the guilt-mongering potential inherent in this omnipresent river of imagery. As in most formal religions, the preaching emphasis is on exhortation and warning to backsliders and recalcitrants. His remarks recall Lasch's observation that modern advertising seeks to promote not so much self-indulgence as self-doubt.

The sudden striking power of technological innocence is a particularly important feature of TV-commercial theology. . . . To attempt to live without technological sophistication is at all times dangerous, since the evidence of one's naiveté is painfully evident to the vigilant. The vigilant may be a waitress, a friend, a neighbor.[10]

Interesting, too, is the implicit parallel between Postman's conceptualization of TV commercials as a secularized form of religious literature and my hypothesis concerning their natural appeal to viewers' ideal selves. In connection with the first curriculum's pictorial, basically anti-intellectual, presentation of its subject matter, and in specific reference to TV commercials, he states, "It is not facts that are offered to the consumer but idols, to which both adults and children can attach themselves with equal devotion and without the burden of logic or verification."[11] In terms of their wider sociocultural ramifications, these observations likewise suggest the deification of technology, the worship of materialism, and the TV as the altar where the worship of this secularized American credo is taking place. They also bring to mind Tony Schwartz's concept of the media as a second god, perhaps even a bit more literally than he had intended.

Another element in this discussion of the implicit religiosity of TV commercials ties in with Ellul's commentary on the broader issue of modern technology. Postman suggests that the childlike public mentality encouraged by commercial TV is neither the intent nor the fault of the executives who control the TV networks. Rather, this unfortunate spin-off results from the penchant among network executives to use TV as they find it, to exploit it to its fullest extent. Thus it is the character of the medium and not the character of its users that tends, over time, to stunt the intellectual level of the viewing public. One of Ellul's basic criticisms of the technological society has to do with the commitment to "know-how," the continuing quest for improved means to *carelessly examined ends*. It is clear that TV commercials, employing the ingenious technologies of modern electronic communications science and the motivational know-how of the advertising firms, have unquestioned power to sell more and more goods and services to the viewing public, many of them already surfeited with stuff. But is the free rein given to its marketing capability an optimum use of the most powerful social invention of the twentieth century, particularly in light of such potential associated problems as those discussed by Postman and other serious thinkers? By passively allowing TV this unchecked commercial reign, are we, in our fascination with accumulating stuff, inadvertently mortgaging our children's futures, as many professional economists warn? And in the same stroke, are we allowing the beguiling river of irrefutable pictures to insidiously undermine our children's ability to reason, let alone pay the accumulated bills, as Postman warns? Is this yet another instance of modern humans, momentarily intoxicated by the spectacular effectiveness of an aspect of their technology, turning a blind eye to the ultimate moral-ethical value issues that are inevitably involved, as Ellul predicts? To these worrisome and complicated questions, I would have to answer first no, followed by three yesses, respectively.

CONFUSION IN THE INFORMATION SOCIETY

In thinking about the problem of personal demoralization in modern America, I have invoked the related concepts of the experiential bind and chronically irritated self-ideal discrepancy as the primary factors feeding this pervasive individual predicament. But confusion is clearly another major source of personal distress in our technology-dominated society. Modern Americans live in confusion right up to their proverbial eyeballs, although for transparently ego-defensive reasons few of them are willing or able to admit this, even to spouses and trusted friends. Oddly, this appears to be a condition of life in the information, or technetronic, society, the latest phase of Western industrial civilization. Data and information exist in superabundance. On the other hand, knowledge and understanding, which arise from adequately processed information, are much less abundant, even to the point of becoming vestigial. Information is verging into disinformation. Paradoxically, it is serving in a general way to confuse and demoralize its recipients rather than to enlighten and enliven them. Why? Because there is just too much of it, coming, as it does, in avalanche proportions from all sides simultaneously. Further, much of it is ill prepared, although it is packaged in such a way as to give it a veneer of authenticity. This slapdash quality is particularly characteristic of media presentations, put together, as they are, on a daily basis. While the media are a prime source of information blitz, the rising tide of disinformation is ubiquitous. It is an inevitable consequence of two of the major institutions within modern society working in synergistic tandem: applied science and free-enterprise capitalism.

The reader might well question my reference to science, asserting that it is inherently intellectual and devoted to the accumulation of knowledge for its own sake. To this objection, I would suggest that it is necessary to distinguish between applied and pure science, something that is easy to do conceptually, less easy to do practically. Pure science is, admittedly, devoted to the increased understanding of our natural world. It is, in fact, the evolved manifestation of natural philosophy. Both philosophy and the fine arts have always been fundamentally oriented toward understanding for its own sake in their respective quests for ultimate truth and beauty. Applied science is, however, innately more pragmatic in its fundamental mission.

Western science reemerged from antiquity in the Renaissance. It was intimately bound up with the emergent humanism of this period, touched upon by Ellul. At this time Western humans began to turn away from a life dominated by preparation for a more perfect afterlife and to concern themselves with their earthly existence—the here and now, the sentient and tangible. Integral to this change of focus was the impulse to modify and improve the earthly realm, to mold it more closely to human needs and desires. The scientific method, as an incubator of appropriate technologies, has served this modifying impulse well. In fact, this latter has always been the central raison d'être of the scientific method, at least that of applied science. The purpose of applied science is to create technologies. The purpose of technology is to change the environment (human and physical) and thus to improve the earthly lot of humanity. It can be generally interpreted as an active, though possibly unconscious, cultural effort to forge a paradise here on earth, rather than waiting and preparing for the one in the afterlife promised by Christianity. This postulated grand objective fits with Freudian, Adlerian, and Frommian, insights into the deeper wellsprings of human motivation. And as Ellul shows, the process has gradually picked up momentum over the ages, accelerating sharply during the late-nineteenth and the twentieth centuries.

The ends of applied science are prediction, control, and manipulation of the environment. Scientific theory and data are means to these ends, and as technology marches on, these means gradually become obsolete and irrelevant. Despite the distinction between its applied and pure forms, science as a methodology is unconcerned with values. Further, it is not important that scientific models of the moment lack verisimilitude—point by point congruity—with their subject matter. As long as they stimulate more research, they have a certain utility; it is called heuristic value. Atomic theory is a good example. As physicists explore the structure of atoms more deeply, they find them to resemble less and less the ringed spheres of earlier conceptions. Nevertheless, that model has facilitated research and improved engineering techniques since before the beginning of this century. And the data and information flowing from these models do produce change, new technologies, and money.

James McGregor Burns makes a nice distinction between intelligence and intellectuality. According to him, the former analyzes, adjusts, orders, and modifies; the latter speculates, wonders, imagines, and concerns itself with ultimate values. With the evolution of the technological society, particularly since the beginning of the present century, valid thought is seen as practical and technical; it seeks to analyze, adjust, and modify things; it strives for action that leads to change and improvement; it is intelligent, but not deeply intellectual.

In modern America the link-up between applied science, technology, and business is natural. The scientists compile the data and invent the models; the engineers and technicians create the new products; and the businesses mass produce and distribute these products to the media-mesmerized, technology-worshiping public. At the key connections within this cycle, profit serves as a barometer; it indicates that thought is being productive and fruitful, bringing fair weather, so to speak.

Modern society has followed the lead of applied science and technology as medieval society followed that of divine revelation. Then, superstition was rampant; now, data production and processing are equally widespread and compulsive in their operation. As a consequence, crushing complexity exists everywhere—in business, law, politics, industry, medicine, sports, health and beauty care, and so on. A natural development within this megatrend is the computer, the electronic file clerk. Utterly desireless and insensitive, but untiring and infinitely fast, it can be programmed to wade through the morass of data, producing apparent edification in the form of tables, graphs, averages, and correlation coefficients. There are questions concerning its ultimate impact on society, but it can crunch data, and it is here to stay.

The psychological hook in all this lies in the fact that in Western technological society, information is perceived as having fundamental value. It has a quality of divinity in the unconscious. Thus, it must be accepted, sought, stored, utilized, extended, and desired. Although there are individual differences, all people, to some extent, revere information, are drawn to it tropistically, as a moth is drawn to the light. If, for any reason, individuals are obtuse to or inept in their response to the information environment, they naturally fall into some measure of self-devaluation. In terms of the influence of the experiential bind, I see this confusion as contributing to chronically irritated self-ideal discrepancy primarily through deflation of the actual self.

Earlier, a distinction was made between information and knowledge. The latter comes from the former but not necessarily. Useful knowledge requires that data and information be digested—accommodated and assimilated in Piagetian terms—and this takes both time and the proper intellectual skills. But in contemporary America there is little time available for intellectual thought in the average person's daily routine, for the construction of anything as intangible as a knowledgeable outlook, a personal apperceptive mass that is seasoned and fortified by the best means to judicious understanding.

I believe that this widespread individual confusion is largely related to the burgeoning influence of Postman's first curriculum, although it is further stimulated by the print media as well. But at base, it is an unintended consequence of life in American high-tech society, with its basic scientific-business engine running full blast twenty-four hours a day. This engine generates data and information as any overdriven mechanical engine generates heat. In the latter case the heat is commonly a symptom of immoderate use, or a functional defect that requires repair. The confusion-breeding flood of data or information can be similarly interpreted as a symptom of immoderacy in the American pursuit of material success via technological progress. It brings to mind Ellul's perception of the basic error of the technical impulse so deeply rooted in human nature, that is, the preoccupation with the best means to the achievement of ill-considered ends, the deification of know-how.

Undigested information is apt to become disinformation, just as undigested food is apt to become a physically noxious, toxic substance in the body. The latter produces discomfort, and it has the potential for causing serious illness; the former contributes to confusion rather than enlightenment, and it has a seriously demoralizing potential. However, given the megatrends within the American version of technetronic society, the force-feeding will continue.

$E_{TV} = MC^2$

The reader will note that the heading of this section is a slight variation on Einstein's famous equation, which states the fundamental relation between energy and matter in scientifically rigorous, quantitative terms. This equation illumines, for the interested student, one of the most basic, and dangerous, relationships in the physical universe. Ironically, as a tool of applied science, one of its first uses—if not *the* first use—was in the development of the atomic bomb.

Along with Ellul's concern over technology's preoccupation with means over ends is his belief that "It is . . . the *essence of technique to compel the qualitative to become quantitative*, and in this way to force every stage of human activity and man himself to submit to its mathematical calculations."[12] In making this statement he does not point an admonitory, or blaming, finger at any group within advanced technological society. Rather, he is simply describing how things work therein.

I don't know whether his formulation is correct in the general case, but to me there is undeniable evidence of its applicability in respect to contemporary American consumerism. Hence, my perverse rendition of Einstein's equation, which, stated verbally, reads: The electronic media, spearheaded by television, contribute irresistibly to mindless consumerism squared, raised to grossly excessive amounts. In fact, the determinism of the one by the other is so complete that it is legitimate to express this relationship as an equation, rather than in some more tenuous formula, such as $E_{TV} \rightarrow MC^2$.

The TV-driven, guilt-ridden preoccupation with accumulating more stuff that characterizes modern Americans depletes their energies and saps their interest in a fuller, better-balanced development of their human potentials. This value orientation undermines their capacities for resisting the system by seeing through it and cultivating other, more creative interests. After all, these latter take time, and they are essentially intellectual pursuits.

Reinforced continually by advertising and having primary narcissistic relevance, this technology-nurtured acquisitive drive is both compulsive in its operation and exceedingly difficult to control or extinguish, either personally or in formal treatment. Further, it is in no way related to need or reasonable requirement; it operates across socioeconomic classes, whether personal income is unlimited, plenteous, adequate, tight, or virtually nonexistent. Worse yet, it frequently gets completely out of hand and in its compulsive spasms becomes a source of trouble-cum-ruination to those caught in its web. Bearing witness to this last instance are the hordes of overextended credit card junkies, some of whom crop up on talk radio as they anonymously solicit the advice of the various air-wave financial counselors on how to curb their additive spending habits; the increasing number of people who, enticed by the lure of the city and state lotteries, regularly gamble away monies needed for family necessities after they have compulsively wagered away their skimpy discretionary funds; and the sinister specter of overcrowded local and state jails literally bursting at the seams with apprehended criminals, not to mention the vaster legion of those who have slipped through the law's utterly inadequate net.

Recently in one of the many magazines devoted to reporting on and depicting the lives of the rich and famous there was an article on the sale of a well-known art masterpiece for a mind-boggling sum in the neighborhood of $75 million. As part of his/her text the author quoted the responses of a number of New York's cognoscenti/litterati to the question "Why would anyone pay $75 million for a painting?" One well-known writer opined, "Why, for self-validation," or words to that effect. I believe that this gentleman hit the nail right on the head. Self-validation is another term for self-affirmation, the inevitable human reaction to self-ideal congruent behavior. It is the antithesis of guilt, self-disappointment, self-contempt, self-hate, and so on. It momentarily buffers the individual against feelings of inferiority or their close variant, feelings of inadequacy. Our writer's remark is in agreement with the fundamental thesis of this book, namely, that the experiential bind forces millions of Americans into the condition of chronically irritated self-ideal discrepancy, with its inevitable freighting of corrosive guilt. Further, his assessment of the buyer's deeper motivation is also congruent with Adler's concept of the striving for superiority, the "great upward-drive" from minus to plus, as the basic motive underlying all human behavior. In the gelidly exclusive social atmosphere of the super-rich in America, where money is as plentiful as oxygen, this drive provides the deepest level of motivation for the daily round of carefully orchestrated social and business activities. In this privileged and surfeited in-group, the ability to purchase the art in question provides the buyer with the heady, intoxicating, but fleeting sense of being in the plus position with respect to his/her confreres/competitors. Even here, mindless consumption, or "conspicuous consumption" as Thorstein Veblen called it some eighty years ago, is the name of the game. It is how the players keep score, as the twentieth-century Adam Smith reminds us.

I believe that in contemporary America this is the natural consequence of the country's unquestioning deification of technology, with its corollary faith in good old American know-how. This practical materialism permeates all socioeconomic strata, as it has throughout America's short national history. But the current frenzied consumption exceeds that of earlier eras by virtue of the endless, irresistible , reality-denying, though ostensibly harmless influence of the tube, the pièce de résistance of modern communications technology. Employed by commercial institutions for essentially economic reasons, TV either plugs products directly through advertisements, or it seeks profit indirectly by featuring a steady docket of prime-time drivel calculated to appeal to lowest common denominator of viewer taste and hence to the largest audience of prospective consumers.

I have seen TV referred to in scholarly articles as the most powerful social invention of this century. I concur. In assessing its supposed innocuous presence in American society, I would direct the reader's attention to Neil Postman's educational concept of the "first curriculum." Recall that Postman defines a curriculum as a specially constructed information system whose purpose, *in its totality*, is to influence, teach, train, or cultivate the mind and character of our youth, as a total learning system. Also, bear in mind that he sees TV as the major educational enterprise now being undertaken in the United States.

Again, I am in total agreement with Postman. And with these two ideas—TV as the century's most powerful social invention, and Postman's first curriculum—buttressing my notion of the experiential bind, the fact of the accelerating rate of juvenile and adolescent crime taking place in American cities today comes as no mystery. Nor is the grisly, adult aspect that much of this juvenile delinquency is assuming particularly mysterious, especially in light of Postman's thoughts concerning TV's role in the disappearance of childhood.

Consider, again, the all-too-common scene of an average lower-class, or ghetto-dwelling, urban, juvenile/adolescent male watching prime-time TV at home in circumstances that can at best be described as modest and more probably as frankly squalid. First, it is a safe assumption that he is not tuned into PBS's program "Nova" or Bill Moyer's "World of Ideas" this average evening. More than likely, the tube is massaging him with imagery from "Miami Vice" or "Knots Landing" or worse. Interspersed at regular intervals are the carefully contrived, artful, technology-exalting, parables providing him unmistakable glimpses of the Salvation of Product Ownership and Consumption. During this "class" he will be plied with a seemingly unending, breathtakingly rapid, flow of lurid, sexually tempting, violence-advocating, action-packed pictures, together with their emotion-intensifying musical background, of people, unlike himself, who have achieved social position and money. You may be certain that the lesson, which states in effect "Get money, so that you can get things," will be clearly learned.

Later in the evening the "subject" will switch to one of the commercial networks' eleven o'clock evening news programs—or depending on our student's class schedule, it may have been the five o'clock news that was studied first—(Doom Imagery 101). Again, it is reasonable to assume that our learner is not tuned into the PBS equivalent. On the commercial network news programs he will be massaged with a rapid sequence of lurid picture stories whose essential lesson can be summed up in the phrase "Life is a bloody battle in which anything goes and everyone cheats." This lesson will be taught by attractive newscasters whose upbeat demeanor and unruffled, seamlessly professional rendering of the material will convey, metacommunicatively, to him their tacit approval, or at least

their lack of personal concern and repugnance. And, again, incongruous-
ly, there will be regular breaks featuring the technology-exalting parables.

The admixture of the academic and religious elements of the first curriculum brings to mind the same admixture inhering in the curricula of
the famous British public schools—Eton and Harrow being the best-known
examples—in terms of its capacity, if not its intent, to mold both the minds
and souls of its students. One basic difference, among many, to be sure,
concerns the narrow repetitiveness of Postman's very real first curriculum.
Whereas the British public school curricula represented all of the diversity of a true educational curriculum and were, in fact, nonpareil models
of same, the first curriculum drones on with monomaniacal fixity about
the all-saving graces of money, no matter how it is obtained and the
mindless consumption of stuff. What is more, it has access to the most
modern and powerful teaching technology known to humans, for its
essential brainwashing purposes: the irrefutable picture tube. No wonder
so many of our youth, particularly the disadvantaged ones, are getting
the message.

Both the print media and the electronic media, by way of daily newspapers and evening city TV news programs, inundate us with the doleful
accounts bearing testimony to the effectiveness of the first curriculum.
And despite the inherent sensationalism of the imagery of doom, we know
that there is a fundamental element of truth in these increasingly grisly
and frequent horror stories. The growing numbers of students in many
urban school districts who now regularly bring lethal weapons—knives
and guns—to school for use in holding up their hapless quarries are in
search of money for expensive clothes, the latest and most expensive
athletic footwear, fancy jewelry, even gold-inlays for their teeth, and of
course drugs, the chemical express ride away from life's inescapable
stresses, particularly for those at the bottom of society. All the way up
the rest of the socioeconomic ladder, from the working-class lotto junkies
through the middle- and upper-middle-class overextended credit card
junkies, to the ostentatiously sybaritic Trumps and Helmsleys at the very
top of the pecuniary heap, the materialist lessons of the first curriculum
are being internalized and acted upon by Americans of all ages. If you
doubt me, recall Alfred Malabre's analysis of our national indebtedness—
exceeding today (by God knows how much) the 1985 figure of $7 trillion.
At the time this figure was equivalent to the indebtedness of every person in the nation, children included, in the amount of $35,000, with in-
dividual debt exceeding both corporate and public debt as separate percen-
tages of the grand total.

My point here is not to remind readers yet again of America's overweening materialism but rather to try and focus their attention on what
I believe to be the ultimate source of this national value orientation, namely, runaway technology. I find Ellul's criticisms of the technological society

convincing. Neil Postman, an educator, sees evidence of influences stifling to the intellectual fiber of America, stemming from the nation's deification of technology. As a psychologist, I believe there is incontrovertible evidence that this self-same apotheosis of technique is the ultimate root of the present dehumanizing of America. And again like Postman, I believe that the electronic media, or perhaps better, their misuse by the commercial interests, are the more proximal, temporally contiguous, culprits.

Ellul asserts over and over again that technology comes to dominate the very people who invent it. Humans in machine-ridden industrial societies eventually begin to act like machines themselves, unconsciously internalizing the machine. In this long-term, subtle, and difficult to discern process, they progressively damage their basic humanity and capacity to feel truly alive. I have tried in the foregoing chapters to show how the specific technologies involved—those of the electronic media together with those of the advertising industry—using the human tendency to identify with and idealize imaginary cultural models as a psychological lever, so to speak, are manipulating the American public into the compulsive accumulation of more and more material possessions that they often don't need and frequently cannot pay for. In discussing this latest example of the domination of people by their own technologies, I have leaned heavily on Postman's concept of the first curriculum because I think it uniquely conveys the power of the electronic media over the public mind, particularly that aspect of the public mind made up by people under the age of thirty or so. I believe that here we have a subtle, but apical, example of Ellul's principal criticism of the technique-deifying society: the overweening concern with improved means to carelessly examined ends. I use the term "overweening" with specific intent again here, because it carries the implication of arrogance, of undue confidence.

George Bernard Shaw once said that science is always wrong; each time it answers a question, it uncovers three more, or words to that effect. We Americans live in the most scientific society the world has ever known, one that is allowing modern technology the fullest possible authority to control its destiny, according to Neil Postman. Most of us are awed by the achievements of modern science, and for the most part utterly confused by its inner complexities. But we quickly and trustfully employ the resulting stream of new technological products in our lives. I think that in the back of most Americans' minds there exists a sense of national superiority based on our technological sophistication relative to other countries, particularly those of the Third World. A basic faith in the ability of technology to successfully confront the inevitable problems of life as they arise feeds this sense of national grandiosity. We are, it seems, not unlike children swaggering securely in the company of their parents, while being entirely in the dark as to how their parents manage from day to day. Only when they have grown up do they begin to question the grounds of their infantile security and learn to avoid their parents' mistakes, as well as to revere and emulate their parents' strengths and wisdom.

As a public, we need to ask some questions about the directions that modern-day technologies are taking us. Certainly, the free use of the electronic media by commercial interests is a powerful way to sell and distribute products, to maintain capitalistic growth, to employ and remunerate large numbers of motivated and appropriately trained members of the work force, even to the point of making them comfortably affluent or rich. But are these benefits a reasonable trade-off when compared to the socioeconomic problems that result from, or at least are fostered by, this insidious process of electronic, dream-making hardsell? I am of course referring to such seemingly intractable problems as America's mountain of personal debt, with its portents of national economic collapse (Malabre); the disappearance of childhood in America, with its ramifications concerning the explosion of sinisterly violent juvenile delinquency, and the worrisome loss, among the young, of traditional academic motivation and skills (Postman); the "narcissification" of America, with its troubling questions concerning America's potential as a nation to maintain its present position of primacy and influence among the international community by virtue of meaningful competitiveness in that arena (Lasch), to name but three issues discussed by other authors. I believe that in its integral contribution to the experiential bind, the untrammeled commercial use of television in America over the past fifty years is intimately hooked to all of the above problems and many more as well. Any social issue traceable to chronic personal demoralization and its probable dehumanization of behavior is a possible consequence, so pervasive is the experiential bind, in my opinion. Further, commercial television is both the spearhead and the battering ram of media blight in contemporary America.

All of the above problems can be seen, more abstractly, as related to the massive and rapid post–World War II "technologizing" of America. Admittedly, such connections are not easily perceived and understood a posteriori, and they are that much more difficult to anticipate a priori. But they are there; they are more difficult of solution the longer they have to fester and ramify; and they are ultimately causal of serious problems that detract from the quality of life in many ways, in America or in any other country where their own antecedent causes exist. And while such problems are difficult for the uninformed to detect or foresee, they are by no means beyond the ken of the informed, thoughtful, and concerned citizen.

THE THERMOSTATIC INTELLECT

We live in a culture in which less and less value is attached to intellectual and philosophical thought. Spurred by the dynamism of applied science, modern Americans are becoming increasingly practical and technical in mentality. In this atmosphere, the assumption is that valid thought should lead to change, should produce workable technologies, should generate profits. While dating back 500 years, this mind-set is gaining momentum at an exponential rate; it is accelerating faster and faster with the passage of time. Applied science and business are growing, cancerlike, in modern America.

It is thus not difficult to see why another application of the human capacity for rational thought, intellectuality, is dwindling within, perhaps even vanishing from, the national mentality. This mode of thinking seeks understanding, not change. It aspires to thorough description of its subject matter, not control. It seeks perspective on the complexity of life, on its "thickness" to use William James's term, rather than the ability to manipulate some minute aspect of life. Its fruits are rather subtle when compared to the implicit promises of applied science and business, that is, to the systematic applications of practical and technical thought. Balance, perspective, deepened sensitivity, greater harmony between self and overarching cosmos; these are some of the commoner fruits of this second, intellectual, mode of rational thought. Art and philosophy are basically intellectual pursuits. They both seek to study the world as it is, in its immanent fullness, rather than change it. They aspire to understanding and wisdom as ends. One part of their value lies in helping people get into a better relationship with the larger order of things, in helping them better to flow, as it were, with the endless vicissitudes of experience. This is an ancient ideal of Eastern philosophy.

But this mental attitude also seems to be the ultimate fruit of Postman's second, thermostatic curriculum: a curriculum that advocates presenting all subjects as stages in humanity's development; teaching he philosophies of science, history, language, and religion; and one in which there would be strong emphasis on classical forms of artistic expression. Ideally, young adult Americans thus educated would have a highly refined capacity for judging societal issues in terms of their wider historical, technical, and moral-ethical perspectives. They would have the ability to see the forest as well as the trees, the larger picture. Such a capacity for perspective is absolutely necessary to, the sine qua non of the thermostatic intellect. It acts, in effect, like a cultural compass. And what is more relevant than a compass when one is lost on a stormy sea? Further, such persons would also have the capacity for effective communication of their thermostatic intuitions vis-à-vis potentially troublesome societal trends, as well as for generally creative self-expression during quieter moments.

Ellul's writings of nearly thirty years ago—before commercial TV shifted into overdrive, with 100 percent color and round-the-clock programming—produces an uncannily accurate picture of the current American version of the technological society's "economic man," particularly in regard to the narrow-minded obsession with money. He writes, "He who has money is the slave of the money he has. He who has it not is the slave of a mad desire to get it. . . . Money is the principal thing; culture, art, spirit, morality are jokes and not to be taken seriously."[13] This bottom line mentality, according to Ellul, had its origins in the evolution of the technological society that occurred during the second half of the nineteenth century. Postman's first curriculum, exemplifying the most recent example of technology's inexorable societal impress, can be seen as inflaming this mind-set with virtually maniacal intensity in contemporary America. This obsession with money can, in turn, be further understood if one considers the first curriculum as a principal element within the experiential bind infesting the consciousness of most of these self-same people. Ever since humans first appeared on earth as a distinct element within the evolutionary chain, they have distinguished themselves from the rest of living creatures through one unique specieswide trait: their capacity to form values, ideals, and gods, together with their unreasoning, often obsessive, devotion to these ideals and/or gods. While the religiophilosophical concept of the "deity/ideal" is universal in human existence, the specific manifestations of same change from society to society, as well as across temporal epochs. In modern America the basic, repetitious, unwavering premise or precept of the first curriculum (catechism) is that salvation in life comes through the accumulation of money to be used for technology-wise consumption of more and more stuff. Thus exists prevailing bottom-line mentality and morality of contemporary Americans.

Both Ellul and Postman have, with rare insight, thrown the venerated societal dynamism of applied science and technology into a questionable light. Postman's concept of a thermostatic second curriculum, offering a corrective, balancing educational experience to children in opposition to the electronic first curriculum, seems to me to offer the best hope for avoiding the deeper abysses of continued national enrollment in the first curriculum.

Of course, the notion of thermostatic balancing is key here. We cannot abolish technology; nor should we give a moment's serious thought to such. None of us wants to go back to cold evenings sitting around a fire in a cave, worrying about where the bears are tonight. Nor would we be capable. The dependable stream of new products and services is just too comforting, liberating, and too exciting. As a society, we have nestled in the lap of technological innovation too long to even consider a 180-, or even a 90-degree change in the direction of cultural evolution. And looking around, we can see most of the undeveloped nations straining at the bit to emulate our example. But everything in life is a trade-off. Everything has its dark side, including the life within modern technological society. The evening TV news programs dependably remind us of life's inescapable tragic aspect, even as we discount their sensationalistic, seemingly thanatophilic biases.

Effective public educational programs built on Postman's specifications would engender the thermostatic intellect in a broad way and, I believe, provide at least some of the inner, personal, moral-ethical balance needed to thwart the further disastrous influence of the first curriculum and the experiential bind, as well as any similar malign by-products of later technological advances. Formally trained from the inception of their public education to see the larger historical and philosophical picture, such a citizenry could also bring intelligent political pressure to bear against the distant, murkily perceived vested interests threatening momentarily to swindle the public, be they commercial, religious, governmental, or scientific.

Thus far, the discussion does not portend any exceptional stresses or responsibilities to any of the groups naturally party to the plan: educators, students, or parents. However, it is necessary here to point out to parents their critical role in the whole undertaking. Depth psychologists since Freud have laid especial emphasis on the importance of the infantile period—from birth to 5 or 6 years of age, when the child normally begins his/her public education—for the whole period of life thereafter. Fortuitous though it may seem, children's experience during this early period, when they are helpless, dependent, and impressionable in the extreme, serves to fix the most basic elements of the personality into a lasting, immutable configuration. Such critical psychical variables as individuals' psychosexual identity; their basic self-esteem; trust in others; capacity for autonomy and autonomous, self-directed effort; and comfort with the two conflicting social-interpersonal motivations, competition and cooperation, have their essential foundations laid down during this crucial period. As suggested repeatedly in foregoing chapters, these critical elements of character are acquired over time, largely through the slow, unconscious process of identification, the principal mechanism of psychogenetic development during these crucial early years. While I am not talking about the development of specific intellectual skills and interests such as those comprising the mind of an educated, thoughtful adult, I am referring to characterological elements which undergird the adult thinking ego, be it intellectual, pragmatically intelligent, or not given to careful thought in general.

In addition to having the natural advantage in best providing their children with healthy infusions of mirroring and the opportunity for realistic idealization, to use Kohut's terms, concerned and loving parents are also in a position to protect their children from the disappearance of childhood, to draw on Postman's cogent analysis. Both of these overlapping and arduous child-rearing tasks are critical to the resultant emotional health, thinking habits and deeply personal values of the mature adult citizen. I repeat, there is no complete eradication of the traces of human experience during these first crucial years; they are there, once and for all, in the memory bank, psychologically, and in the neural circuitry, physiologically. And in general there are no substitutes in all of creation for concerned, loving, joyful and proud parents in terms of heightening the probabilities that an individual's experience of infancy will, on balance, be of a quality that prepares him/her for a happier and more productive adult life.

Educating children along the lines of Postman's second curriculum, or for that matter along those of today's public school curricula, is a complex, demanding task. Teachers cannot be expected to achieve this goal successfully with children who come to the first grade weighted down with personal emotional problems, problems which, in many cases at least, are destined to worsen and ramify as the child attempts to cope with the ever-increasing demands of life. Teachers cannot be expected to be effective educators if they are simultaneously saddled with problems in the classroom that require them to act, secondarily, as personal counselors, drug and alcohol counselors, or professional disciplinarians. Put differently, teachers cannot be good teachers *and* parent surrogates simultaneously. As I have suggested in a previous chapter, there are no service professionals available in the whole of our vaunted technological society—public school special services teams; outpatient mental health practitioners in the disciplines of social work; psychology, and psychiatry; teams of similarly trained specialists providing twenty-four-hour-a-day in-patient services at general medical hospitals, neuropsychiatric hospitals, and special institutions for drug and sex offenders and runaways; specially trained clergy working in churches and related religious institutions, to list but a few of the best—who can, in general, fully repair the damages done to infants and children in homes led by disturbed or disinterested or preoccupied parents. Specialists such as the above can help, but they cannot compensate children completely for whatever their parents have not provided. In fear of beating a dead horse, I will conclude this discussion with the following statistically based fact: The most common correlate of all forms of individual behavior disturbance is the *broken home*.

At this point, two important qualifications and a warning are necessary in order to clarify my argument. First, I am not for a moment suggesting that parents should attempt to emulate the various health professionals just mentioned in their child rearing. This would constitute a technologizing of parenthood, and that is the last thing that our children need. A good example of the counterproductiveness that this would bring lies in the area of adult sexual relations. The spate of how-to sex manuals that sprang

up during the 1970s backfired by and large because they induced an excessively technical, cognitive attitude to lovemaking. Primed with
technical information on the achievement of mutual orgasm and determined to succeed efficiently and powerfully, many, if not most, of the
lover technicians were about as relaxed and responsive to the ebb and
flow of each other's romantic and sexual passions as they would have
been during their comprehensive examinations in graduate school.
Although the situations and tasks of lovers and parents are in essence
different, they have basic similarities as well. In both spheres an attitude
of self-acceptant confidence, expressing forgiving, though strong and
joyful, concern for the other person and/or child (Tillich's acceptance
"in-spite-of"), is generally more fruitful than that of a technically sophisticated, but narrow and manipulative concern with a deep mutual orgasm
or a so-called well-adjusted child. It is just those parents who have
achieved realistic self-acceptance, and who, largely because of their self-
affirming natures, can joyfully lose themselves in the task of child rearing,
that provide their children with realistic, attainable models for identification and idealization. This point is of the utmost importance. It is precisely
at this initial, idealizing, model-hungry phase in the child's psychical
development that the battle with Postman's first curriculum is joined and
its outcome essentially prefigured. While in the individual case we can
never predict with certainty the eventual outcome vis-à-vis the first curriculum, we can safely state, generally, that those children who grow up
under the influence of realistic and attainable parental models (self-objects,
in Kohut's terms) will be less susceptible to the powerful pull of electronic first curriculum. They will be less easily subjected to its spell, less
easily mesmerized by it, because they will have developed other interests
that are rooted in idealization of other heros, their parents. On the other
hand, the children who most readily swallow the precepts and premises
of the first curriculum do so because the fantastic figures depicted therein
become their personal heroes, their identification models. They tend to
be the ghetto and lower-class children who live in de facto broken homes
and the poor, lonely couch potatoes hailing from functionally broken
homes across the rest of the socioeconomic spectrum. These unfortunate
adultified children also tend to become the individuals who, as childified
adults, are headed for a life of chronic demoralization; economic trouble,
if not failure; the psychotherapist's office; the psychiatric wards; or prison.

The second qualification has to do with parents' expectations of themselves and their children vis-à-vis Postman's model of the proposed second curriculum. The terms "intellect," "intellectual," and
"philosophical" have been bandied about in the foregoing discussion.
I am not—nor is Postman, I am sure—suggesting that this second curriculum will require that all successful graduates become heavyweight

intellectuals or philosophers. Nothing of the sort. Most of the graduates will undoubtedly fan out across the spectrum of jobs offered by the economy, as they always have. Those with the desire and the talent to become accomplished thinkers will do so too, as they always have. But armed with the fundamentals of Postman's thermostatic curriculum, all of them ought to arrive at adulthood better insulated against the distortions of the first curriculum than most of them are today. And those whose future career and civic paths are constellated by strong, realistic, attainable identifications with loving and concerned parents will be the best protected of all. They are the ones who will have the best chances to experience regular moments of self-ideal congruity, inner peace, and serenity. They will not have to play the catch-up game, running, tongue out, after the elusive symbols of monetary success, and away from their own media inflated, insatiable, guilt-spewing, ideal selves.

My warning has to do with the probable timespan involved. As I see it, this is the only radical solution to the burgeoning sourge of the unfettered first curriculum and the experiential bind in contemporary America. These two intertwined phenomena are unintended results of the technological engine, operating at full throttle here. In terms of this mechanical model, they can be seen as equivalents to the heat of friction that invariably signals trouble to the sensitive mechanic. Switching to an organismic model, they can also be viewed as pathological processes resulting from a more basic disease operating within the body. In the past ten years they have been breeding clear-cut economic symptoms, in the form of excessive personal and institutional debt, on which professional economists, trained to perceive such symptomatology, have commented. In the past year or so the more acute urban crime symptoms ultimately traceable to them have begun to alarm the general public. That something is basically wrong with American society is now clear to all who are interested and concerned.

Most of the remedies being called for—more police on city streets, beefed-up federal drug programs and so on—are superficial. They are oriented toward symptom control. A more radical solution or cure will take more time; just how much is impossible to predict. And it will take more disciplined involvement by individual Americans, particularly parents. Just as a change of life-style—eating better, exercising more, avoiding toxins—is a more radical preventive approach to cardiovascular illness, it is also more time and energy consuming than simply popping blood pressure pills. However, when successfully undertaken, it can contribute to such basic desiderata as improved general wellness and longer life. In addition, it also carries the possibility of unforeseen serendipities based on one's improved vigor and appearance, for example, career advances, new friendships, and the like.

Similarly, changing the mentality of the American public via successful involvement in Postman's thermostatic curriculum can be seen as a more basic antidote to the elemental problem of unbridled technology and the more immediate and society-threatening issues of the first curriculum-experiential bind than hiring more urban police and federal drug agents. However, if carefully and patiently undertaken, it has preventive potential in connection with the basic economic and legal symptoms already overwhelming many urban, suburban, and rural Americans. By way of unanticipated serendipities, it might contribute to a fundamental improvement in the overall quality of commercial television, giving the first curriculum more real educational meaning, as well upgrading its entertainment programming. Remember, one of the basic axioms of free-enterprise capitalism is no market, no product.

Postman, making concluding remarks on the problem of deified technology in *The Disappearance of Childhood*, speculates thus, "Now that the first shock of what we have embarked upon is beginning to diminish, we may yet think ourselves into a more felicitous position and come out resembling something worth saving."[14] As suggested above, we cannot, as a society, turn our backs on five centuries of technological advance. Nor do we want to. But like all things in life, technology has its good and bad sides, its chiaroscuro of darkness and light. We need to balance our impressive national technical intelligence with more intellectual perspective, more of the philosopher's capacity to see the whole as well as unrelated bits of information. If it seems to readers too ambitious to aspire, as a citizenry, to become more philosophical, then they should consider once again the thoughts of William James, who described a philosopher as nothing more than a man who thinks very hard about his subject.

Quoted in George Seldes's *The Great Thoughts*, James's famous remark on the value of the philosophical mind-set to the members of any society is:

Philosophy is at once the most sublime and trivial of human pursuits. . . . It "bakes no bread," as has been said, but it can inspire our souls with courage; and repugnant as its manners, its doubting and challenging; its quibbling and dialectics, often are to common people, no one of us can get along without the farflashing beams of light it sends over the world's perspectives.[15]

I believe that clear thinking, of the kind extolled by both James and Postman, is our most adaptive national recourse in the face of the dehumanizing of contemporary America. It lies within the capacity of all Americans to build up this natural propensity, not necessarily to the Olympian level of a William James, but to some point exceeding our present individual level. At present most of us want to be richer and healthier. Why not wiser as well? Such a personal goal could, under the right circumstances, multiply rapidly across individuals and become a national priority, as has the present health consciousness of Americans. If the lantern of the intellect can be lit in America on a truly broad scale, it will gradually (such a project cannot be hurried) serve to provide a thermostatic balance to some of our current, potentially unhealthy national goals, ideals, and values. Then and only then will we as a nation be healthier, stronger, and better able to compete successfully in the international arena in the twenty-first century. We might also be happier. But as John Updike suggests, "Happiness . . . is something that is best seen out of the corner of the eye."[16] Like a mirage, it vanishes when stared at too intently, or pursued too hotly, for its own sake.

NOTES

1. Jacques Ellul, *The Technological Society* (New York: Alfred A. Knopf, 1964), vi.
2. Ibid., 27.
3. Ibid., 34.
4. Ibid., 45.
5. Ibid., 24.
6. Erich Fromm, *The Anatomy of Human Destructiveness* (New York: Holt, Rinehart & Winston, 1973), 225–26.
7. William James, *The Principles of Psychology* (Chicago: Encyclopedia Britannica, 1952), 7.
8. Fromm, *Anatomy of Human Destructiveness*, 226.
9. Neil Postman, *The Disappearance of Childhood* (New York: Delacorte Press, 1982), 146.
10. Ibid., 110.
11. Ibid., 108.
12. Ellul, *The Technological Society*, xvi.
13. Ibid., 221.
14. Postman, *The Disappearance of Childhood*, 145.
15. Qtd. in George Seldes, *The Great Thoughts* (New York: Ballantine Books, 1985), 204.
16. John Updike, *Self-Consciousness* (New York: Alfred A. Knopf, 1989), 254.

6

Concluding Thoughts

I believe that America's overweening hedonistic materialism is its Achilles' heel, the national trait that may well lead to its eclipse as a leader within the international polity of the twenty-first century. Ultimately traceable to our deification of technology, the trait under question is kept red-hot, so to speak, by a combination of the first curriculum and the imagery of fantasy pervading the burgeoning vicarious realm of experience. These two abstract terms refer, of course, to elements within the most recent phase of technology's inexorable, undeniably impressive evolution in Western culture, namely, electronic communications technology.

Impressive though it may be at first glance, under scrutiny our vaunted technological dynamism reveals a darker side to those, like Jacques Ellul and Neil Postman, who take the trouble to look and who have the intellectual depth and sensitivity to perceive the hazards of this multifaceted human enterprise lurking subtly within its noisier, blinding, ever-accelerating outpouring of life-enhancing goods and services. I, for one, find the written works of these and similarly inquiring minds to be both interesting and reassuring; and I am thankful for their willingness to formally send their far-flashing, Jamesian beams of philosophical light across the modern world's complex and frenzied perspectives.

Persons such as these manifest shining examples of the balancing, philosophical, thermostatic intellect. As a nation, we need to cultivate this mentality on a broad scale for one cardinal reason: to help us stay connected with our long, hard-won, spirit-redeeming, humane cultural traditions. Put differently, we need this mentality to help us keep from getting lost, as a society, in the uprushing night of uncontrolled change and improperly assimilated freedom.

Existential psychology emphasizes the primary importance of the concept of freedom within the human condition. But like all of the basic human desiderata, freedom is a Janus-faced issue. On the positive side it promises a heady lack of constraint or limitation. On the negative side, however, it also carries the threat of responsibility, failure, and guilt. Persons enjoying freedom are necessarily saddled with the responsibility of using their freedom effectively, productively, and profitably and with the potential burden of guilt for personally perceived failure. As I have labored to show throughout this book, pathological guilt is common to all forms of functional psychopathology; it is the keystone of this multiform source of human suffering and debilitation. Further, I have also presented in a number of places in my discussion the standard psychological formulation illustrating that the degree, or intensity, of the guilt is directly related to the degree of self-ideal discrepancy. Where the idealized figures are utterly unattainable, the guilt is invariably intense and intractable and corrosive in its influence on complex patterns of adaptive, socially responsible behavior. In the extreme, such severe pathological guilt carries the potential for inducing psychotic derangement in the afflicted individuals. When the form of this derangement centers on depression, there exists the ever-present danger of suicidal impulses.

Ernest Becker argued that humans must embark on heroic acts in order to deny the specter of death. These acts need not be grand in design, but they must constellate people's energies, providing them with the basis for feeling effective and triumphant. In a similar vein, Paul Tillich taught that one of the principal human methods for dealing with the existential anxiety of death, which is psychologically overwhelming when confronted directly, involves replacing it with lesser, objective, more tangible objects of fear that can be faced and conquered through the courage to be.[1] Both men held the conviction that the need for a sense of heroic adequacy vis-à-vis the inevitable threats to life runs deep in the human soul.

However, according to Becker, in fashioning their heroic themes, people are faced with the crucial task of selecting idols.

It seems to me that we have, then, evolutionarily and historically, a common problem for men of good will in all fields to work on: in their own lives if they so chose, and in the social and political sphere. Basically . . . it is a problem of the identification of idols. To what powers has a man given himself in order to solve the paradoxes of his life? On what kind of objective structure has he strung out his meanings and fenced off his own free eneregies? As [Max] Scheler points out, each person *has* an idea of the absolutely real, the highest good, the greatest power; he may not have this consciously, in fact he rarely does. The idea grows out of the automatic conditioning of his early learning, he *lives* his version of the real without knowing it, by giving his whole uncritical allegiance to some kind of model of power. So long as he does this he is truly a slave, and Scheler's point is that not only is he unconsciously living a slavish life but he is deluding himself too: he *thinks* he is living on a model of the true absolute, the really real, when actually he is living a second-rate real, a fetish of the truth, an idol of power.[2]

That the idols populating the imagery of unreality within the first curriculum are false goes without saying. In fact, they are doubly so. They are false in the ethical sense that the basic values they advocate or symbolize can be seen as essentially inimical to human survival and social cohesion. In addition, they are false in the sense that they are utterly contrived, consisting of pure fantasies artfully presented in the guise of reality to an increasingly undiscriminating public. It is their fantastic nature, commuicating essentially to the wishful, pleasure-loving side of our mentality—the Freudian id, psychologically; the right brain, neurologically—that gives them their mesmeric appeal. This, together with their omnipresence in contemporary America, makes them irresistible models for solving the eternal paradoxes of many people's lives, for constellating their death-denying heroic acts, in Becker's terms.

It seems clear to me that we, as a society, must break their hypnotic grip on us if we are to hold our position of leadership on the international scene, maintain our general standard of living, and collectively grow in a healthy, balanced way as the twenty-first century unfolds. In the previous chapter I suggested formal adoption of Postman's proposed second, thermostatic curriculum as the most radical step in this direction that I am aware of.

Such a radical prophylactic approach to this problem will take time. How much is difficult to say, but one can estimate roughly a period of twelve years or so—the time for a generation of schoolchildren to complete the thermostatic curriculum—will be needed before any attempts at assessment, either formal or informal, can be meaningfully done.

Second, it will take work and determination, probably in staggering amounts. As I suggested previously, parents are absolutely critical to the success of the plan, as they are to any systematic attempt to educate and mold their offspring. They are equivalent to the fulcrum in a mechanical lever system, the point around which the various forces rotate and give the lever its mechanical advantage. To use another analogy, their input provides the psychological foundation to the edifice of the child's character structure. If the foundation is strong, then the chances are heightened that the whole personality will also be strong, capable of dealing competently and responsibly with the demands of life.

Psychologically speaking, human life has a fortuitous or contingent aspect at its core. To use existential terms, at birth we are thrown into life without our consent; and we are thrown out of life, usually without our consent, at the time we die. In between, we have to try to do the best that we can with our personal and situational resources. During the first years of infancy we have experiences that are ineradicable. Whether they be essentially good or bad, they will have a permanent, lifelong, influence on our entire repertory of responses, both overt and covert. This is why good, healthy, loving, proud parents are so quintessentially important. They literally hold the future of society in their hands.

The challenge to parents in the above plan is that they will have to make the decision to ignore the press of the imagery of fantasy in their own lives, at least until their children have all reached the age of six, at which time the period of infancy and early childhood is past and children normally begin public school. Given the enormous power of the first curriculum, or imagery of fantasy, this will not be easy. But concerned parents will have to make the choice between getting everything immediately for themselves or providing their children with a solid psychological foundation upon which to build their own lives during the next generation. This applies maximally to mothers, although it also applies critically to fathers as well. Day-care centers, baby-sitters, preschools or nursery schools for three-to-five-year-olds notwithstanding, there are no really satisfactory substitutes for good, healthy, loving, proud biological parents in terms of adequately meeting infants' and children's mirroring and idealizing needs. At the risk of beating this point to death, I will repeat, once more: to the extent that children make strong, positive, primary identifications with their parents, they will be protected from making them with the fantastic models infesting the first curriculum. This in turn is the most powerful antidote in existence to the child's pathological engulfment in the first curriculum. We humans have an elemental need for idols; we tend to learn ineradicably the lessons coming from our personal idols; to the extent that our initial idols are real and realistically emulable we are protected from the curse of corrosive, pathological guilt and the sad, wasteful, self-destructive compensatory behaviors it invariably feeds.

Bearing me out here is the tragic fact that those children in contemporary America who are most involved in the first curriculum and who are emulating their TV idols most dramatically by actively preying on their victims, weapons in hand, are the young ghetto-dwelling males whose biological fathers, for all practical purposes, no longer exist as a functional familial entity. The maxim that nature abhors a vacuum applies here. These prematurely "adultified" children will find their idols where they will. It is a grotesque irony that the profit-driven drivel of the first curriculum is so irresistibly available to them.

Alvin Toffler has already published *Power Shift*, the last book of a trilogy on the subject of change in modern postindustrial society. His study of this basic phenomenon began twenty-five years ago. His epoch-making *Future Shock*, which appeared in 1970, examines the process of accelerating, technology-spawned, societal change; *The Third Wave*, appearing in 1980, looks at the directions of this runaway phenomenon; and now *Power Shift* deals with the control of changes yet to come—who will shape them and how.

As one would expect, Toffler sees power as the ultimate source of societal change. Ominously, from the standpoint of this discussion, his analysis focuses on the crucially changed role of knowledge in relation to power. Enlarging on this basic point, he states,

Today, in the fast-changing, affluent nations, despite all inequalities of income and wealth, the coming struggle for power will increasingly turn into a struggle over the distribution of and access to knowledge. . . . This is why, unless we understand how and to whom knowledge flows, we can neither protect ourselves against the abuse of power nor create the better, more democratic society that tomorrow's technologies promise. . . . The control of knowledge is the crux of tomorrow's worldwide struggle for power in every human institution.[3]

Toffler is a futurist. Like Ellul and Postman, his thought exemplifies the operation of the synthesizing, perspective-seeking intellect at its very best. His trilogy on change is edifying millions of people all over the world. His books, despite their being packed with subtle insights into the complexities of the uprushing future, are eminently readable and entertaining. All concerned adults, particularly parents of infants and young children, should read him carefully and be guided toward the future by his presciece.

The present discussion is, in the final analysis, a plea for balance in the way we as individuals lead our lives and as parents prepare our children ultimately to lead their own lives. Life in the world's most technological society is simultaneously more plenteous and more dangerous than in other societies with less inner dynamism, running with their belts less tight and their bearings less hot, to borrow another of William James's inimitable metaphors. Careening down the highway of life at future-shocking speed, we run the peril of losing our direction, perhaps losing our sanity, as a society. The psychoanalytic definition of a psychologically traumatic, potentially psychosis-inducing experience centers around the individual being helplessly subjected to excessive amounts of intense stimulation. In the commonest, prepsychotic case this stimulation is drive related, and it is the consequence of an abrupt loss of repression. However, there is ample documentation in connection with traumatic war neuroses to the effect that excessive stimulation originating outside the person can have equally debilitating, though typically shorter-term consequences. Whether the source of the overstimulation is internal or external, it can put the controlling ego out of commission, reducing the individual, either momentarily or permanently, to invalid status.

I see media blight, stemming from powerful commercial interests, as a prime source of such potentially traumatic overstimulation operating endlessly and pervasively in America today. Employing the omnipresent tube as its spearhead and battering ram, this malign spin-off of technological progress is steadily and insidiously sapping our adaptive potential as a nation. The threat of national decline is not immediate, to be sure. However, as the influence of media blight accumulates, via its longer-term effects on the nation's youth, the symptoms of national deterioration will become more acute. In its contribution to the experiential bind, I believe that it is fostering the dehumanizing of America. Spurred on by the profit motive to attract larger and larger and younger and younger audiences, and increasingly using luridly sexual-aggressive contents toward this end, it is inadvertently contributing to the development in millions of young Americans of something like an "id-ified" superego, incongruous as this may sound.

Neil Postman sees commercial TV, in its creation of the first curriculum, as a major cause of the atrophy of traditional, left-brain intelligence among American schoolchildren. Complicating this downward pull on the intellectual development of the nation's youth is commercial TV's tendency to "disappear" childhood, thereby fostering a generation of adultified children. In Postman's view, this latter maleficent influence serves to aid and abet the former, thus adding insult to injury.

When one adds to this picture Toffler's futuristic adumbrations concerning the importance of knowledge in the twenty-first century's struggle for power, the outlook for America dims perceptibly. Further, when one stirs in the notion that, because of the global dimensions involved, Americans will be competing with Europeans and Asians in this informational power struggle, the images relating to this outlook take on an even darker hue. Finally, when one considers that the demoralization caused by the experiential bind weakens even further the flaccid intellectual curiosities of American youth, then our anticipations of America's future international competitiveness may well become alarmingly bleak, and rightfully so.

We know from formal psychology that all degrees of depression undermine intellectual motivation and capability. To the extent that humans are depressed they are robbed of both the taste and talent for complex learning. Depression, already described as the common cold of mental illness in contemporary America, is also the modal affective accompaniment to intractable demoralization. Thus we are confronted with the familiar vicious cycle that tends to characterize patterns of maladaptive human behavior: demoralization fosters academic inadequacy, which in turn fosters further demoralization, and so on.

How to break the loop, particularly when it involves millions of people to one degree or another? In Chapter 4, I outlined a theoretical approach to treating the bind-induced demoralization in the context of formal psychotherapy. In addition, I briefly suggested a condensed version of same for those persons who, for a variety of reasons, chose to go the self-help route. As stated in the introduction, to the extent that individuals can transcend their own demoralization, the wider dehumanizing of America should also be meliorated. Admittedly, this approach to the wider problem is incremental, and glacial in terms of movement toward the goal of rehumanizing America. But as I suggested in the introduction, there are no large-scale, programmatic solutions to the problem of the adult bind-induced demoralization.

On the other hand, work against the stupefying effects of the first curriculum among the nation's schoolchildren can, reasonably, assume large-scale, programmatic dimensions and efficiencies. Schoolchildren, being younger, more impressionable, and more malleable, should be more amenable to programmatic attempts at weaning them away from the imagery of unreality pervading the vicarious realm of experience and comprising the contents of the first curriculum, particularly if parents are also firmly denying unrestricted TV watching and thoughtfully critiquing the programs allowed on the home front. To the extent that this weaning process succeeds, it should both encourage academic-intellectual proficiencies *and* insulate the growing child against the bind-induced demoralization. Also, as these developments occur, those in charge should be able to discern the operation of a virtuous cycle serving to perpetuate the child's healthy behavior pattern: academic interest and proficiency foster enthusiasm and self-esteem, which, in turn, foster further academic proficiency, and so on.

Of course, I am not talking about observing new, improved, shinier widgets coming off an assembly line at a faster rate. Nothing of the sort. To the degree that programmatic solutions become too standardized, they will begin to fail. I am talking about programs for improving the education of American children so that they can better cope with the inevitable demands of life as adults and in the process help keep America strong. This cannot be totally standardized. While everything I have suggested follows from formal psychology, the teachers will still have to feel their way along with students, helping them discover their individual strengths and weaknesses and where they will fit in the larger scheme of things as adults. And in the end, all parties will have to guard against the formation of unrealistic expectations, stimuli to which are, in the final analysis, the essential pathogens infesting the imagery of unreality.

I have made it clear that I favor the adoption of Postman's second, thermostatic curriculum, as he outlines it in *Teaching as a Conserving Activity*, in this public educational approach to the personal repudiation of the first curriculum by the nation's schoolchildren. His curriculum is well planned to strengthen the philosophical, perspective-seeking attitude in those who successfully graduate as young adults. Not only should this habit of thought protect them from the deceptions of the first curriculum and the imagery of fantasy, it ought also to help them as successive waves of young adult citizens to judiciously consider how, and whether, they will use each technological innovation as it comes along. Put differently, it ought to help them to better control the technological engine of Western culture, while retaining both the unique and common elements of their cultural traditions. And it ought also to guide and motivate them in exercising an attitude of prudent, loving stewardship toward the ever-beautiful, ever-shrinking blue and white planet, our delicate home within the cold, dark, infinite, seemingly unconscious cosmos.

NOTES

1. Paul Tillich, *The Courage to Be* (New Haven: Yale University Press, 1952). This, to my knowledge, is the best distillation, from among his voluminous theological writings, of Tillich's views on the problem of human anxiety. Tillich was greatly absorbed with such worldly subjects as art, philosophy, and mental health; in fact, he was criticized by the Protestant theological orthodoxy as being virtually atheistic in some of his views. He was well aware of the centrality of anxiety and its relation to guilt, in human experience. His treatment of anxiety as an existential fact of life is required reading for anyone interested in understanding this troubling human emotion form the existentialist's point of view.

2. Ernest Becker, *The Birth and Death of Meaning* (New York: Free Press, 1973), 185–86.

3. Alvin Toffler, *Power Shift* (New York: Bantam Books, 1990), 20.

Bibliography

Adler, Alfred. *See* Ansbacher and Ansbacher.

Allen, Gay. *William James*. New York: Viking Press, 1968.

Ansbacher, Heinz, and Rowena Ansbacher, eds. *The Individual Psychology of Alfred Adler*. New York: Harper & Row, 1956.

Bandura, Albert. "Social Learning through Imitation." In *Nebraska Symposium on Motivation*, edited by Marshall Jones. Lincoln: University of Nebraska Press, 1962.

——— . "Vicarious Processes: A Case of No-Trial Learning." In *Advances in Experimental Social Psychology*, edited by Leonard Berkowitz. Vol. 2. New York: Academic Press, 1965.

——— . "Social-learning Theory of the Identification Processes." In *Handbook of Socialization Theory and Research*, edited by David Goslin. Chicago: Rand-McNally, 1969.

Barzini, Luigi. *The Europeans*. New York: Simon & Schuster, 1983.

Batra, Ravi. *The Great Depression of 1990*. New York: Simon & Schuster, 1985.

——— . *Surviving the Great Depression of 1990*. New York: Simon & Schuster, 1988.

Becker, Ernest. *The Birth and Death of Meaning*. New York: Free Press, 1962.

——— . *The Denial of Death*. New York: Free Press, 1973.

Bettelheim, Bruno. *Surviving and Other Essays*. New York: Alfred A. Knopf, 1979.

Cameron, Norman. *Personality Development and Psychopathology: A Dynamic Approach*. Boston: Houghton Mifflin, 1963.

Colm, Hanna. *The Existentialist Approach to Psychotherapy with Adults and Children*. New York: Grune & Stratton, 1966.

Combs, Arthur, and Donald Snygg. *Individual Behavior: A Perceptual Approach*. Rev. ed. New York: Harper & Row, 1959.

Comstock, George, with the assistance of F. G. Christen, M. L. Fisher, R. C. Quarles, and W. D. Richards. *Television and Human Behavior: The Key Studies*. Santa Monica: RAND Corporation, 1975.

Cousins, Norman. "Modern Man is Obsolete," *Saturday Review of Literature* 28 (August 18, 1945): 5–9.

Dollard, John, Leonard Doob, Neal Miller, O. Hobart Mowrer, and Robert Sears. *Frustration and Aggression*. New Haven: Yale University Press, 1989.

Ellul, Jacques. *The Technological Society*. New York: Alfred A. Knopf, 1964.

Fischer, David, *Growing Old in America*. New York: Oxford University Press, 1977.

Frankl, Victor. *Man's Search for Meaning*. Boston: Beacon Press, 1959.

Freud, Sigmund. *A General Introduction to Psychoanalysis*. New York: Permabooks, 1935.

Fromm, Erich. *The Art of Loving*. New York: Harper & Row, 1956.

——— . *The Anatomy of Human Destructiveness*. New York: Holt, Rinehart & Winston, 1973.

Galbraith, John Kenneth. *Money: Whence It Came, Where It Went*. Boston: Houghton Mifflin, 1975.

Gaylin, Willard. *Feelings: Our Vital Signs*. New York: Harper & Row, 1979.

Gazzaniga, Michael. *Mind Matters*. Boston: Houghton Mifflin, 1988.

Goldenson, Robert. *The Encyclopedia of Human Behavior: Psychology, Psychiatry, and Human Behavior*. New York: Dell, 1975.

Greenberg, B. S., and B. Dervin. *Use of the Media by the Urban Poor*. New York: Praeger, 1970.

——— . "Mass Communications Among the Urban Poor." In *Advances in Communications Research*, edited by C. D. Mortensen and K. K. Sereno. New York: Harper & Row, 1973.

Halberstam, David. *The Reckoning*. New York: William Morrow, 1986.

Hall, Calvin, and Gardiner Lindzey. *Theories of Personality*. New York: John Wiley & Sons, 1970.

Hamill, Pete. "Crack and the Box," *Esquire*, May 1990, 63–66.

Havighurst, Robert, Myra Robinson, and Mildred Dorr. "The Development of the Ideal Self in Childhood and Adolescence." In *The Self in Growth, Teaching and Learning*, edited by Don Hamachek. Englewood Cliffs, N.J.: Prentice-Hall, 1965.

Heilbroner, Robert. *The Nature and Logic of Capitalism*. New York: W. W. Norton, 1985.

Hooper, Judith, and Dick Teresi. *The 3 Pound Universe*. New York: Dell, 1986.

James, William. *The Principles of Psychology*. Chicago: Encyclopedia Britannica, 1952.

——— . *The Varieties of Religious Experience*. New York: Mentor Books, 1958.

Kernberg, Otto. *Borderline Conditions and Pathological Narcissism*. New York: Jason Aronson, 1975.

Kohut, Heinz. *The Analysis of the Self*. New York: International Universities Press, 1971.

——— . and Wolf, Ernest. "The Disorders of the Self and Their Treatment: An Outline." *International Journal of Psychoanalysis* (1978): 59, 413–25.

Lasch, Christopher. *The Culture of Narcissism*. New York: W. W. Norton, 1978.

——— . *The Minimal Self*. New York: W. W. Norton, 1984.

Malabre, Alfred. *Beyond Our Means*. New York: Random House, 1987.

Mead, George H. *Mind, Self, and Society*. Chicago: University of Chicago Press, 1934.

Menaker, Esther. "The Ego-Ideal: An Aspect of Narcissism." In *The Narcissistic Condition: A Fact of Our Times*, edited by Marie Nelson. New York: Human Sciences Press, 1977.

Mills, Charles Wright. *The Power Elite*. New York: Oxford University Press, 1956.

Murray, Henry, and Clyde Kluckhohn. " Outline of a Conception of Personality." In *Personality in Nature, Society, and Culture*, edited by Clyde Kluckhohn, Henry Murray, and David Schneider. New York: Alfred A. Knopf, 1956.

Postman, Neil. *Teaching as a Conserving Activity*. New York: Delacorte Press, 1979.

——— . *The Disappearance of Childhood*. New York: Delacorte Press, 1982.

——— . *Conscientious Objections*. New York: Alfred A. Knopf, 1988.

Robinson, J., and P. Converse. "The Impact of Television on Mass Media Usages: A Cross-National Comparison." In *The Use of Time: Daily Activities of Urban and Suburban Populations in Twelve Countries*, edited by A. Szalai. The Hague: Mouton, 1972.

Rogers, Carl. "A Theory of Therapy, Personality and Interpersonal Relationships as Developed in the Client-centered Framework." In *Psychology—A Study of a Science*, vol. 3, *Formulations of the Person and the Social Context*, edited by Sigmund Koch. New York: McGraw-Hill, 1960.

Rogow, Arnold. *The Dying of the Light*. New York: Putnam, 1975.

Rotter, Julian. "Trust and Gullibility," *Psychology Today*, October 1980, 102–11.

Schwartz, Tony. *Media: The Second God*. New York: Random House, 1981.

Seldes, George. *The Great Thoughts*. New York: Ballantine Books, 1985.

Siegel, A. E. "The Influence of Violence in the Mass-Media Upon Children's Role Expectations." *Child Development* 29 (1958): 35–56.

——— . "The Effects of Media Violence on Social Learning." In *Violence and the Media: A Staff Report to the National Commission on The Causes and Prevention of Violence*, edited by R. K. Baker and S. J. Ball. Washington, D.C.: U.S. Government Printing Office, 1969.

"Skinner, B. F." *U.S. News and World Report;*, November 3, 1980.

Smith, Adam. *The Roaring Eighties*. New York: Summit Books, 1988.

Spitz, Rene. *The First Year of Life*. New York: International Universities Press, 1965.

Stein, Jess. and Laurence Urdang. *The Random House Dictionary of the English Language: The Unabridged Edition*. New York: Random House, 1966.

Stern, Aaron. *Me: The Narcissistic American*. New York: Ballantine Books, 1979.

Strachey, James. "The Nature of Therapeutic Action in Psychoanalysis." In *Psychoanalysis Clinical Interpretation*, edited by Paul Louis. London: Collier-Macmillan, 1963.

Suzuki, D. T., Erich Fromm, and Richard DeMartino. *Zen Buddhism and Psychoanalysis*. New York: Grove Press, 1960.

Symonds, Percival. *The Ego and the Self*. New York: Appleton-Century-Crofts, 1951.

Tannenbaum, P., and B. Greenberg. "Mass Communication." *Annual Review of Psychology* (1968): 351–86.

Thomas, Lowell. "Good News from Lowell Thomas." *Newsweek*, July 7, 1980. 9.

Tillich, Paul. *The Courage To Be*. New Haven: Yale University Press, 1952.

Toffler, Alvin. *Future Shock*. New York: Random House, 1970.

—— . *The Third Wave*. New York: William Morrow, 1980.

—— . *Power Shift*. New York: Bantam Books, 1990.

Tuchman, Barbara. *New York Times Magazine (Sunday)*, November 12, 1980.

Turiell, Elliot. "An Historical Analysis of the Freudian Concepts of the Super-Ego." *Psychoanalytic Review* 54 (1967): 118–40.

Updike, John. *Self Consciousness*. New York: Alfred A. Knopf, 1989.

Upjohn, W. E., Institute for Employment Research. *Work in America: Report of a Special Task Force to the Secretary of Health, Education and Welfare*. Cambridge, MIT Press, 1972.

Veblen, Thorstein. *The Theory of the Leisure Class*. New York: Modern Library, 1934.

Weakland, John. "The Double-Bind Hypothesis of Schizophrenia." In *The Etiology of Schizophrenia*, edited by Don Jackson. New York: Basic Books, 1960.

Weintraub, Sidney. "The Human Factor in Inflation," *New York Times Magazine (Sunday)*, November 25, 1979.

Weiss, W. "Effects of the Mass Media of Communication." In *The Handbook of Social Psychology*, edited by Gardiner Lindzey and Elliot Aronson, Vol. 5. *Applied Social Psychology*, 2d ed. Reading, Mass.: Addison-Wesley, 1969.

—— . "Mass Communication," *Annual Review of Psychology* 22 (1971): 309–36.

Index

ABOUT THE AUTHOR

WILLIAM K. SHRADER received his doctoral training in clinical psychology from the University of Massachusetts, and has twenty-five years of experience in psychotherapy and counseling. He is the author of several published works on related topics.